Birth of the Persian Empire

Birth of the Persian Empire

Volume I

Edited By

Vesta Sarkhosh Curtis
and
Sarah Stewart

in association with The London Middle East Institute at SOAS
and
The British Museum

Published in 2005 by I.B.Tauris & Co Ltd
6 Salem Road, London W2 4BU
175 Fifth Avenue, New York NY 10010
www.ibtauris.com

In the United States of America and Canada distributed by
Palgrave Macmillan a division of St. Martin's Press
175 Fifth Avenue, New York NY 10010

Copyright © 2005 Vesta Sarkhosh Curtis & Sarah Stewart

The right of Vesta Sarkhosh Curtis & Sarah Stewart to be identified as editors of this work has been asserted by the editors in accordance with the Copyright, Designs and Patent Act 1988.

The publication of this book was generously supported by the Soudavar Memorial Foundation.

All rights reserved. Except for brief quotations in a review, this book, or any part thereof, may not be reproduced, stored in or introduced into a retrieval system, or transmitted, in any form or by any means, electronic, mechanical, photocopying, recording or otherwise, without the prior written permission of the publisher.

ISBN 1 84511 062 5

EAN 978 1 84511 062 8

A full CIP record for this book is available from the British Library
A full CIP record for this book is available from the Library of Congress

Library of Congress catalogue card: available

Typeset by P. Fozooni

Printed and bound in Great Britain by TJ International Ltd, Padstow, Cornwall from camera-ready copy edited and supplied by the editors

Contents

Introduction	1
Cyrus the Great and the Kingdom of Anshan	7
An Archaeologist's Approach to Avestan Geography	29
The Achaemenids and the *Avesta*	52
The Contribution of the Magi	85
The History of the Idea of Iran	100
Iron Age Iran and the Transition to the Achaemenid Period	112
List of Abbreviations	132
Bibliography	133

List of Figures

Map showing the principal sites in southwestern Iran mentioned in the text	10
Persian nobleman at Persepolis wearing the "Elamite" dagger	12
Bath-tub coffin of Kidin-Hutran, son of Kurlush, from the Neo-Elamite tomb at Arjan	17
Modern impression of a cylinder seal in the Louvre, bearing the legend "Parsirra, son of Kurlush" (after Amiet 1973)	17
Composite drawing of impressions on Persepolis fortification texts 596–695 and 2003 by M.C. Root and M.B. Garrison	18
Map according to Gnoli (adapted from Gnoli 1980)	32
Map according to Vogelsang	33
Map according to Humbach	34
Map according to Witzel	35
Map according to Frantz Grenet	44
Aerial photograph of the Hellenic town of Ai Khanum	46
Pottery vessel in the form of a humped-backed bull from tomb 18 at Marlik, National Museum of Iran. Photograph J.E. Curtis	113
Horse's breastplate from Hasanlu, National Musem of Iran. Photograph J.E.Curtis	114
Bronze drinking-cup in the form of a ram's head from Hasanlu, National Museum of Iran. Photograph J. E. Curtis	115
Dish in "Egyptian blue" with bird's head on rim, from excavations at Ziwiyeh in 1977, National Museum of Iran. Photograph J. E. Curtis	117
Drawings of seals and a sealing from Tepe Nush-i Jan	120
Drawings of possible Achaemenid period material from Tepe Nush-i Jan	122
The base and the top part of a bronze stand found in an Elamite tomb at Arjan, National Museum of Iran. Photograph J. E. Curtis	124

Acknowledgements

This proceedings of the first series and the planning of future series have developed with the support and invaluable advice of a number of people. The editors would like to thank Fatema Soudavar Farmanfarmaian, Ardavan Farmanfarmaian, Susan Salmanpour, Narguess Farzad and Nazi Mahlouji.

This book could not have been published without the dedication and expertise of Parvis Fozooni, who typeset and formatted all the papers and scanned the images.

The editors are also grateful to Iradj Bagherzade and staff at I.B.Tauris for their support.

Introduction

Vesta Sarkhosh Curtis (The British Museum)
and
Sarah Stewart (The London Middle East Institute at SOAS)

This volume contains a series of six lectures delivered at the School of Oriental and African Studies in the spring and summer terms 2004 organised by the London Middle East Institute at SOAS and the British Museum. As a result of the tremendous success of the first series, the Soudavar Foundation has generously agreed to support further series.

The Lecture series "The Idea of Iran: from Eurasian Steppe to Persian Empire" was prompted by a desire to explore the multifarious ideas about the notion of "Iran" beginning with the origins of Achaemenid hegemony. The first half of the title was borrowed from Gherardo Gnoli's collection of essays entitled *The Idea of Iran* (Rome, 1989), in which he discussed the complex question of Iran and its national identity from a historical perspective. The title of the present volume, *The Birth of the Persian Empire*, broadens the approach and takes into account research undertaken during the past fifteen years. It enables scholars from different subject disciplines; archaeology, history, religion and philology, to debate various issues concerning the nature and origin of Iran as a political, religious and/or ethnic entity.

The importance of Iranian studies cannot be underestimated. It is our hope to re-invigorate the subject, which for many years has been neglected. This would require ending its vulnerability due to changes in the international political environment or fluctuations related to government funding. As well as providing a forum for academic debate, our aim in organising this series is to attract young people to the field of Iranian studies and encourage them to think beyond contemporary geo-political boundaries. Iranian cultural heritage spans a vast area of what is now a region divided by nation-state borders, religious ideology and political conflict. There is a need for a coherent approach to Iran's historical cultures that is free from contemporary pressures to reinterpret the past in ways that conform to present norms of whatever nature.

We are extremely fortunate to be able to bring together a collection of papers by eminent scholars, all of whom are experts in their field. The editors have, therefore, respected the fact that their research sometimes involves pushing back the boundaries of conventional terminology and challenging existing translations.

The first paper by Daniel Potts deals with the contribution of the Elamites to the formation of an ethnic and cultural identity which is usually associated with the foundation of the Persian Empire under Cyrus the Great in 550 BCE. The author discusses the question of "cultural diversity" in the pre-Achaemenid period and the role of the Elamites as the non Iranian inhabitants of present-day southwestern Iran. The Elamite contribution to the culture and civilisation of Iran has been neglected. The main core of the Elamite cultural zone, according to Potts, consisted of Elam and Anshan, which comprised the Deh Luran plain, Bushire, and Marv Dasht in Fars. Anshan consisted of the eastern highland, with the city of Anshan located at the site of Tal-e Malyan, north of modern Shiraz in southern Iran. This site was excavated in the 1970s under the directorship of Professor William M. Sumner of Ohio State University. Elam also included Shushan, the area around Susa. It was within a Neo-Elamite cultural and political milieu in the region of Anshan, modern Fars, that Cyrus the Great and his family emerged. Potts discusses the genealogy of Cyrus in connection with his royal title "king of Anshan", which appears in the Cyrus Cylinder. He dismisses any connection between Kurash of Anshan and Kurash of Parsumash, the latter mentioned in Assyrian annals of Assurbanipal of 643 BCE, and argues that Cyrus may have been "an Anshanite, with an Elamite name". Potts argues that inspiration for the cultural and political unity of Iran came from the Elamites rather than the Persians. When Darius seized the throne after the death of Cambyses, he replaced "the Anshanite Teispid family of Cyrus" with "the Persian line of Achaemenes". This gave cause to a rebellion by three Elamites, Açina, Martiya and Athamaita, as described by King Darius in his Behistun inscription.

From Elam and the west we move east to Central Asia and the Hindu Kush. In Chapter 2, Frantz Grenet discusses the geography of the *Avesta* with particular reference to the list of countries contained in the *Vidēvdād*. The paucity of evidence regarding the homeland of the prophet Zarathuštra and his early followers has resulted in a variety of scholarly theories based on the tantalisingly scant allusions and references contained in the *Young Avesta*. The positioning of the countries listed in the *Vidēvdād* is an important factor in determining when the migration of Avestan peoples from east to west began and, therefore, whether or not the early Achaemenids are likely to have been Zoroastrians. At the centre of the debate has been the location of the country Ragha referred to in the *Vidēvdād*, which has been variously identified with the holy city of Ragā in ancient Media (modern Ray near Tehran), and a region to the east of the Iranian plateau with a cognate name.

Grenet approaches the subject from an archaeological as well as a philological perspective. He looks at the natural topography of the region in relation to the text asking: "Do the descriptive words of the *Avesta* make sense on the ground." Each of the countries in the list is blighted with an Ahrimanic plague and so it is possible to speculate for example, where would winter have lasted ten months? Where is there likely to have been excessive heat? Where did non-Aryan masters rule and where grew "thorns fatal to cows"? The basis for Grenet's discussion is the logical sequence of the countries contained in the *Vidēvdād* list according to their geographic location. He charts the progress of this sequence with reference to the arguments presented by Gerhardo Gnoli, Willem Vogelsang, Helmut Humbach and Michael Witzel and traces the process by which the Median city of Ragā came to be associated with Zarathuštra's legend. In the second part of his paper Grenet proposes his own sequence in which the countries of the *Vidēvdād* are divided into four groups fanning out from around the same area which is that of "Airyanem Vaējah of the Good River" (central Afghanistan). After identifying the location of the "Good River", he gives a detailed analysis of each of the four groups of countries with reference to the geography of the region and textual sources including the ancient *Yašts*.

The idea of Iran from a religious perspective is addressed by both Oktor Skjærvø and Albert de Jong. The question of whether or not the early Achaemenid kings were Zoroastrian has long been a subject of scholarly debate and raises the important question of how and when the *Avesta*, a collection of oral texts compiled in an eastern Iranian dialect, came to be understood, adopted and interpreted by priests in the west. The religion of the Achaemenid kings, therefore, is directly linked to the broader question of east/west relations during the early Achaemenid period, and the time immediately preceding it, and to whether or not we can see in the religion of this period a coherence that can be said to contribute to a sense of Iranian identity.

One of the advances of modern scholarship in the field of Zoroastrianism is research into the character and composition of oral texts. The corpus of Zoroastrian extant literature is small. It had been in oral transmission for well over a millennium before being written down in the mid-Sasanian period by which time, with the probable exception of the *Gāthās* and ancient prayers, it had been through many redactions and translations. In discussing the religion of the Achaemenid religion both Skjærvø and de Jong give insights into the difficulty of dealing with such texts. While both scholars are broadly in agreement that the Achaemenids were Zoroastrians, they reach their conclusions via very different routes and do not agree on certain issues. For example Skjærvø suggests there are parallels between Avestan texts and Persian inscriptions that show that the king (Darius) "...unites in one and the same person the functions of supreme king, prototype Yima ..., and supreme sacrificer, prototype Zarathuštra." Conversely, de Jong maintains that the roles of king and priest were entirely separate: "There is no evidence at all to suggest that the Persian kings were in any way interested in possessing authority in religious matters ...."

Oktor Skjærvø deals with the question of the religion of the Achaemenid kings by looking at the religious significance of the Persian inscriptions with reference to Avestan texts. He finds the parallels so convincing that it soon becomes a foregone conclusion that the Achaemenid kings were Zoroastrian.

The more interesting question, in Skjærvo's view, is whether the early Achaemenids had become Zoroastrians or whether the faith was part of their religious heritage.

Skjærvø begins by outlining the Zoroastrian worldview with reference to the *Gāthās* and the *Yasna haptaŋhāiti*; Ahura Mazdā as creator, the assault upon the cosmos and the central ritual of the sacrifice by which the world is renewed and the powers of darkness banished. He draws our attention to Avestan *sə̄ṇgha-* "announcement" which is used with reference both to Ahura Mazdā and the sacrificer. Whereas the announcements of the former are effective in fighting the Lie, the sacrificer, through his announcements becomes a *saošiiaṇt-*, "revitaliser", one who will help to rejuvenate the world. It is these quintessentially Zoroastrian elements contained in the *Gāthās* that provide the basis for the parallels that Skjærvø finds in the "announcements" of the king in his inscriptions. For example at Naqsh-e Rostam Darius is shown sacrificing to Ahura Mazdā whom he acknowledges as the creator of the ordered cosmos. Here, as in the *Yašts*, the sacrifice is a reciprocal arrangement between man and god. At Behistun the king declares himself an enemy of the Lie in various contexts. He also shows himself to be responsible for maintaining social order and the welfare of the land, cattle and men under his rule. In the final section of his paper, Skjærvø focuses on the similarity between the role of the king and that of Zarathuštra. In the *Fravardīn Yašt*, the prophet functions as priest, charioteer and husbandman. It is these functions that Skjærvø suggests were assimilated by the king: "whom we have already seen sacrificing, is, of course, a supreme charioteer and fighter, but he also pays attention to the well-being of his subjects and his land".

In Chapter 4, *The Contribution of the Magi*, De Jong focuses his discussion on what is meant by Zoroastrianism at the time of the early Achaemenids beginning with the interesting concept of magic and the meaning of the term *magus*. With reference to Greek sources he illustrates the way in which the word and the concept acquired an ambiguity being understood both to mean a Zoroastrian priest and a sorcerer. While there were some who appeared to have a correct understanding of the function of a Persian priest, for others the term *magus* was associated with "private, non-social types of ritual activity, often with sinister overtones, harnessing unseen powers to reach concrete goals".

The Magi were the repositories of the religion, at least according to the available evidence, and De Jong proceeds to trace images of the Magi through the Iranian traditions of western Iran where the term is attested from the Achaemenid period onwards. In so doing he challenges the view, long held by some scholars, that the Magi were a Median tribe. He also discusses the subject of Gaumata the *magus* suggesting that Darius deliberately used this title to emphasise Gaumata's priestly status thereby challenging his right to the throne. Evidence from the Elamite Persepolis tablets agrees with Greek sources as well as the later history of the priesthood in depicting the magi as ritual specialists, the role with which we are most familiar. They were also responsible for transmitting the oral religious texts and played an important role in education and as theologians. It is priestly speculation, during the Achaemenid period, concerning the division of time that De Jong suggests is the most important contribution of the Magi and one which was to have lasting impact on the Zoroastrian religion and Iranian civilisation.

Shapur Shahbazi attacks the theory that the idea of Iran went back only to the Sasanian period and argues that the idea of Iran as a national entity had already originated in the Avestan period. "The empire of Iranians" was a solid concept in the Avestan period and did not, as suggested by Gerhardo Gnoli, start in early third century CE with the Sasanian king Ardashir I. Shahbazi shows that Professor Gnoli's idea was already formulated in the second half of the 19th century by the German Iranist Friedrich Spiegel. Shahbazi firmly believes that there is no reason to support such a hypothesis. He sees the evidence for the existence of a sense of unity, "of belonging to a nation" in the Avestan hymn dedicated to Mithra (*Mihr Yašt*). The idea of Iran was known to the Achaemenids, but as the Achaemenid empire included non Iranians as well as Iranians, it was not possible to use the term "empire of Iran". However, he argues, that at the time of Darius, the Iranian (Aryan) countries formed a unit that consisted of Parthia, Aria, Bactria, Sogdia, Choresmia and Drangiana. In the Parthian period the province of Nišapur, with its capital Abaršahr, was occasionally called Ērānšahr, and according to some Islamic sources, even Sistān was part of it. The Parthian empire, like that of the Achaemenids, included various provinces with a non Iranian population, e.g. Mesopotamia. It was therefore not possible to use the term "the empire of the Iranians", but this did not mean that the term disappeared. The re-emergence of the term Ērānšahr in the Sasanian period was necessary in order to unify all the Iranian peoples. It was a political move to restore national pride amongst the Parthians, Persians and other Iranians. Under Shapur I, when large areas of the empire, inhabited by non Iranian, were conquered, the royal title "King of Kings of Iran" was extended to "King of Kings of Iran and un-Iran".

John Curtis' paper underpins the cultural diversity which contributed to the formation of Iranian culture and civilisation. He deals with the archaeological evidence in Iron Age Iran in the second and first millennia BCE, the so-called period of migrations of people speaking Indo-Iranian languages. He discusses the evidence from a number of important sites including Marlik Tepe in northern Iran and Hasanlu in western Iran. He discusses Assyrian influence as a result of the campaigns of the Late Assyrian kings in the Zagros Mountains of western Iran which are described in Assyrian annals. Although Assyrian influence seems to be absent at Hasanlu, it is evident in the area of Bukan, where the design on polychrome tiles include human-headed winged figures, lions, ibexes and birds of prey.

Although little is known about the material culture of the Medes, they first appear on the historical scene in the 9th century BCE and Assyrian reliefs of the 8th century BCE depict Median fortresses. While some scholars have denied the existence of Median art, more recently young scholars have re-addressed the problem and have tried to show that the Median material culture can be identified through artefacts and costumes shown on the reliefs at Persepolis.

The Median-period site of Nush-i Jan in western Iran, its architecture and material culture is examined in detail, which leads to the suggestion that the site was perhaps closed down around 550 BCE. If so, this would indicate, contrary to the view held by some scholars, that there was "no hiatus in the occupation of Median sites." From the pre-Achaemenid evidences, Curtis draws together the various contributions to development of the Achaemenid art style. "The tradition of stone bas-reliefs...well-known in Assyria, ...finds a completely different sort of expression at Persepolis. The reliefs are on the outsides of buildings, rather than the inside, and the composition is exclusively Persian." He concurs with the suggestion that there was Persian influence in Greece, particularly noticeable in the Parthenon friezes.

1

Cyrus the Great and the Kingdom of Anshan

D.T. Potts (University of Sydney)

Introduction

The fact that a lecture series on the "Idea of Iran" commences with the Elamite contribution to Iranian identity is, to say the least, anomalous. For it is no exaggeration to state that, traditionally, the subject of Iranian cultural identity has been examined through an Indo-European or more specifically Indo-Iranian lens, leaving the Elamites entirely out of the equation.[1] In the course of preparing this essay I was led to a re-examination of Cyrus the Great's relationship with the kingdom of Anshan, and more broadly with the Elamite cultural crucible in which, as I will argue, what we call the Persian empire was forged. To begin with, however, I would like to say a few words about the study of Cyrus, the Persians and the Elamites.

Working broadly from a 19th century model of Indo-European origins which has been gradually modified over the years, most scholars have either tacitly assumed or actively asserted that Iranian-language speakers were not native to the area we call the Iranian Plateau; rather, they were immigrants. This is a view which is based generally on notions, few of which are demonstrable in fact, about the existence and location of an original Indo-European homeland, with the implicit understanding that wherever this may have been, it most certainly lay *outside* of Iran proper, be it on the steppes of the Ukraine and southern Russia, in the Urals, in Central Asia or, as Lord Renfrew has argued, in Anatolia.[2]

Coupled with this belief is an assertion that Iranian speakers – proto-Iranians, as they are sometimes referred to, and later Medes, Persians and perhaps others – did not enter Iran until the 2nd or early 1st millennium BCE. Greyware, the cult of fire and etymologically Old Iranian personal names in Mesopotamian and Neo-Elamite cuneiform sources have all been adduced as cultural markers which flag the arrival of this new population. The fact that no cultural uniformity can be demonstrated across Iran in either the late 2nd or the early 1st millennium BCE, however, has scarcely diminished the zeal with which some scholars seem to pursue those elusive first Iranians on Iranian soil.

Of course, a belief that the Iranians were not present in Iran until some time in the 2nd or early 1st millennium BCE in no way conflicts with a view that the region was nonetheless inhabited prior to their arrival. Archaeological evidence of settlement in Iran extends well back into the Pleistocene period and certainly there is ample evidence of Neolithic, Chalcolithic and Bronze Age occupation across the length and breadth of Iran,[3] proving that the region was inhabited long before the first people bearing Iranian names – mentioned in Assyrian cuneiform sources of the 9th century BCE – appeared in the western Zagros mountains on the eastern frontier of Assyria.[4] It is important to stress, however, that the archaeological assemblages of Neolithic, Chalcolithic and Bronze Age Iran are far from uniform. On the contrary, they provide ample evidence of cultural diversity in pre-Iron Age Iran. Ceramic styles alone should never be used to identify ethnic groups, but when ceramics, architecture, seals, metals and the other forms of material culture that have survived in the archaeological record show such marked regionalism as is the case in Iran, I think it is fair to interpret that diversity of material accoutrements as a genuine reflection of *cultural* diversity.

This cultural diversity may also be reflected in the toponymy of Bronze and Iron Age Iran. From the time when regions east of Mesopotamia begin to appear in the cuneiform record in the late 3rd millennium BCE to the period of the Assyrian campaigns in the Zagros and Khuzestan, we see a substantial increase in the number of place names and ethnic names which must, judging by the context in which they occur, have lain to the east of the Tigris, even if most remain unidentified. The summary accounts of Tiglath-Pileser III's campaigns in the Zagros region, for example, include references to no fewer than 41 different toponyms.[5] Of course a multiplicity of place names does not necessarily denote a multiplicity of cultures or differentiated social groups, but I think that, on analogy with what we know from the Achaemenid period, when Herodotus could characterise the provinces of the Persian empire by dress and armament, we may take the diversity of material culture attested archaeologically, in tandem with the numerous place names and ethnic names known from the cuneiform sources, as an indication of a fairly high degree of group differentiation in Iran at this time.

You will note, however, that while I have used the term "cultural diversity" I have intentionally said nothing about ethnicity or linguistic diversity. Over half a century ago the anthropologist Franz Boas[6] explicitly warned of the dangers of conflating what he referred to as "race, language and culture", which we might nowadays prefer to call biological, linguistic and cultural diversity. I do not share the enthusiasm of some archaeologists for speculating on the linguistic affiliations of archaeological cultures, whether Indo-European or otherwise, having never had a conversation with a potsherd or stone tool. Just how linguistically diverse Iran may have been down through the pre-Achaemenid Iron Age is impossible to say. Was it like the highlands of Papua

New Guinea, one of the most linguistically diverse regions in the world,[7] where mutually unintelligible languages are today spoken in virtually adjacent intermontane valleys? It certainly wasn't monolingual. We have no idea about linguistic diversity in Iran until we reach the late 3rd millennium BCE. From this period, however, we have Sumerian and Akkadian texts which at least provide us with some information on the situation in western Iran.

To be sure, there were almost certainly groups in which languages were spoken which have since died out. Many of the personal names of individuals said to come from Shimashki, Marhashi, Zabshali, Tukrish and other eastern areas in Mesopotamian sources cannot be classified linguistically as Elamite, Kassite or Hurrian and must reflect no longer extant languages, the names of which we do not even know. This would explain the occurrence of names of individuals such as Arzana, described as "Anshanite" in an Ur III text from Lagash; Si/Ziringu, identified as a Shimashkian; and most of the 46 individuals identified in cuneiform sources as Marhashians, none of whom has an Elamite or otherwise classifiable name.[8]

Elam

It is against this backdrop that we must situate Elam and the Elamites (Fig. 1). Even though we have few Elamite texts prior to the late 2nd millennium BCE, the frequent attestation of Elam and the Elamites in Mesopotamian sources from the mid-3rd millennium onwards and the history of Mesopotamian–Elamite military conflict, which can be traced for over 2000 years, both suggest that the Elamites were one of the most important of the indigenous groups[9] in Iran before the formation of the Persian empire. We are, I think, therefore fully justified in at least canvassing the possibility that Elam and the Elamites contributed something which may have been overlooked in previous studies of the formation of Iranian identity and the "idea of Iran". To begin with, however, it may be helpful to say something more precise about the geographical parameters of this inquiry.

Defining the limits of Elam and the Elamite cultural and linguistic sphere is never going to be more than an approximation. If we look for written sources – cuneiform texts, not all of which are contemporary – in conjunction with architectural and ceramic coherence, then the area more or less coterminous with the modern provinces of Khuzestan and the western half of Fars can be considered the Elamite core area. Beginning in the northeast, a Middle Elamite brick of Hutelutush-Inshushinak was discovered only a few years ago on the surface of Tul-e Afghani near Lordegan in the Bakhtiyari mountains,[10] while to the northwest silver vessels with late Neo-Elamite inscriptions on them are known from the Kalmakareh hoard found near Pol-e Dokhtar.[11] The most easterly, pre-Achaemenid Elamite texts come from Tal-e Malyan, on the Marv Dasht plain in central Fars,[12] while the southernmost examples come from

Tul-e Peytul, ancient Liyan, near modern Bushire on the Persian Gulf.[13] The westernmost Elamite texts come from Susa,[14] and in spite of the fact that ceramics and other typically Elamite examples of material culture have been excavated at Tepe Farukhabad and Tepe Musiyan in the Deh Luran plain,[15] which are even further west, no epigraphic finds have yet been made there to my knowledge.

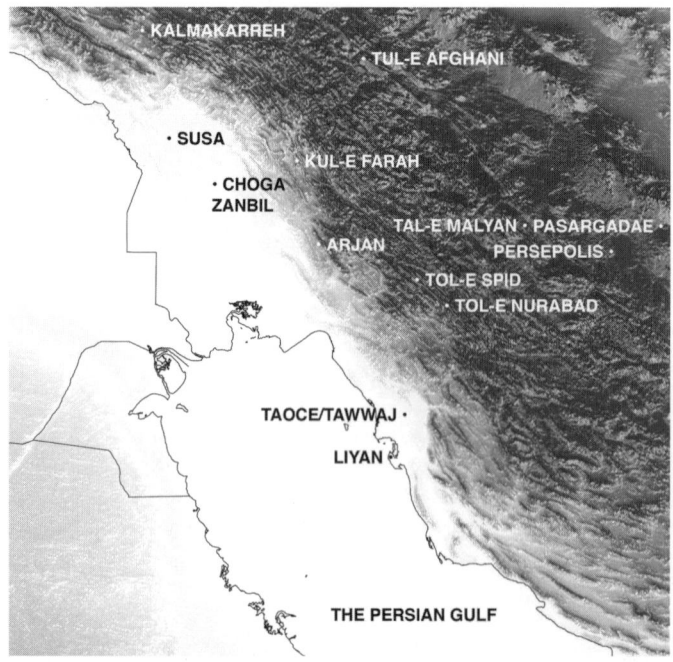

Fig. 1. Map showing the principal sites in southwestern Iran mentioned in the text.

Thus, very crudely, we could delimit the core Elamite cultural zone by circumscribing the area between the Deh Luran plain, Bushire, Marv Dasht and Tul-e Afghani, bearing in mind that the limits of this area will have fluctuated through time. Moreover, we know that this area was identified by more than just one name, but perhaps the two most prominent, supra-regional names here were Elam and Anshan. Although scholars of the late 19th and early 20th century such as de Harlez, Sayce, Halévy and Delattre speculated unsuccessfully on the location of Anshan,[16] and Prášek insisted that the Anshan of the Gudea inscriptions and that of the Cyrus Cylinder (see below) were different,[17] the discovery of inscribed bricks at Tal-e Malyan in the early 1970s proved that this was the location of Anshan the city,[18] while Anshan the region was presumably located around it. Anshan thus constituted the eastern, highland component of what has often been interpreted as a bipartite Elamite state,[19] with Shushan, the area around Susa, its most important western component. Numerous other toponyms, such as Huhnur, Bashime or Mishime and Ayapir,[20] were probably located between Anshan and Shushan, but their precise location is not important for us at the moment. For the present, this definition of the Elamite core area, though crude, suffices to illustrate that a significant overlap exists between it and one of the most important areas of ancient Iranian identity, namely Parsa or Persis, the heartland of the Persians and later Sasanians, with Pasargadae, Persepolis, Naqsh-e Rostam and Istakhr all clustered in close proximity to each other.

In and of itself this proximity, or indeed overlap, need signify nothing. After all, one can point to numerous pre-modern archaeological cultures which were, so to speak, genetically unrelated to those that later occupied the same territory. Connections between successive cultures occupying the same territorial niche must be proven, not assumed, a view which is surely relevant to our examination of the relationship between Elam and Parsa. I also believe that we should acknowledge the existence of very different sorts of data which may be telling us very different things about the relationship between Elamites and Persians. In other words, we may be able to discern links between Elam and later Iranian cultural manifestations on a variety of levels, not all of which should be valued equally.

One could say for example that, at a very basic level, the skills of Elamite metalsmiths, architects, potters and artists all contributed to the fund of technological experience and wisdom from which all subsequent inhabitants of southwestern Iran have benefited. In a sense this is not wrong, but clearly the very generic skills implied may not signify very much. Nor does the fact, stated in Darius Susa f (DSf), that the stone used to make the columns for Darius' palace at Susa came from the Elamite village of Hapiradush or Abiradu necessarily signify much. This can hardly be taken as evidence of an Elamite contribution to Achaemenid stoneworking, particularly as the text goes on to tell us that the masons who actually worked the stone were Ionians and Sardians.[21]

The evidence of writing and administrative technology is another area which has been explored over the years with a view to demonstrating an Old Persian debt to Elamite literacy and accountancy. It is now generally accepted that the Old Persian writing system was developed, indeed "invented", in the reign of Darius.[22] Clearly Neo-Elamite was the written language at Susa and in the highlands around Izeh-Malamir during the years leading up to the crystallisation of the Persian empire, and the very fact that Darius' Behistun monument began with an Elamite text, which was later rendered in Akkadian and Old Persian, strongly suggests that Elamite was an important source of inspiration for the drafters of the Old Persian syllabary. At another level, moreover, Elamite account-technical praxis, best exemplified by the fortification and treasury texts recovered at Persepolis, reveals an unquestionable Elamite legacy in Old Persian administrative procedure. The very scribes themselves were probably still Elamites, writing in Elamite, yet serving Persian masters. The onomasticon of the texts, on the other hand, shows clearly that the administrative personnel receiving rations and running the show were largely endowed with Persian names, and indeed Manfred Mayrhofer's analysis of the onomastic evidence in the Persepolis fortification texts showed that only about 10 per cent of the c. 2,000 individuals named in the texts bore Elamite names.[23] Statistics such as these make it moot whether the Achaemenids adopted the duck-headed bow from the Elamites, as Hinz suggested, and the curious dagger with extended guard, known as the "Elamite dagger", worn by many Persian noblemen (Fig. 2) on the Persepolis reliefs.[24]

Fig. 2. Persian nobleman at Persepolis wearing the 'Elamite' dagger.

Similarly, the fact that Elamite deities continued to receive rations at Persepolis is of questionable significance in light of Darius' Behistun inscription, which calls the Elamites "felons" who "do not worship Ahuramazda" (DB §72). Clearly then, one ought not to look to formal religion for signs of an Elamite legacy in Iranian religious practice. In many ways, if one wishes to adopt a cynical perspective, all of the traits just mentioned, whether daggers or scribal conventions, can be regarded as just so many cultural epiphenomena: undoubted examples of Elamite survivals in the brave new, Iranian world of 6th and 5th century Parsa, but epiphenomena nonetheless which fail to convince one of any meaningful Elamite contribution to the idea of Iran or Iranian identity. But here I wish to approach the problem from quite a different standpoint, not from the highly visible cultural signature of Achaemenid Persia, i.e. the Persia forged by Darius, the first "true" Achaemenid, but from the much less well-known vantage point of Cyrus II, or Cyrus the Great, and his family, about whom much has been written but less is in fact known.

Cyrus the Great

At the outset, let me make it clear that I do not intend to undertake an exegesis of the Classical and late antique sources: Herodotus, Xenophon, Ctesias, Dinon, Diodorus, Strabo, Justin or Nicholas of Damascus.[25] Rather, I wish to look at the Babylonian sources which are far closer in date to the lifetime of Cyrus himself. These are: the so-called Cyrus Cylinder, discovered by Hormuzd Rassam in the Esagila, or great temple of Marduk, at Babylon in 1879 and published the following year by Rawlinson, to which we must add BIN II 32, in the Yale Babylonian Collection, which duplicates lines 36–45; second, the Nabonidus Chronicle, known from a large tablet in the British Museum (BM 34381) and first published in 1924;[26] and finally, UET 1.194 from Ur. Of these three texts, the Cyrus Cylinder is the only one to give us genealogical information. In this text, composed almost certainly by the Marduk priesthood at Babylon,[27] Cyrus is called "son of Kambuziya [Cambyses], great king, king of Anshan, grandson of Kurash [Cyrus], great king, king of Anshan, great-grandson of Shishpish [Teispes], great king, king of Anshan".[28] In addition to the Cyrus Cylinder's testimony on the family of Cyrus the Great, we should also remember that the Ur text published by Gadd refers to Cyrus as "son of Kambuziya, king of Anshan",[29] while the Nabonidus Chronicle, as well as the Nabonidus cylinder from Sippar, calls him, in the first instance, "king of Anshan".[30]

The significance of this genealogy resides in the references to Anshan and in the personal names attested. Yet in spite of the fact that these sources are well-known and straightforward, they have been consistently, if unconsciously, embellished by most commentators who read them through what might be termed a Herodotean or Hellenic lens. Examples of what I mean abound and can be found in the literature extending right back to the 1880s when the Cyrus Cylinder was first published. Without making any pretence at completeness, I offer merely a selection to illustrate what I mean.

- Nöldeke suggested that Anshan was the *Familiensitz* of Cyrus[31] and the *first Achaemenids*.[32]
- Prášek assumed that the original kingdom of the Achaemenids was limited to the tribal territory of the Pasargadai and that the title "king of Anshan" reflected the extension of *Achaemenid rule* to other areas, though he disputed that the Anshan attested in the 3rd millennium sources was the same as that of the Achaemenid period.[33]
- Wiesehöfer wrote in his entry on Fars in the *Encyclopaedia Iranica* of the formation of an "independent kingdom of Anshan under a *Persian* dynasty".[34]
- Hansman wrote of the "*Achaemenian Kings* of Anshan".[35]
- Dandamaev wrote in the entry on Cyrus in the *Encyclopaedia Iranica*: "That Cyrus' ancestors had ruled the *Persian tribes* for several generations is clear from both his inscriptions and contemporary historical reports".[36]
- De Miroschedji has argued that Cyrus' forebears founded a *Persian* kingdom of Anshan and that Elamite heritage, in the form of an ancient title, was adopted by the "premiers souverains perses".[37]
- Waters, while maintaining that Cyrus and Darius were unrelated, characterised the "coup" effected by Darius and his heirs vis-à-vis the family of Cyrus as a continuation of "*Persian rule*".[38]
- Briant declared in his *Histoire de l'empire perse* that the first *Persian* kingdom arose in the territory of Anshan.[39]
- Stronach has stated that "the Cyrus Cylinder not only provides what is arguably a complete list of those who preceded Cyrus as kings of Anshan, but evidence, in addition, for the conceivably continuous, independent condition of *the early Persian kingdom of Anshan* from the time that it was first founded, presumably somewhere in the years following the fall of Susa to the Assyrians in 646 B.C.".[40]

We thus have authors imputing *Achaemenid* (Nöldeke, Prášek, Hansman, Vallat) or *Persian* rule (de Miroschedji, Waters) to Cyrus' ancestors; writing about a *Persian* kingdom of Anshan (Briant, Wiesehöfer, Stronach); and declaring that Cyrus' family exercised sovereignty over *Persian* tribes (Dandamaev). In fact, I believe all of these scholars, and many more like them, have attributed a meaning to the Babylonian testimony which is unjustified. For the sources refer only to the land of Anshan, *never* qualifying it as a Persian domain or Cyrus and his family as Achaemenids. Cyrus himself is never identified as a Persian king of Anshan, but rather a king of Anshan plain and simple.

Anshan, as we have seen, was the name of an Elamite city and region which, from the 3rd millennium BCE onwards, formed one of the core areas of highland Elam. In the 21st century BCE, two kings of the Ur III dynasty – Shulgi and Shu-Sin – alternately campaigned against and gave their daughters in marriage to the "governors" (**ensí**) of Anshan.[41] The title "king of Anshan", given in the Cyrus Cylinder to Cyrus' father, grandfather and great-grandfather, is first attested in the early years of the 2nd millennium. A seal impression on a tablet from Susa bears the seal of Imazu, son of Kindadu, who is called **lugal Anshan**.[42] If this Kindadu is the same person as the Kindattu mentioned in the so-called Awan/Shimashki king list from Susa, then Imazu was the son of the Shimashkian king who contributed greatly to the fall of the Third Dynasty of Ur and who is referred to in a hymn to Ishbi-Erra, founder of the First Dynasty of Isin, as the "man of Elam" (**lú-Elam**^{ki}).[43] Several generations later, the title "king of Anshan and Susa" and "priest of Anshan and Susa" are attested in the inscriptions of Ebarti II, another ruler of Shimashki.[44] An unnamed "king of Anshan" is also attested in a year formula of Iddin-Dagan, who reigned from 1974 to 1954 BCE, according to the middle chronology, and married his daughter Matum-niatum to a king of Anshan, possibly the aforementioned Imazu.[45]

Around 1400 BCE, the Elamite line of kings beginning with Kidinu began calling themselves "king of Susa and Anshan". These "Kidinuids" were followed by a dynasty claiming descent from Igi-Halki, which likewise boasted of having inherited the "kingship of Susa and Anshan (Anzan)", whereas Untash-Napirisha, the builder of Choga Zanbil and one of the most famous kings in Elamite history, called himself "king of Anshan and Susa", thus reversing the twin toponyms again.[46] The apparent significance of the position of Susa and Anshan in the title lay not in the primacy of one or the other city at any given point in time, but rather in the intended audience for whom the inscription conveying the title was written. A study of the texts containing this title reveals that those written in Elamite always mention Anshan first, while those in Akkadian put Susa first,[47] where, in fact, Akkadian was the more common written language owing to the site's long history of close political ties with Mesopotamia from the 3rd millennium onwards.

But to some extent all of this is ancient history, or certainly was for the ancestors of Cyrus the Great, and to explore the use of the title "king of Anshan" for Cyrus and his forebears in the Cyrus Cylinder and the Nabonidus sources we must consider several of the slightly earlier, late Assyrian military-historical sources that are far closer in date to the period in which Cyrus' ancestors actually lived.

Elam and Assyria

Much attention has been concentrated on the texts reporting on Assurbanipal's campaigns against the Elamites. Another text which has been repeatedly discussed but is still, in my opinion, largely unappreciated comes from the reign of Assurbanipal's grandfather, Sennacherib.

To begin with, it should be noted that, by Sennacherib's time, the titulary of the Elamite kings no longer included Anshan, as in "king of Susa and Anshan" or "king of Anshan and Susa". Indeed, the Babylonian Chronicle consistently refers to the contemporaries of Sennacherib as "king of Elam".[48] Putting these two facts together we might suggest that Elam, in this period, comprised Susa and its hinterland, with the provinces of Nagite, Hilmu, Billatu and Hupapanu, all described as "provinces of Elam" on a prism of Sennacherib now in the Oriental Institute, as well as some important cities like the so-called "royal city" of Madaktu, but that the *political* state of Elam no longer included Anshan. In fact, this interpretation is confirmed later in the same prism inscription of Sennacherib where the events of 691 BCE are described. There we learn that Umman-menanu or Humban-nimena III, called "king of Elam", "gathered to himself a large body of confederates – (the men) of Parsua, Anzan, Pashiru, Ellipi, the whole of Chaldaea, and all the Aramaeans" prior to the battle of Halule.[49]

Twenty years ago Briant suggested that Persian participation in this alliance – which he inferred from the presence of the toponym Parsua – may have come at a high price for the Elamites of the lowlands. He felt that the Persians may only have joined Humban-nimena in return for an acknowledgement of Persian territorial sovereignty over Fars.[50] In fact, notwithstanding the long debate on the location of Parsua,[51] such an interpretation of Sennacherib's rather laconic inscription is by no means obligatory and I would prefer to take a far more straightforward approach to our source. Parsua, after all, is simply named as one member of the anti-Assyrian coalition. It is given no prominence whatsoever, and for this reason I think the circumstantial conclusions drawn by Briant from his reading of the Sennacherib prism are unjustified. What is striking, however, is the fact that Anshan, of which we have heard so little since the Middle Elamite period, appears here as an independent entity, one of Elam's confederates, and this I take to be significant. This suggests to me that while the "kingdom of Anshan and Susa" was no longer a reality,[52] a highland Elamite kingdom or recognised entity led by a chief and identifiable as "Anshan" *did* exist. And it is here, I would argue, that we have a geopolitical locus in which to place the line of Anshanite kings enumerated in the Cyrus Cylinder, even if, chronologically, the eldest ancestor of Cyrus, Shishpish, may not have reigned until about 50 years after the battle of Halule.

The basic point, however, is that the highland polity of Anshan that allied itself with the lowland state of Elam in 691 was the polity in which the family of Cyrus dwelt. Thus, contrary to such scholars as de Miroschedji and, more recently, W. Henkelman, I would see neither the use of the geographical term "Anshan" by Sennacherib nor the title "king of Anshan" in the Cyrus Cylinder and related inscriptions as in any way anachronistic or archaising.[53] Rather, I take the purport of Sennacherib's text to be that the allies of lowland Elam included no fewer than four distinct regions which are to be located in the Iranian highlands, i.e. Parsua, Anshan, Pashiru and Ellipi. And this suggests that, during Sennacherib's reign, a corona of areas can be distinguished outside the control of Elam, by then a lowland rump state based at Susa, which were nevertheless close enough to be worried by the Assyrian threat. One of these areas, I suggest, is the Anshan which the Cyrus Cylinder says was ruled by the ancestors of Cyrus the Great, an Anshan that was culturally *Elamite*, not Persian.

Furthermore, that such smaller polities did in fact exist, and did support local elites, is demonstrated clearly by archaeological and epigraphic evidence. For example, at Kul-e Farah, in northeastern Khuzestan, Elamite inscriptions refer to events such as the suppression of revolts and the capture of rebellious chieftains by Hanni, *kutur* or governor of Ayapir, who was a subordinate of a "king Shutur-Nahhunte, son of Indada".[54] Similarly, the rich burial from Arjan, recently discussed at length by both Stronach and Alvarez-Mon, and attributable to one Kidin-Hutran, son of Kurlush, thanks to inscribed objects found in the tomb (Fig. 3), points to the presence of yet another aristocratic line

Fig. 3. Bath-tub coffin of Kidin-Hutran, son of Kurlush, from the Neo-Elamite tomb at Arjan.

in the Behbehan area of eastern Khuzestan[55] to which a cylinder seal in the Louvre, bearing the legend "Parsirra, son of Kurlush" (Fig. 4), perhaps a brother of Kidin-Hutran, may also have belonged. And finally, the extraordinary Kalmakarah hoard found near Pol-e Dokhtar contained silver vessels inscribed in Elamite which mention no fewer than four kings of Samati.[56] This evidence almost certainly points to the existence during the 6th century BCE of a polity independent of Elamite Susa in what is today southern Luristan, probably in the southern portion of what had been referred to in Assyrian sources as Ellipi.

Although the accounts of Assurbanipal's devastating campaigns against Susa and a host of smaller cities in the mid-7th century

Fig. 4. Modern impression of a cylinder seal in the Louvre, bearing the legend "Parsirra, son of Kurlush" (after Amiet 1973).

BCE contain no reference to Anshan, this need not imply that an independent Anshan no longer existed. Indeed, Anshan's alliance with Elam in 691, culminating in the defeat at Halule, may well have deterred Anshan from proferring further aid to her western neighbour. One issue which must be discussed in this regard, however, arises from the latest edition of Assurbanipal's annals, Edition A from 643 BCE, which refers to two leaders from the Iranian sphere who sent tribute to the Assyrian monarch upon learning of his decisive victory over Elam. Following Assurbanipal's sack of Susa, Kurash, king of Parsumash, and Pizlume, king of Hudimiri, are both said to have acknowledged the Assyrian king with tribute, and Kurash even sent his son Arukku to Nineveh.[57]

In the past many scholars[58] have suggested that Kurash of Parsumash was the same as the Kurash, king of Anshan, mentioned in the Cyrus Cylinder. Chronologically it is entirely possible for Kurash of Parsumash to have been the grandfather of Cyrus the Great, notwithstanding recent attempts to reject this scenario,[59] but two points compel me now to consider this unlikely, indeed impossible. First, I believe it is clear from Sennacherib's prism that Parsua or Parsumash was distinct from Anshan,[60] the region that Cyrus' forefathers are said to have ruled. Second, Kurash is a personal name attested in both Neo-Babylonian sources from Babylon and in late Neo-Elamite texts from Susa,[61] and hence by no means rare or unique. For these reasons I would reject the equation of Kurash of Parsumash with Kurash of Anshan.[62] On the other hand, however, I believe that the well-known seal impressions from Persepolis, found on five of the Persepolis fortification tablets, which bear the legend "Kurash, the Anshanite, son of Shishpish [Teispes]" (Fig. 5), most certainly preserve for us the testimony of a seal which belonged to Cyrus' grandfather and namesake in the Cyrus Cylinder inscription.[63]

Fig. 5. Composite drawing of impressions on Persepolis fortification texts 596–695 and 2003 by M.C. Root and M.B. Garrison, bearing the legend "Kurash the Anshanite, son of Shishpish" (after Garrison and Root 1996).

Much has been written about this piece, and I find myself disagreeing with numerous scholars whom I greatly admire over the interpretation of this important document. Two years ago, for example, T. Cuyler Young discussed this seal impression and claimed that its allegedly Achaemenid style, which he said – following de Miroschedji's 1985 discussion of the iconography – dated it to the time of Darius I or slightly earlier, ruled out any possible association with Kurash of Parsumash.[64] By contrast, several years earlier, in one of the Lukonin seminars, Stronach asserted that the seal used to make this impression was "of a distinctly older date" than the Persepolis texts on which it had been impressed – obviously differing from Young and de Miroschedji on the interpretation of the seal's style. Stronach went on to suggest that, "while there can be no absolute certainty that 'Cyrus of Parsumash' was a direct ancestor of Cyrus the Great, there has to be ... a strong presumption that this was the case", concluding, "it is increasingly tempting to associate this seemingly assertive 'Persian' ruler with the spirited 'Anshanite' Cyrus (or Kurash) of the royal seal impression" from Persepolis.[65] Later, Stronach changed his mind: "Whatever ancestral relationship 'Kurash of Parsumash,' ... is likely to have had with the subsequent Persian rulers of Fars, I now think it preferable to assume that he ruled before the creation of the explicitly-named Anshanite dynasty of Teispes".[66] Still later, he ruled out categorically any equation of Cyrus I and Kurash of Parsumash.[67] And finally, in a recent paper, J. Alvarez-Mon states that Assurbanipal's sack of Susa "obliged Kurash (Cyrus), son of Teispes, to surrender his son Arukku to the court of Assurbanipal",[68] thus conflating the two Kurashes by equating the son of Teispes (Kurash of Anshan) with the father of Arukku (Kurash of Parsumash), inferences which are entirely unwarranted by the sources.

In my opinion, each of these scholars (with the exception of Stronach's recent statements) has conflated *precisely* what I have been at pains to keep separate, namely Parsua or Parsumash and Anshan. If Parsumash and Anshan were distinct entities, as I believe they most certainly were, the former predominantly ethnically Persian and the latter predominantly ethnically Elamite, then Kurash of Parsumash and Kurash the Anshanite cannot have been the same individual and the seal of Kurash the Anshanite cannot be attributed to Kurash of Parsumash. Moreover, following this line of reasoning, Kurash of Parsumash cannot have been a son of Teispes/Shishpish, for this filiation applies only to Kurash of Anshan. While I do not believe that de Miroschedji and Young are correct in their relatively late stylistic attribution of the seal that made these impressions, this does not of course mean that I would use an earlier date, as proposed by Stronach, to argue for the attribution of the seal to Kurash of Parsumash.[69] On the other hand, while I agree with Stronach on chronology, I believe that in his Lukonin lecture he uncharacteristically misunderstood what I consider a critical point.

For the Cyrus Cylinder does not call Kurash and his ancestors kings of Parsumash but kings of Anshan. Therefore I cannot accept that Kurash of Parsumash could possibly be the ancestor of Kurash, founder of the Persian empire, nor can I accept that Kurash and his Anshanite line were *Persian* or

Achaemenid in the sense implied by Stronach and assumed by Nöldeke, de Miroschedji, Vallat, Briant, Wiesehöfer, Dandamaev and many other scholars.

But to explain this more fully we must return to the genealogy of Cyrus the Great (Table 1). It has long been recognised that the genealogy of the Cyrus Cylinder differs from that given by Herodotus for Xerxes and the family of Darius or by Darius himself in the Behistun inscription. Since Rawlinson's original publication of the Cyrus Cylinder in 1880, a host of scholars have tried to harmonise these genealogies, mainly by conflating them. About six years ago, Cyrus' family tree was the subject of an exhaustive study by R. Rollinger who showed – convincingly, in my opinion – that the divergent traditions of Cyrus and Darius, which we see in effect merged by Herodotus, should certainly not be conflated.[70] Darius' attempt to co-opt Cyrus and his line, best exemplified by his forgery of the so-called Cyrus Murghab inscriptions at Pasargadae,[71] was nothing but a political manoeuvre.[72] If we follow the Cyrus Cylinder, however, then his eponymous ancestor was Shishpish, or Teispes, as Herodotus called him. Hence, the line of Cyrus should be qualified as "Shishpishid" or "Teispid", whereas that of Darius alone, descending from Achaemenes, should be properly considered "Achamenid".[73]

Cyrus cylinder	*Behistun*	*Herodotus*
Kurash [Cyrus II]	Darius	Xerxes
Kambuziya [Cambyses I]	Hystaspes	Darius
Kurash [Cyrus I]	Arsames	Hystaspes
Shishpish [Teispes]	Ariaramnes	Arsames
	Shishpish	Ariaramnes
	Achaemenes	Teispes
		Cyrus
		Cambyses
		Teispes
		Achaemenes

Table 1. Genealogies of Cyrus (Cyrus Cylinder), Darius (Bisotun) and Xerxes (Herodotus 7.11).

Recently, David Stronach wrote: "For those who are interested in the formation of the Achaemenid Persian empire it ... remains not a little mysterious that Cyrus I, Cyrus II, and even Cambyses II (530 BCE–520 BCE) can each be shown to have insisted on the 'Anshanite' identity of their ancestors".[74] I believe we can conclude that the members of this Teispid line were, just as Cyrus claims, and as Sayce and others argued in the late 19th century, kings of Anshan, and that the Anshan in question was a more or less independent polity in Fars, distinct from Parsua, Parsumash and Parshiru, which were predominantly Persian. I suggest that Anshan in this period was: 1) linguistically and culturally Elamite; 2) independent of the lowland "Elamite" kings of Susa attested in the Assyrian sources; yet 3) willing to join in an anti-

Assyrian coalition against Sennacherib when called upon to render service. I reject as an oxymoron the description of the realm ruled by Shishpish and his descendants, and proferred by generations of scholars, as a *Persian* or *Achaemenid* kingdom of Anshan[75] and instead would insist that the adjective Persian be replaced, as Sennacherib's text implies, by Anshanite (rather than Elamite, which in the later Assyrian period tended simply to describe lowland Susiana and its immediate environs). As to the objection, raised by de Miroschedji 20 years ago, that the site of Tal-e Malyan, the city of ancient Anshan, has no evidence of late Neo-Elamite occupation which we may associate with the period in which Cyrus' ancestors lived,[76] I would simply note that Tal-e Malyan is a very large mound, only a small portion of which has been explored to date. Thus there is every chance that a Neo-Elamite settlement is present somewhere on the site. But even if it isn't, Teispid rule over Anshan could have been based at any number of other sites in the region of Anshan with early 1st millennium BCE occupation.

The Elamite or Anshanite nature of the Teispids can also be examined from the standpoint of their personal names. Several years ago Jean Kellens asserted, "Les trois noms de la lignée de Cyrus ne s'expliquent ni dans le cadre iranien ancien, ni dans le cadre indo-iranien, ni même, pour deux d'entre eux, par l'étymologie indo-européenne".[77] Let us begin with Teispes. The Belgian Iranologist Jan Tavernier, whose dissertation dealt with Old Iranian personal names in non-Iranian texts of the Achaemenid period,[78] lists Teispes, or Chishpish, as one of those non-Iranian names which is normally classified, erroneously, as Iranian but which must belong to an Elamite, Aramaic, Babylonian, Lydian or other linguistic milieu. In its Elamite form the name is written Z/Shishpish, as it appears in Darius' Behistun inscription (DB I 4; DBa 5) and in two of the Persepolis fortification texts (PF 388: 3–4; 524: 3), incorporating the Elamite verbal stem *pish-* meaning "renew, restore".[79] With respect to Kambuziya [Cambyses], the situation is more complex. Although Hüsing suggested in 1908 that the name might be Elamite and Frye suggested in 1962 that Cambyses "may carry a non-Iranian name",[80] some scholars have emphasised the Sanskrit and Avestan parallels for the initial *Kam-* and compared it with the Indian ethnic and toponym Kamboja.[81] Skalmowski has suggested that the name is an adjectival form from a compound like **kamp + auj-ias-* (cf. Sanskrit *kampate* "he trembles", Avestan **auj*, as in *aojyah*, "stronger than"), meaning "unshaken, stronger than trembling, *intrepidus*",[82] although this is not considered very likely by some scholars.[83] Finally, and perhaps most importantly, we come to Kurash or Cyrus. Tavernier classifies this as "pseudo-Iranica" and follows F.C. Andreas' suggestion, made in 1902 at the International Orientalist Congress in Hamburg,[84] that Cyrus was "kein Perser", but an Anshanite, with an Elamite name. The putative Iranian etymology of Kurush as "youth, child" is contradicted by the Elamite and Babylonian transcription of the name, which is always Kurash, never Kurush. Particularly given the fact that Elamite names ending in *-ush*, such as

Hutelutush, are well known, it is unlikely that, if Kurush were the original, Babylonian or Assyrian scribes would have transcribed it using a final *-ash*. Rather, it seems more plausible to suggest that Elamite Kurash sounded alien to Persian ears and was transformed in Persian usage to Kurush, or that there was an Old Persian name Kurush, as distinct from Elamite Kurash, a name already attested in the Ur III period.[85]

The implications of Cyrus' Elamite identity

If Cyrus was indeed an Anshanite, with an Elamite name, then our conception of the Elamite contribution to Iranian identity, of the formation of the Persian empire and of Cyrus' achievements generally must be seriously re-evaluated. But before considering some of the wider implications of this thesis, I would like to raise a few more issues which suggest that a nuanced approach is required to understand the late Elamite cultural phenomenon. We know from the onomasticon of the Susa Acropole texts, which probably date to shortly before Cyrus' formation of the new empire, that Iranian speakers were present in Elamite territory during the mid-6th century BCE, and we have Neo-Assyrian sources as well which attest to their presence in the western Zagros several centuries earlier.[86] We have, likewise, numerous Assyrian references to Median groups in the Zagros. My point here is merely to underscore the fact that, by the 6th century BCE, southwestern Iran was even more multicultural and multilingual than it had been in the past two millennia, thanks to the presence of Indo-European speakers in ever-growing numbers, something we see clearly in the onomasticon of Neo-Elamite and Royal Achaemenid Elamite texts.[87] Certainly we know that names do not tell the whole story of a person's ethnicity. Several centuries later, for example, Babylonian mothers and fathers at Uruk occasionally gave their children Greek names. But, for the sake of argument, let us assume for the moment that Cyrus was indeed an Elamite-speaking Anshanite, as were his grandfather and great-grandfather. His father, on the other hand, Kambuziya, *may* have an Indo-European name.

Even if we cannot be certain that these names reflect ethnic identity, we do know that Iranian speakers were present in the region. The Sennacherib prism shows that the culturally Elamite polities of Susiana and Anshan were already neighbours of groups led by Iranian-speaking chiefly families, and intermarriage, for purposes of alliance-building, with attendant cultural blending, was almost certainly a by-product of such a situation. Cyrus' own family, therefore, while it probably had a far more Elamite cast than Darius', was not necessarily monocultural or monoethnic or even monolingual. Nor should we think that Fars was simply bi-cultural either. There were almost certainly groups in which non-Iranian and non-Elamite languages were spoken which have since died out.[88] For Kellens, intermarriage with Iranian-speaking groups on the part of the indigenous Elamite substratum contributed to "l'iranisation progressive de toutes les ethnies de l'Elam".[89] Cyrus' Anshanite identity may also find a reflex in Nicholas of Damascus (Frag. 64) and Ctesias, who say that Cyrus was a Mardian.[90] Rather than assimilating this with the Amardoi of the northern Zagros,[91] it is more likely that these authors were referring to the same group called the "Mardoi" by Strabo, who identified them as "brigands" (*Geog.* 15.3.1) inhabiting that part of Persis known as Mardene (Arrian, *Ind.* 40; Curtius 4.12.7.5, 6). Forbiger located Mardene north of Taocê – medieval Tawwaj and modern Borazjan – and Spiegel concurred, putting it in "etwa das Gebiet der jetzigen Mamasseni".[92] As Briant noted over 20 years ago,[93] it is tempting to identify Mardoi/Mardene with the Elamite toponym Mardash, which Hinz, Koch and Vallat situated somewhere in Persis.[94] If Forbiger and Spiegel were correct in placing Mardene in western Fars, i.e. in the Mamassani region north of Taocê (a possibility but by no means a certainty), then it was located in an area rich in monuments where the joint expedition that Kouroush Roustaei and I have been directing for the past two years is working.[95] Our excavations have focused on two large mounds, Tol-e Nurabad and Tol-e Spid, where recent excavations have revealed Neo-Elamite and Achaemenid as well as much earlier occupation dating back to c. 6000 BCE.[96]

Finally, if what we today call the *Persian* empire was, in fact, originally an *Anshanite* empire, established by Kurash, king of Anshan, then its creation must be seen not as a new creation *ab novo* but as a major *revival* in the political fortunes of a group which had not risen to such heights since Shutruk-Nahhunte brought about the downfall of the Kassite dynasty. Already a force in Sennacherib's time, the kingdom of Anshan may well have been aided by Assurbanipal's crushing attack on Susa, an act which could have enabled the increasing ascendancy of the Teispids in highland Anshan,[97] a region which remained beyond the reach of Assyrian military operations.

By the same token, if the kingdom so brilliantly expanded by Cyrus was Anshanite, then Darius' seizure of power upon the death of Cyrus' son Cambyses emerges as a Persian *coup d'état* which replaced the Anshanite, Teispid family of Cyrus with the Persian line of Achaemenes headed by Darius. In this context, therefore, the attempts by no fewer than three Elamite leaders – Hashshina/Açina, Martiya and Athamaita[98] – to rebel against Darius are suggestive of a very real Elamite attempt to throw off the Persian interloper and to maintain an Elamite regime (albeit a lowland one) which Cyrus had made a world power.[99] Darius' reign, I would argue, marked the commencement of the Achaemenid or Persian empire, while that of Cyrus marked the ascendancy of an Anshanite state, the existence of which can be detected during the reign of Sennacherib and the remote ancestry of which went back to the unified kingdom of Anshan and Susa in the early 2nd millennium BCE.

Notes:

1. This essay is a slightly modified version of a lecture delivered on 29 April 2004 at SOAS on the Elamite contribution to Iranian identity. I would like to express my sincerest thanks to all those involved in the lecture series, particularly Prof. Robert Springborg, Director of the London Middle East Institute at SOAS; Dr Sarah Stewart (SOAS), who dealt with many of the practical arrangements associated with my visit; Dr Vesta Sarkhosh Curtis (British Museum); and all of the members of the Soudavar Memorial Foundation, whose generosity contributed enormously to the success of my visit. I would in particular like to mention Dr Abolola Soudavar, who kindly sent me several offprints of relevance to my topic. Subsequently, I delivered a variant of the original lecture at the University of Pennsylvania, Harvard, the University of Michigan, UCLA and the University of California (Berkeley), and benefited enormously from the questions and comments of many scholars, in particular Prof. Ran Zadok, Prof. P.O. Skjærvø, Prof. P. Michalowski, Prof. G. Windfuhr, Prof. R. Shayegan, Prof. E. Carter, Prof. M. Feldman, Prof. N. Veldhuis and Prof. M. Schwartz. I am grateful to all of these scholars and numerous students who also commented upon the central thesis of the lecture, particularly J. Alvarez-Mon, but remain solely responsible for the views expressed here. Waters 2004 appeared after the completion of this article and I have not attempted to deal with each and every point made in that important article but simply with those issues that seemed most germane to my own arguments.
2. Bellwood 2001: 196; Parpola 2002: 233–48. See Lamberg-Karlovsky 2002 for a recent summary.
3. Voigt and Dyson 1992.
4. Zadok 2002.
5. *Ibid.*: Table 1.
6. Boas 1940.
7. The highlands of Papua New Guinea exhibit "By far the greatest linguistic diversity in the modern world ... with 1000 of the modern world's 6000 languages, and with dozens of language isolates or families that have no demonstrable relationship to each other or to any language outside New Guinea", according to Diamond and Bellwood (2003: 600).
8. See Zadok 1991: 226, 229.
9. In actual fact we do not know for certain that the Elamites were "indigenous", but they were certainly present in southwestern Iran from the beginning of recorded history. Whether they represent a group which coalesced out of still older, prehistoric groups inhabiting the region or entered the area some time prior to the beginnings of writing, we simply do not know.
10. Unpublished; personal communication from Mr Norouzi, ICHTO, Shahr-e Kord.
11. See e.g. Henkelman 2003b: 214–27.
12. Stolper 1984.
13. König 1965.
14. *Ibid.*
15. See Carter 1981: 218.
16. See de Harlez 1882, 1883; Sayce 1882, 1886; Halévy 1883; Delattre 1883a–b.
17. See Prášek 1912: 6.
18. Reiner 1973.
19. Vallat 1980.
20. S.v. Vallat 1993.

21. See Potts 1999: 328.
22. Stronach 1990, 2000.
23. Mayrhofer 1973: 310.
24. See Potts 1999: 342ff.
25. Cf. Dandamaev 1993a: 517.
26. Smith 1924.
27. Dandamaev 1993b: 521.
28. Berger 1975: 197, l. 21.
29. Gadd, Legrain and Smith 1928: no. 194, ll. 1–3.
30. Grayson 1975: 106, ii 1; cylinder text cited from Beaulieu 1989, where it appears as text 15. The assertion, "In a Babylonian text Cyrus II gives his line of descent from Achaemenes, the eponymous founder of the family, as Teispes, Cyrus, and finally Cambyses" (Hansman 1975: 289), is utterly baseless. Hansman also draws the equally unfounded conclusion that Parsumash = Anshan, since he equates Kurash of Parsumash with Kurash, king of Anshan (*ibid.*: 290).
31. Nöldeke 1887: 15.
32. I have this reference via Briant 1984 but have only been able myself to consult the 1896 French translation of this work, which appeared as Nöldeke T. 1896. *Études historiques sur la Perse ancienne*. Paris: Ledroux. Cf. Weissbach 1924: col. 188, "Die Dynastie des K. war von einem elamischen Lande oder Grenzlande (Anšan) ausgegangen", without commenting on the ethnicity of Cyrus and his forebears.
33. Prášek 1912: 6. He also suggested, apropos the Anshan of the Achaemenids, "wir werden nicht fehlgehen, wenn wir mit ihm den gräzicierten Flussnamen Andanis und den landschaftlichen Namen Assan arabischer Geographen in Zusammenhang bringen" (*ibid.*).
34. Wiesehöfer 1999.
35. Hansman 1975: 294.
36. Dandamaev 1993a: 516.
37. De Miroschedji 1985: 298–9.
38. Waters 1996: 18.
39. Briant 1996: 27.
40. Stronach 2000: 684.
41. Potts 1999: Table 5.2.
42. *Ibid.*: 145.
43. *Ibid.*: 142–5.
44. *Ibid.*: Table 5.5.
45. Thus Vallat, see Potts 1999: 149.
46. Potts 1999: Table 7.7.
47. *Ibid.*: 211.
48. *Ibid.*: 268.
49. *Ibid.*: 272; Luckenbill 1924: 88.
50. Briant 1984: 82; Potts 1999: 273.
51. See most recently Rollinger 1999, Zadok 2002: 29–33.
52. Cf. Stronach 2003b: 251.
53. Cf. Stronach 1997a: 38; *contra* Henkelman 2003b: 193. Stronach has noted: "it is of special interest that so much is made, through clearly conscious repetition, of the distinctive Anshanite titulary of Cyrus' own blood line. While the argument is sometimes advanced that Cyrus only introduced the toponym 'Anshan' instead of 'Parsa' in his Mesopotamian inscriptions in order to give his Persian homeland a name that would have been more readily recognisable to a Mesopotamian audience,

such an interpretation is, in the end, highly improbable. As early as 547 B.C. the Babylonian Chronicle already refers to 'Parsu' (the Akkadian form for 'Parsa') and, as the annals of the Near East make plain, royal rulers do not lightly depart from their established titulaturies." (Stronach 2000: 684)

54. Potts 1999: 302–303; Henkelman 2003a: 258.
55. Potts 1999: 303; Stronach 2003; Alvarez-Mon 2004.
56. Henkelman 2003b: 214–27.
57. Potts 1999: 287.
58. E.g. Weidner 1931–2; Harmatta 1971a: 5; Hansman 1975: 290; Briant 1984: 81; Shahbazi 1993: 516; Waters 2004: 94. More examples are cited in Potts 1999: 287.
59. See de Miroschedji 1985: 283–5; Briant 1996: 28. Shahbazi (1993: 516) argued against the chronological impossibility of such a scenario. A modern example also warns against assuming that such long reigns could never have occurred. In Kuwait the first Shaikh Sabah reigned from c. 1756 to 1762, while his grandson by the same name reigned from 1859 to 1866. See the genealogical table in the back of Dickson 1956. Bollweg (1988: 55–7, n. 16) has gone into the question of age in depth, but it is all so speculative, and the conflated genealogy offered (following W. Nagel) so fanciful, that I shall not comment upon it.
60. Harmatta (1971b: 222) writes: "Whatever our judgement about the relationship to each other of the geographical positions of Anšan and Parsumaš may be, the report of the Assyrian royal chancellery relies upon the mission of the son of Cyrus I, thus it can very likely be regarded as authentical. Therefore, the predecessors of Cyrus bore the title 'king of *Pārsvā (>Pārsā)'. Its original Old Persian linguistic form is not known so far, but at the time when Cyrus marched against Babylon it might have been already replaced by the form *xšāyaθiya Pārsaiy*. This could then be rendered by the Babylonian compiler of the edict [Cyrus Cylinder] with the phrase *šar* uru.*an-ša-an*." The logic of this statement defies me.
61. Zadok 1976: 63.
62. Whether Parsumash = Parsua and whether these should be distinguished from Parsa, *pace* de Miroschedji 1985: 268, cf. Bollweg 1988: 53, I shall not attempt to say. This is by no means the only line of argumentation which one can use here to refute the identification of Kurash of Parsumash with Kurash of Anshan.
63. Cf. Stronach 2000: 684–5, n. 13; 2003: 257. Also Dusinberre 2002: 43.
64. See Young 2003: 245.
65. Stronach 1997a: 39.
66. Stronach 2000: 684.
67. Stronach 2003b: 257–8.
68. Alvarez-Mon 2004: 205.
69. Stronach (1998: 237) dates it to the late 7th century, "shortly before 600 B.C.".
70. Rollinger 1998.
71. Stronach 1997b.
72. Cf. Waters 1996, 2004: 91. This had already been suspected by Hüsing (1908: 322).
73. Rollinger 1998; cf. Stronach 1997a: 37–8.
74. Stronach 2003b: 258.
75. Cf. Shahbazi 1993: 516, "Cyrus I was a Persian prince ruling over some localities that included Anshan"; or Dandamaev 1993a: 516, "That Cyrus' ancestors had ruled the Persian tribes for several generations is clear".
76. Waters (2004: 92 and 94) assumes that the Anshan ruled by Cyrus was a town, i.e. Tal-e Malyan, not a region. He does not seem to recognise the difference between Anshan the region and Anshan the capital of that region.

77. Kellens 2002: 422. I would like to thank Mr Abolola Soudavar for kindly bringing this article to my attention.
78. Tavernier 2002.
79. Cf. Grillot and Vallat 1978; *contra* Harmatta 1971a: 8, who views all of the names of Kurash's family as Iranian.
80. Hüsing 1908: 320–22; Frye 1962: 87.
81. Tavernier 2002: 333.
82. Skalmowski 1993: 74–5.
83. E.g. P.O. Skjærvø, pers. comm.
84. Andreas 1904. Cf. Hoffmann-Kutschke 1907: 182, "Kurusch [Kyros] ist kein persischer, sondern elamischer Name".
85. Zadok 1991: 237, citing Forde, *Nebraska cuneiform texts*; cf. Tavernier 2002: 753, with references.
86. See, most conveniently, Zadok 2002.
87. Zadok 1991: 224.
88. Discussing the onomastic and toponymic evidence from Neo-Assyrian sources relevant to western Iran, the prolific Israeli scholar Ran Zadok has stressed the difficulty of segregating "the pre-(Indo-)Iranian substratum among the local population" from "the advancing (Indo-)Iranianization of the territory" since the "substratum is heterogeneous and varies from region to region" and "much of it belongs to entirely unknown dialects" (Zadok 2002: 15). He writes: "Only a minority can be identified with various degrees of plausibility with recorded languages, like Hurro-Urartian and Elamite. Another segment is identical or related to the onomasticon of the Kassites" (*ibid.*: 16). To these must be added the names associated with "the two most ancient groups of the territory ... viz. the Qutians and Lullubians" (*idem*). He concludes pessimistically: "On the whole, a clear-cut differentiation of the considerable linguistically unaffiliated onomasticon cannot be attained as a specific ascription to the languages of the autochthones is generally impossible" (*idem*).
89. Kellens 2002: 427.
90. I cannot, of course, follow Ctesias or Herodotus (i.98–125), who say that Cyrus was born of two Mardian parents, his mother Argoste, a goatherd, and his father Atradates, a brigand. Obviously if we believe the testimony of the Cyrus Cylinder then this is fictitious. On this evidence cf. Sayce 1882: 550. Briant (1984: 75) has suggested it is Median propaganda.
91. Cf. Marquart 1891–3: 642.
92. Forbiger 1844: 577; Spiegel 1878: 528.
93. Briant 1984: 107.
94. See Vallat 1993: 171, with references.
95. Roustaei and Potts 2004.
96. A full, monograph-length report on these excavations, in Farsi and English, has been completed and should appear in the course of 2005.
97. Cf. Kellens 2002: 425.
98. Or Atta-hamiti-Inshushinak of EKI 86–89, as argued convincingly by Waters 2000: 85–7; cf. Henkelman 2003a: 262 and supported on linguistic grounds by Tavernier.
99. As R. Shayegan pointed out to me, many other regions, besides Elam, rebelled against Darius as well, making the Elamite rebellions less amenable to the interpretation given here. While this is true, the fact that simultaneous or slightly later rebellions occurred in other regions does not necessarily mean that the rebellions in Elam were not an attempt to regain the paramount position enjoyed

briefly by the Elamites and Anshanites under Cyrus. What later tradition did with Cyrus and his family affiliation, e.g. in the association with Kai Khosrow of the Kayanids (Yarshater 1983: 389; Wiesehöfer 2002: 115, n. 25; Kellens 2002: 428ff), is of no relevance here.

2

An Archaeologist's Approach to Avestan Geography

Frantz Grenet (CNRS / Ecole Pratique des Hautes Etudes, Paris)

When in 1980 Gherardo Gnoli published his *Zoroaster's Time and Homeland*, it would appear as if definitive progress had been made in the definition of the geographical horizon of the *Avesta*. All the countries mentioned there (especially in *Vd.* 1, the first chapter of the *Vidēvdād*) were identified, precisely or with a limited range of approximation, on the basis of a scrupulous discussion which took a century of research into account. All the countries were drawn into a coherent picture, firmly grouped around the Afghan mountains. The last ties with the western-centred tradition of Pahlavi commentaries seemed to have been severed for good.[1]

But instead of resulting in a pause, as one might have expected, Gnoli's synthesis reactivated the debate. One now has to take into account three other systems, more or less at variance with Gnoli as well as with each other: they were proposed by Helmut Humbach (1991), Willem Vogelsang (2000) and Michael Witzel (2000). At the same time Jean Kellens (1999–2000) expressed a strong (and, despite the call for unanimity, quite isolated) protest against the positivist approach shared by all rival systems: "Il serait aberrant que nous poursuivions l'analyse dans cette perspective historiquement connotée et que nous avons tous, en traitant d'autres questions, abandonnée".

What can an archaeologist working in the Central Asian field (in Afghanistan from 1975 until 1981, in Uzbekistan from 1989) bring to the debate? Probably a bias towards the "perspective historiquement connotée", at least as long as the identifications withstand not only the test of philology (i.e. arguable comparisons with toponyms attested in historical times) but also some practical issues. Does the proposed order of countries not just look nice on a large-scale map but correspond to attested historical routes? Were not some regions which today look insignificant well situated on transhumance itineraries? Do the descriptive words of the *Avesta* make sense on the ground? To take just one small example: the "thorns" mentioned in *Vd.* 1.4 as the Ahrimanic plague of "Gava inhabited by the Sogdians"[2] might appear trivial compared with the other counter-creations, but to somebody walking on ancient

Sogdian sites the shrub *alhagi camelorum* is a widespread nuisance and of concern to cowherds. In the same perspective, the recurrence of the formula *srīrąm ərəδβō.drafšąm*, "beautiful, with uplifted banners", for Bactria and Arachosia[3] is certainly influenced by rhetorical choices (the "mirror composition" of this chapter, evidence by Kellens). However, for a specialist of the Iron Age, Bactra and Kandahar, the capital of Arachosia, obviously match each other on both sides of the Hindukush: they were the largest fortified sites in this period, towering above rich plains, and hence suitable for military and/or religious gatherings.[4] In contrast, both Nisāya (Juzjān) and Ragha (in my opinion, in Badakhshān) lack a central plain and a fixed capital, and the recent reinterpretation of their common plague *uparō.vimanō.hiia-* as "neighbourhood discords" appears perfectly justified in a "realistic" perspective. It will be no surprise, eventually, to find out that I often side with W. Vogelsang, who is also an archaeologist, the main difference between us being that I reconstruct an overall order for the list of countries, while he does not for the second half of the list.

The state of the research

It has long been recognised that some of the *Yašts* have a very precise setting in some eastern Iranian countries, albeit different ones in each case. The *Mihr Yašt* is clearly centred on the Bāmiyān and Band-i Amir area, upon which Mithra's gaze takes in those "Aryan countries" stretching along the rivers which spring from the central Hindukush.[5] A non-Buddhist painting which adorned the vault of one of the Bāmiyān Buddhas, until it was destroyed by the Taliban, actually showed Mithra riding his chariot across these mountains.[6] In a different setting, the *Zamyād Yašt* continuously celebrates the country now known as Sistān, with its rivers flowing into the Hāmūn lake; here the ultimate Saviours will eventually come on Mount *ušiδarəna*, the mountain "with reddish cracks"[7], a fitting descriptive epithet for the Kūh-i Khwājah basaltic island where an important Zoroastrian sanctuary was to stand in later times.[8]

Besides these pieces of regional patriotism, the "Younger *Avesta*" contains what purports to be a comprehensive list of countries (*šōiθra-*) created by Ahura Mazdā, each affected by a specific plague sent by Ahriman. This list constitutes the first chapter of the *Vidēvdād*. It starts with the country called Airyanem Vaējah, where winter lasts ten months, and it ends with another country affected by the same discomfort, the Raŋhā. Of a total of sixteen countries, seven have always been identified beyond doubt, as they kept their name until historical times or even to the present day. Five of these countries are at the beginning of the list, directly following Airyanem Vaējah: Gava "inhabited by the Sogdians", Merv, Bactria, Nisāya said to be "between Margiana and Bactria" and therefore corresponding at least in part to medieval Juzjān in northwest Afghanistan.[9] Then comes the sixth country, Harōiva, the

Herāt region. In addition, the tenth and eleventh countries are respectively Arachosia, the Kandahar region, named by its river Harahvaitī, and Sistān, named by the Hilmand river. In the following table I list, in the first column, the name of the country (under its modern form when it is known for certain); in the second column, its "Ohrmazdian" qualification (positive or neutral); and in the third column, its Ahrimanic plague.

Airyanem Vaējah	"Aryan rapids(?) of the Good (river) Dāityā"	red snake (or dragon), demonscreated winter (gloss: which lasts ten months)
Gava	inhabited by the *suγδa* "Sogdians"	thorns fatal to the cows
Merv	strong, supporting the religious order	[*unclear*]
Bactria	beautiful, with uplifted banners	Barvara people and [*unclear*]
Nisāya	which is between Merv and Bactria	evil [neighbourhood] discords
Herāt	[*unclear*]	[*unclear*]
Vaēkereta	inhabited by the *dužaka*	the *pairikā* Khnathaitī whom Keresāspa seduced
Urvā	rich in pastures	evil masters
Khnenta	inhabited by the Vehrkāna people	sodomy
Arachosia	beautiful [with uplifted banners]	neglectful abandonment of corpses (*nasuspaya*)
Hilmand	rich, possessing the Khvarenah "fortune, glory"	evil sorcerers
Ragha	of the three cantons	evil neighbourhood discords
Chakhra	strong, supporting the religious order	cooking of the carrion
Varena	with four corners (gloss: birthplace of Thraētaona who killed Azhi Dahāka)	untimely menstruations, non-Aryan masters
Hapta Hendu		untimely menstruations, excessive heat
Over (...) the Ranhā		demons-created winter, plunderer overlords

As can be seen, almost all identified countries are situated beyond the present borders of Iran, to the east and northeast. The only exception is Sistān, and only for its westernmost part. It is only possible to draw the Iranian plateau into the picture of early Zoroastrianism by recognising one or several of its regions in the remaining countries on the list. This has been the regular tendency of Zoroastrian scholarship since the Sasanian commentators of the *Avesta* and all modern scholars have followed suit, up until Arthur Christensen (1943). But in the last decades Gherardo Gnoli (most elaborately in 1980) (Fig. 1) has brilliantly argued for a scheme that pushes the list definitively outside the boundaries of Iran and substantially into Pakistan. Willem Vogelsang (2000) has presented what purports to be an improvement on this scheme. Discordant voices were heard at once, however, and after criticisms by Helmut Humbach[10] and Michael Witzel (2000) it now seems that the pendulum is again swinging back towards Iran, through Gurgān all the way to Ray near modern Teheran.

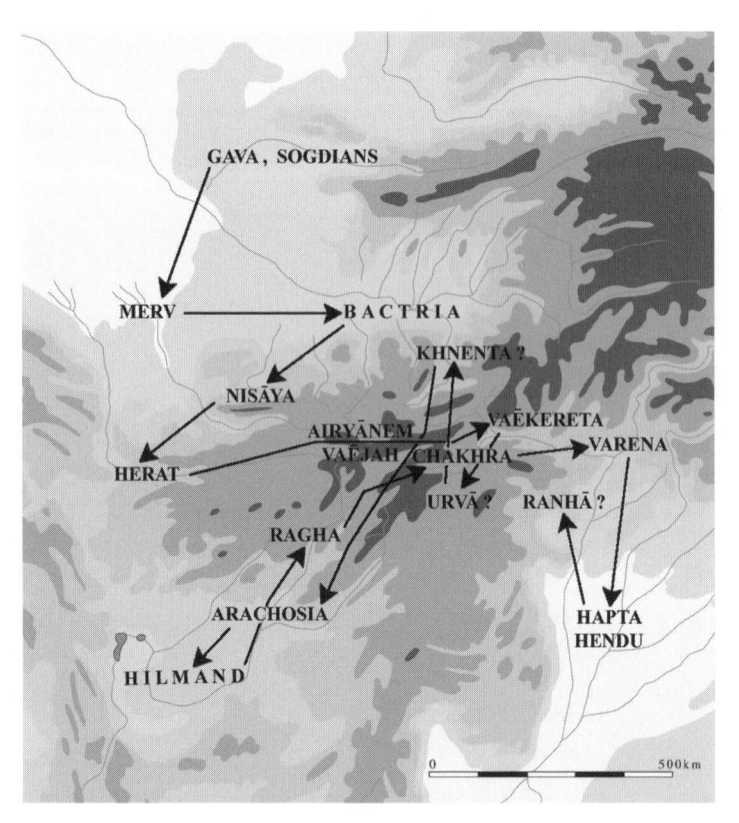

Fig. 1: Map according to Gnoli (adapted from Gnoli 1980; this map and the following one have been drawn by François Ory, CNRS, Paris)

In the present contribution I would like basically to suggest a return to Gnoli's and Vogelsang's conclusions, keeping in mind that some improvements can still be made using the same principles as they did. These principles are, first, a sceptical attitude towards identifications in Pahlavi texts, most of which were clearly motivated by a wish to transfer as much as possible of the tradition to more central regions of the Sasanian empire. Secondly, great attention has to be paid to the geographical characterisation of the countries as they appear in the list: sketchy as they are, they sometimes offer precious clues to anybody familiar with natural conditions in these regions. To these points of method I would add the recognition of a simple and logical order. This was in fact the weak point in Gnoli's system, as Witzel did not fail to point out in his article, which otherwise recommends itself by many pertinent comparisons with the Rgvedic material. In particular, the middle part of the list as Gnoli reconstitutes it seems to proceed in huge zigzags, for example moving from Urvā in the Ghazni region to Khnenta, put in eastern Bactria, then leapfrogging to Arachosia and Sistān. Also, the sequence Ragha – Chakhra – Varena is made to go in the opposite direction from the preceding one, because Gnoli wants to put the particularly religious place Chakhra as close as possible to Sistān, which he takes as the real focal point. Vogelsang, though less committed in his identifications of countries south and east of the Hindukush, also does not claim to present a logical order as far as this part of the map is concerned (Fig. 2).

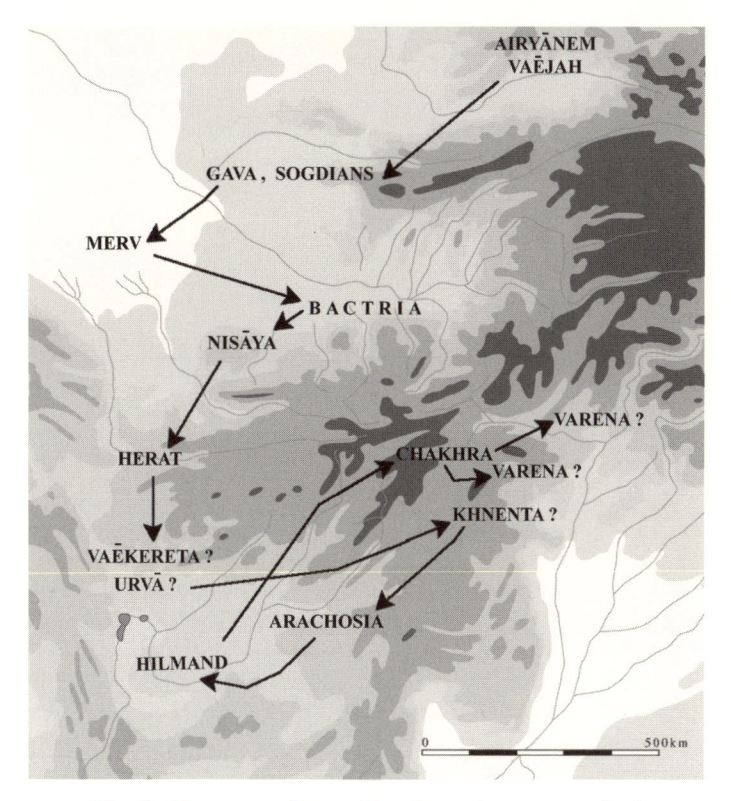

Fig. 2: Map according to Vogelsang (reconstruction)

Humbach stretches to the west as far as Hyrcania and Ray (which he considers the "obvious" candidates for Khnenta and Ragha). For the rest his system stands apart from all the others in that he puts in eastern Bactria the countries Varena and Hapta Hendu, which are held by all modern scholars (and, in the case of Hapta Hendu, even by the Iran-centred Pahlavi tradition) to be in northwest India (Fig. 3).

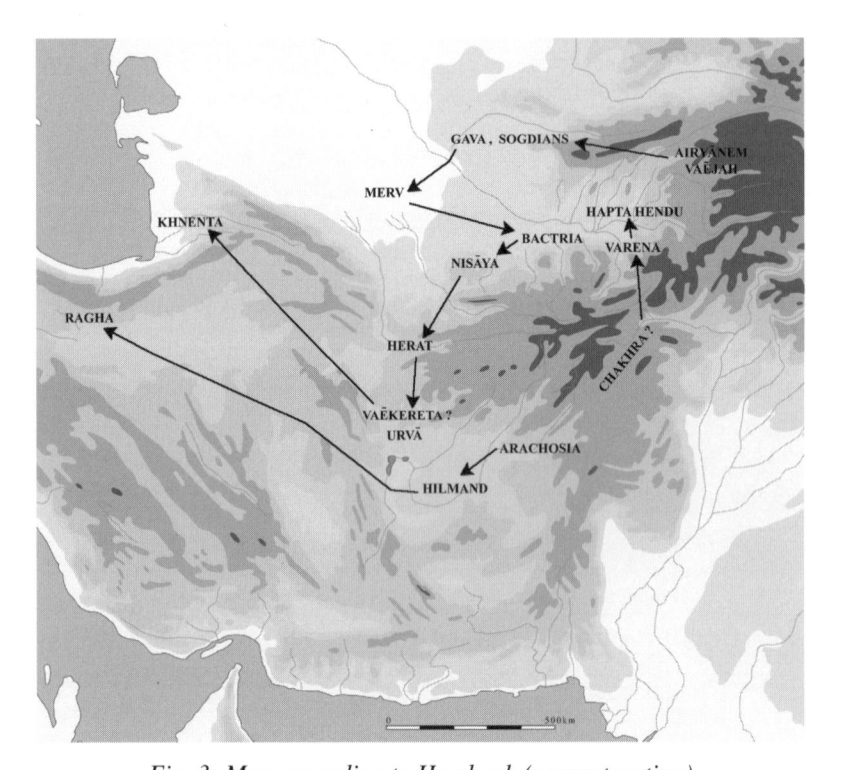

Fig. 3: Map according to Humbach (reconstruction)

He does not bother about recognising an overall order, but Witzel, adopting some of his identifications, does. His own scheme appears extremely complicated, although purporting to look like a spread-out *maṇḍala* (Fig. 4). One is invited to start from the highlands of central Afghanistan, to move northeast (to Sogdiana), northwest (to Hyrcania), then southwest (to Sistān), and finally to move right across from west (Ray) to east (Panjāb). This scheme would structurally correspond to that of the seven continents (*kišwar*) as expressed in Pahlavi texts, but in a reverse, anticlockwise order, and in addition each branch of the list would be affected by a pulsatory movement to and fro. One wonders whether it would not be simpler to assume that there is no order at all.

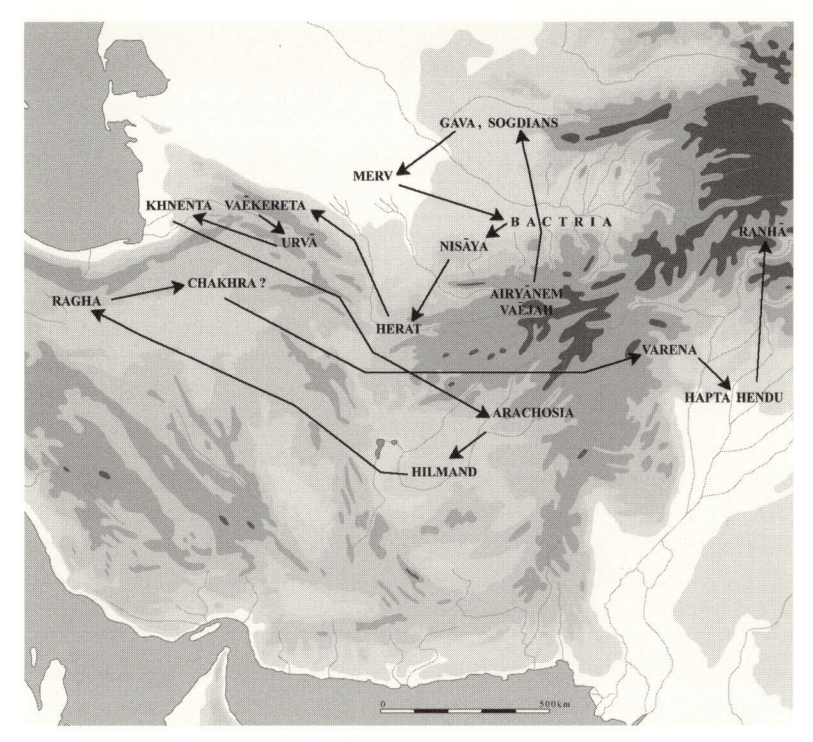

Fig. 4: Map according to Witzel (reconstruction)

The starting point of the list: Airyanem Vaējah

Before reconsidering the list entirely, it might be worth examining the starting point, namely the Airyanem Vaējah, more precisely the "Airyanem Vaējah of the Good River". If this country is central Afghanistan, as assumed by Gnoli and Witzel, one wonders what the "Good River" can be. This difficulty has been challenged only by one scholar, the Russian Iranologist Ivan Steblin-Kamenskii, in a short article published 27 years ago which has remained largely unnoticed.[11] He drew attention to the fact that the name of the "Good River", Vahvī, had tenaciously survived until the early 20th century under the form Vakh, known to the Greeks as the "Ochos" and designating the river today known as the Daryā-i Panj on the upper course of the Oxus (it is now reduced to its uppermost section, the Vakhān = Vakh + ān). The name Oxus, which eventually spread to the whole river, originally belonged to a right-hand-side tributary that is still known locally as the Vakhsh. Consequently, the cold country of the *airyanəm vaējō vaŋhuiiā dāitiiaiiā*, best translated as "the Aryan rapids of the (river) Dāityā",[12] would rather correspond to the water system of the Pamirs and the pre-Pamirian highlands (that part of Badakhshān which is now in Tajikistan).

The Ragha question

We shall encounter the Good River again in connection with another problematic country, Ragha, which comes twelfth on the list. This country, identified as Ray in the Pahlavi commentary of the *Vidēvdād* (but not in the *Bundahišn*), has always been the focal point of those who wished to recognise in the *Vidēvdād* list an echo of the Median empire and of its reception of the Zoroastrian faith. Some interesting details are in fact mentioned concerning Ragha. Its Ahrimanic plague is *uparō.vimanah-*, generally translated as "extreme doubts". Moreover, in another Avestan passage from the *Yasna* (*Y.* 19.18) it is stated that Ragha is the only country that has only four *ratu-* (patrons) instead of the usual five: one for the *nmāna-* (family/house), one for the *vis-* (clan/village), one for the *zantu-* (tribe/canton), and above them Zoroaster himself, but no master for the *daiŋ́hu-* (people/country) as such; consequently it is called *zaraθuštriš* "belonging to Zarathuštra" or maybe just "Zoroastrian". These two sets of characteristics have provided the foundation for an imposing edifice, initiated by Martin Haug in 1857[13] and then built up step by step by successive scholars. In the most extreme elaboration of this theory, formulated by Humbach, Ragha, city of Media, would become "a sort of Mazdayasnian Vatican whose pope called "Zarathuštra" is simultaneously the worldly ruler of the country and its supreme religious authority". As for the "extreme doubts", they would refer to "an early religious disagreement, a schism between the Mazdayasnians of the east, represented by the majority of the geographical names in the list of lands, and those of the west".[14]

But these theories have recently been exposed to philological criticisms which I consider decisive. Jean Kellens has recently discovered that the expression understood as "extreme doubts" instead means something more mundane, probably "neighbourhood discords".[15] In fact the same epithet is met with for Nisāya (Juzjān), where no modern scholar ever proposed to locate a great Zoroastrian theological school. As for the country belonging to Zoroaster or to some carrier of this title, Xavier Tremblay has convincingly proposed that the information should be reduced to a mechanical consequence of the state of political fragmentation.[16] The successive stages can be viewed as follows:

a) Descriptive epithet. In *Vd.* 1.15, Ragha is simply qualified as *θrizantu-*, "of the three tribes/cantons", which implies a divided or partitioned country not organised above the tribal level; this detail, perfectly consistent with the Ahrimanic plague of "neighbourhood discords", might have been chosen in order to distinguish this Ragha from homonymous countries which did not share the same political

characteristics (as aptly stressed by Tremblay, Media with its kings and chief city Ragā surely were in the latter category).
b) Scholarly development. In *Y*. 19 (a word-by-word exegesis of the prayer *Ahuna vairiia*), paragraphs 14–18 offer a formalistic digression about various things expressed in numbers. One of them appears to be the formula *θrizantu-*, found in *Vd*. 1.15 and brought to its seemingly logical consequence in paragraph 18: as Ragha has no organised social level above the *zantu-*, it has no *ratu-* ("patron")[17] for the *daiŋhu-* and people are referred directly to everybody's *ratu-*, i.e. Zoroaster; hence the new epithet given to the country, *raya zaraθuštri-*.[18]
c) Historicisation. This last qualification gave rise in its turn to the idea that Ragha was Zoroaster's homeland. In the Zoroastrian literature that has come down to us, this idea is expressed only in Pahlavi texts. In the commentary of *Vd*. 1.15 it is given as a non-unanimous opinion, "Rag (. . .); some say: Zoroaster was from this place", no doubt because of Azerbaijan's rival claim (the contradiction was solved by some exegets who plainly stated that Rag, i.e. according to them Ray, was in Azerbaijan).[19] The concept of Ragha as Zoroaster's country can also be traced in the seventh book of the *Dēnkard* (*Dk*) and in the *Wīzīdagīhā ī Zādspram* (*WZ*), and this is all the more interesting as these two books draw from the *Spand Nask*, the Avestan book which contained the legend of Zoroaster, now lost but still in existence in the 9th century (as shown by its short summary in *Dk*. 8). They use its *zand* version (Pahlavi translation with glosses), which they either quote (*Dk*) or rephrase (*WZ*). In *Dk*. 7.2.9–10 we read that Zoroaster's mother, in order to be married, was sent "to the village (*deh*) of the Spitāmān, on the *rōstāg* of *'l'k* (. . .), to the house (*mān*) of Padīragtarasp". As noted by Humbach, *'l'k* appears to stand for *l'k*, the usual Pahlavi transcription of Ragha. Normally *rōstāg* means "district", but as in translations from the *Avesta* it is regularly used for *šōiθra-*, "country", one can conjecture that the underlying Avestan text of the *Spand Nask* had *rayąm šōiθrəm. The regular transcription *l'k* appears in the formula *Rāg ud Nōdar* (*Dk*. 7.2.51, 3.19; *WZ* 10.14–15), which is best interpreted as uniting the names of Zoroaster's country and Vīshtāspa's clan.[20]

Besides these direct mentions of Ragha in connection with Zoroaster's legend, there are undirect ones.[21] Both the *Dēnkard* and the *Selections of Zādspram* describe how Zoroaster had his great vision of Wahman (Vohu Manah). These accounts are loaded with very precise topographical details that provide a decisive clue to the actual location of the Ragha country.

"It is revealed that after the passing away of thirty years since he existed (. . .), after Nowruz, there was a festival called Wahār-būdag, in a place particularly well known where people from many directions had come to the festive place (. . .). On the passing away of the five days at the festive place (. . .) Zoroaster went forth to the bank of the river Dāityā in order to squeeze the *hōm* (. . .). The river was in four arms and Zoroaster crossed them, the first one was upto the feet, the second upto the knees, the third upto the parting of the two thighs, the fourth upto the neck (. . .). When he came out of the water and put up his cloth, he saw the Amahraspand Wahman in human form." (*WZ* 20.1–4) In the parallel passage *Dk*.7.3.51–54 (where the crossing of the four arms is marked as a quotation), it is stated that Wahman comes from the south, from which we can infer that Zoroster has crossed the river from the north.

Nothing in the logic of the narrative calls for this material detail of the "four arms", and Zādspram's gloss is clearly a scholastic addition ("This was a sign that religion will come to the height four times, the manifestation of which will be through Zoroaster, Ushēdar, Ushēdarmāh and the Sōshāns"). If we now look along the actual course of the Daryā-i Panj, to which the name of the Vahvī Dāityā was attached since at least the Achaemenian period (as shown by the Greek transcription Ochos, already found in the historians of Alexander), then we find one ford that corresponds very well to the description. This ford, known as the Samti or Badakhshān ford, always had great importance as it provided the main passage between the Kulyāb plain in the north and the valleys of western Badakhshān in the south. I quote the description given in the *Gazetteer of Afghanistan*: "The river which is here divided into four channels, 109, 207, 680 and 1012 paces, respectively, in breadth, with only a few paces of dry land between them is fordable. The current is rapid in the two middle channels, and the water waistdeep".

Even more interesting for our purpose is the fact that the region immediately to the southeast of the ford is still known as Rāgh. It was probably mentioned (as the "kingdom" of *Heluoho*) by the 7th-century Chinese pilgrim Xuanzang.[22] In the late 19th century, Rāgh was described as a cluster of valleys, six eventually uniting into one (the Sadda or Āb-i Rāgh) and two others (the Turghān and the Āb-i Rewinj) independently flowing into the Daryā-i Panj. This rings a bell when one remembers the "three cantons" of *Vd.* 1.15.[23] Further to the southwest there is a local toponym Rāgh Dasht, 20 kilometres north of the bend of the Kokcha river, the Rūd-e Badakhshān. In the only fragment of Zoroaster's legend preserved in the Avestan language, in the late passage *Vidēvdād* 19.18 (a recycled fragment of the *Spand Nask*?), Ragha is not named, but Zoroaster's father's house is said to stand "on the bend of the *darəjī*". It is tempting to identify this river with the *Dargoidos* / *Dargidos* mentioned by Ptolemy (6.11.2), in a position corresponding to the present Kokcha. Actually in *WZ*. 23.7-8 the last of the seven interviews between Zoroaster and the Amahraspands takes place at the confluence of the Darjēn (i.e. the *darəjī*) with the Dāityā; here "winter lasts five months", an indication which shows that this region lies out of what is properly called Aiyanem Vaējah where winter lasts ten months.

One cannot escape the conclusion that the redactors of the *Spand Nask*, probably in the Achaemenid period,[24] had precise knowledge of eastern Bactria.

The list as a whole

a) Along the Oxus

We can now reconsider the entire list of countries. If we take the Pamirian region as its starting point, it appears that the first part of the list, in which all countries can easily be identified, displays a simple order. There are neither to-and-fro movements nor important gaps, but rather several continuous sequences arranged in an anticlockwise order. The first chain of countries comprises "Gava inhabited by the Sogdians", then Merv. Gava, if its name survives in *Gabai* (Arrian, *Anab*. 4.17.4), should be looked for in the Bukhārā oasis or on the lower Kashka-daryā valley, in any case near the Oxus, which Achaemenid Sogdiana (a broader concept) also bordered.[25] In the Iron Age, the oasis of Merv reached closer to the Oxus than in later periods.[26] Therefore this first sequence moves along the Good River, the Oxus. The statement in the *Great Bundahishn* (XI A.7) according to which "the river Dāityā comes out of Ērānwēz and proceeds to *Gōbedestān" is consistent with the interpretation of Gōbed as **gauua-pati-*, "lord of Gava".[27]

b) North of the Hindukush

The second chain, starting again from near the Pamir, comprises Bactria, Nisāya (Juzjān) and Herāt. It proceeds along the northern foothills of the Hindukush.

c) South of the Hindukush

After this section come the countries Vaēkereta, Urvā, Khnenta, followed by the more familiar Arachosia and Sīstān.

In the case of Vaēkereta, the identification with "Kābul" unanimously proposed in the Pahlavi tradition seems, for once, well grounded. In a decisive article, Sylvain Lévy showed a long time ago that this identification is mirrored by the *Mahāmāyūrī*, a Buddhist list of countries considered an excellent source, which gives Vaikṛtika as the name of the spirit (*yakṣa*) of Gandhāra.[28] This proposal has since been generally accepted, the only challenge having come from Humbach, who writes that "its place in the list does not favour this equation" (see below on this particular question). Should an attempt be made to displace Vaēkereta to the north of the Hindukush (for his own part Humbach would put it between Sīstān and Herāt), one could play with a comparison with Wēshgird <**vayuš-kṛta-*, "made by Vayu", the ancient name of an important town near Dushanbe, in the easternmost part of Achaemenid Sogdiana. But the etymology Vaēkereta <**vayu-kṛta-* upheld by several authors, including Humbach, is at least questionable.[29] To sum up, no credible alternative has been proposed to the firm testimony of the *Mahāmāyūrī*. A possible specification would be to consider the western part of historical Gandhāra (Kapisa, the Kābul region), rather than the eastern part, as the "Seven Rivers" of India (Hapta Hendu in our list) included the Kābul river. This brings us back again not far from Pamir, while the two last names in this section, Arachosia and Sistān, invite us to look for an itinerary in the southern foothills of the Hindukush.

The arguments for locating the following country, Urvā, in the Ghazni region were excellently presented by Christensen[30] and endorsed by Gnoli.[31] The epitheth *pouru.vāsta-,* "rich in pastures", echoes the 19th-century travellers who were very concerned about the military potential of Afghanistan and mentioned the exceptional capacity of the plain immediately to the north of Ghazni for maintaining cavalry; 60 kilometres westwards, the Dasht-i Nawur was still in the 1970s a major gathering point of Pashtun nomads in summer.[32] The name Urvā reappears in the *Zamyād Yasht* (*Yt.* 19.67) as the river Urvadhā (with the same epithet, *pouru.vāstra-*), listed among the tributaries of the Hāmūn lake. Historically, though it does not correspond any more to physical reality, the Ghazni-rūd was considered to be linked to the Arghandāb through the lake Āb-i Istāda and the Lōra river. The alternative identification proposed by Humbach and Vogelsang (between Sistān and Herāt) is based upon a speculative localisation of the river Urvadhā.[33] The solution suggested by Witzel (on the Kopet-dagh foothills) is a *petitio principii*.

Next comes Khnenta "inhabited by the Vehrkāna" (*vəhrkānō.šaiiāna-*). As the coupling of these names has always been the core of the argument, one should perhaps begin with a preliminary evaluation of the particular meaning of *šaiiāna-* (in principle "inhabited by") in this context. The word also appears with Gava (*suγδō.šaiiāna-*) and Vaēkərəta (*dužakō.šaiiāna-*). The *dužaka-* is a problem,[34] but there is no doubt that *suγδa-* is the name of the people known as the Sogdians through history. The *Mihr Yašt* (*Yt.* 10.14) also associates "Gava, Sughdha", but on an equal footing, suggesting two adjacent areas, as is surely the case with "Ishkata, Pouruta". As Gava appears to correspond to the western (lowland) part of Achaemenid Sogdiana, one could suggest that the Sughdha inhabited the eastern (highland) part of the region and used the plains as winter pastures.[35] I think a similar reasoning might help in clarifying the situation with Khnenta "inhabited by the Vehrkāna".

The name Khnenta (*xnənta-*) is not recorded elsewhere in historical geography. Humbach proposes to emend it to **xrənda-*, later Hirand, today the river of Gurgān (given as a people in Ptolemy 6.9.5: Khrendoi). As Gurgān, ancient Hyrcania, carries the same name as the Vehrkāna, the solution seems attractive and Witzel eventually adopts it. But there are difficulties. Leaving aside for the moment the huge consequences for the geographical cohesion of the list, the form *xnəntəm* is given by all manuscripts. Though the initial cluster *xn-* is indeed atypical for Indo-Iranian words, there is one other case in Avestan, and it is surely no coincidence that it is Khnathaitī (*xnaθaitī*), the name of the *pairikā-* (evil female being, witch) of Vaēkereta (Kabul). Therefore the form Khnenta, however non-Indo-Iranian it may be, is not so easy to discard. Vehrkāna, ultimately from *vr̥k-*, "wolf", undoubtedly underlies "Hyrcania". But it is also attested in Waziristān, a hilly region on the Indo-Afghan border, with the town Urgūn (Pashtun Wərgūn < *vəhrkāna-*).[36] The name seems to be mirrored on the Indian side by the *Vr̥cīvant* people, whom the *Ṛg-Veda* (6.27.5) locates just to the south of Waziristān, on the Haliāb and Zhob rivers; Witzel briefly contemplates them as a possible alternative to Gurgān.[37] Vogelsang, for his part, accepts the identification Vehrkāna – Urgūn as "a distinct possibility".[38] Gnoli once inclined in the same direction but eventually rejected it in favour of southeast Bactria, at great cost to the coherence of his system (see Fig. 1) and on the sole evidence of the imprecisely situated Barkanioi mentioned by the court physician Ctesias, who probably never set foot in those eastern regions.[39]

But did Khnenta occupy the very same spot? If we suppose the same sort of relationship between Khnenta and Vehrkāna as between Gava and Sughdha, we are allowed a certain latitude. In fact, assuming that Urvā/Urvadhā is the Ghazni-rūd, the position of Khnenta between Urvā and Harahvaitī (the river of Arachosia, i.e. the Arghandāb) leads us to the Tarnak valley, where today the main centres are Mukur (upstream) and Kalāt-e Ghilzai (downstream). Confirmation of this identification can be found by comparing the list of rivers given in the *Zamyād Yasht* (*Yt*. 19.67) as tributaries of the Hāmūn lake.[40] Thanks to the conservatism of local toponymy, the first five rivers (Khvāstrā, Hvaspā, Fradathā, Khvarenahvaitī, Ushtavaitī) are safely identified as northeastern and northern tributaries of the lake, enumerated in anticlockwise order (merely with interversion of the last two). Then come Urvadhā, Erezī, Zarenumaitī and Haētumant. Gnoli rightly recognises the first and third ones as eastern tributaries, not flowing directly into the lake but eventually collected by the Haētumant (Hilmand) and again enumerated anticlockwise: the Ghazni-rūd (continued by the Lōra) and the Arghandāb.[41] Strangely enough, he leaves the intermediate Erezī out of this group and without a firm identification. It can be no other than the Tarnak "sandwiched between the Arghandāb and Arghastān [the lower course of the Lōra]",[42] a straight river, which is precisely the meaning of *ərəzī-*. Therefore the sequence Urvā – Khnenta – Harahvaitī – Haētumant in *Vd*. 1 corresponds to Urvadhā – Erezī – Zarenumaitī – Haētumant in *Yt*. 19.76.

The town Urgūn is 130 kilometres east of Moqur. In the 19th century, nomadic groups belonging to the Ghilzai confederation used to ascend every year from the plains beyond Urgūn, via the Tochi and Gomal valleys, to "spread out in small [summer] camps over the countryside, usually on the stretch south of Ghazni to Muqur and Kalât [i.e. the Tarnak valley]".[43] The fort at Kalāt-e Ghilzai indicates military organisation. There is no question of asserting that migration patterns remained unchanged in this sector over two and a half millennia, but I would suggest "Khnenta inhabited by the Vehrkāna" should be visualised in such a way.

d) The path to India

The last chain of countries starts with Ragha and eventually brings to northwest India, the Hapta Hendu (the *Sapta Sindhavas* of India, i.e. the five rivers of Panjāb, plus the Kābul river, plus the Indus). Humbach's attempt to shift this country to the upper Oxus basin is rightly rejected by Witzel[44] (and ignored by the others) in view of the Ahrimanic plague of Hapta Hendu: the "excessive heat". The preceding country, Varena has been identified with Bunēr on the unanimous testimony of Pāṇini and the Buddhist literature, including the authoritative *Mahāmāyūrī*, which has already provided the identification of Vaēkereta with Gandhāra.[45] Between Ragha and Varena comes Chakhra, which in this perspective would probably correspond to Chitrāl.

There is, however, a possible alternative more to the south, as the chief town of the Lōgar valley south of Kābul is called Chakhr (the name is attested since the 14th century).[46] From here, heading east towards the Kurram valley, one could eventually reach the Indian plains through Bannu whose name, like that of Bunēr, reflects Varena. Though only the northern Varena was recorded in Indian literary and scholarly tradition, the original form of the southern one is attested by Xuanzang (*Falana*, with indications of distances which correspond only to Bannu).[47] But if so, one would have to assume a severe disturbance in the order of countries. The road between Kapisa–Kābul (Vaēkereta) and Ghazni (Urvā) goes through Lōgar, which therefore should have been mentioned at this place. The same remark applies for the position of Kapisa–Kābul between Badakhshān and Lōgar. In the latter case, one cannot *a priori* exclude the possibility that the Ragha of the *Vidēvdād* (*raya θrizantu-*) was a different country from the Ragha the redactors of the *Spand Nask* had in mind (obviously Badakhshān), the more so if the first text is pre-Achaemenid and the second one late Achaemenid. But such a hypothesis does not get us very far. Where should we put "Ragha of the three cantons"? Just after Sistān, which precedes it in the list? This is Gnoli's choice, "with a fair degree of approximation . . . in an area that includes the modern districts of Zamīn-Dāvar and Qalʻat-i Gilzai".[48] But at this stage of our argument it seems that all this sector is already distributed between the basins of Tarnak (Khnenta), Arghandāb (Harahvaitī) and Hilmand (Haētumant). Or should we place Ragha next to Lōgar? The only possible direction is to the west and there is hardly any room there, except in the small valley of Wardak.[49]

All things considered, the sequence Badakhshān – Chitrāl – Bunēr seems more coherent than the Zamīndāvar – Lōgar – Bunēr proposed by Gnoli, while Vogelsang is committed to none of the three names (Ragha is not situated, Lōgar "may be correct" for Chakhra, Varena is either Bunēr or Bannu). One should keep in mind that regional names travelled in groups across the Hindukush and across the Kābul river: as the couple Khōst–Warnu of eastern Bactria is mirrored by Swat–Bunēr to the north of Gandhāra,[50] by Khōst–Bannu in the Kurram valley, the possibility that there once existed a Chakhra to the west of Swat should not be discarded. Badakhshān communicated with Chitrāl through the Kokcha valley (probably the *darejī* of the *Avesta*, see above) and several high passes, mainly the Dorah pass and those leading to the Pech valley. The fact that specific religions related to an archaic Indian stratum survived in Chitrāl and in the higher valleys until recent times does not rule out ancient attempts at spreading Zoroastrianism. Chakhra's positive and negative characteristics are, respectively, the best and the worse possible ones : on the one hand *aṣ̌auuan-* "upholding the religious order", an epithet shared only with Merv, on the other hand *nasu.spačya-* "cooking of the carrion", a term which can refer to various inexpiable sins: anthropophagy, cynophagy, defilement of the (sacrificial ?) fire with impure dead matter[51] Such a contrast suggests the coexistence of several populations, some of them religiously controlled and some of them not at all. Also, traditional communications between Chitrāl, Swat and Bunēr did not necessarily use the valley of the Kābul river.

In any case the list eventually ends up near its starting point with the last country, Ranhā, Sanskrit Rasā, where winter lasts ten months like in the Airyanem Vaējah. This country is endowed with mythological features but also, as Witzel rightly argued, it has some basis in reality, namely some upper tributary of the Indus.[52]

* * *

The relative uncertainty about the last section does not break the logical construction of the list (Fig. 5). Far from reflecting an elaborate cosmogony like that of the list of the seven parts of the world, it is a group of four sequences, each starting from roughly the same area and each arranged according to the principle of continuity. This is exactly the underlying principle of the list of countries in most of the inscriptions of Darius,[53] except that the general order is clockwise in the inscriptions and anticlockwise in the *Vidēvdād*. Witzel draws attention to the fact that, in Indo-European concepts and rituals, the counter-clockwise order is in principle associated to inauspicious contexts, and puts forward the interesting suggestion that its use in the *Vidēvdād* should be linked with the fundamentally exorcising character of this book.[54] At the same time, the selection of countries in the first section directly results from them bordering on the Vahvī Dāityā, which flows through Airyanem Vaējah, and this initial choice could well have dictated the overall order.

A second observation, on which I side entirely with Gnoli and Vogelsang, is the total exclusion of the Iranian plateau. Everything stops on a line Merv – Herāt – Sistān. As a cluster of countries, it seems to prefigure two historical constructions that were later created by horsemen descended from the north: the Indo-Scythian kingdoms in the 1st century BCE, then the Hephtalite empire in the 5th century AD.[55]

The early list in the *Vidēvdād* bears witness to a period when the main focus of the Zoroastrian priests, or maybe the rulers, was still along the Indian border, with combined or alternating phases of defence and encroachment.[56] This impression is reinforced by the mention of "non-Aryan masters" as the specific plague of Varena or "plunderer overlords" in Ranhā,[57] maybe the "evil masters" in Urvā. No wonder the *Avesta* associates these southeastern countries with typical "frontier heroes": the dragon-slayer Thraētaona, born in Varena; Keresāspa, lover of the witch from Vaēkereta and whom his exploits against bandits and a *gandarəuua-* (loanword from Sanskrit *gandharva*?) bring to Lake Pishinah, the name of which survives today in the Pishin plain to the south of the Lōra river (lower Urvadhā).[58] The grazing lands of southeastern Afghanistan are in fact over-represented in the list, suggesting a horizon centred rather on Arachosia and the neighbouring valleys. The more landlocked east-west valleys of the Hindukush, today Afghanistan's "central road", are left out of the picture, though they are mentioned in the *Mihr Yasht* : Ishkata (the Bāmiyān and Band-i Amir region), Pouruta (Ghōr).[59] As Vogelsang aptly writes: "While in this part of the Iranian world [i.e. south and east Afghanistan] the composer names a number of obscure districts that otherwise remain unknown, his series of lands mentioned at the beginning of the list (nos. 1–6) is remarkable by the mentioning of merely the most famous lands".

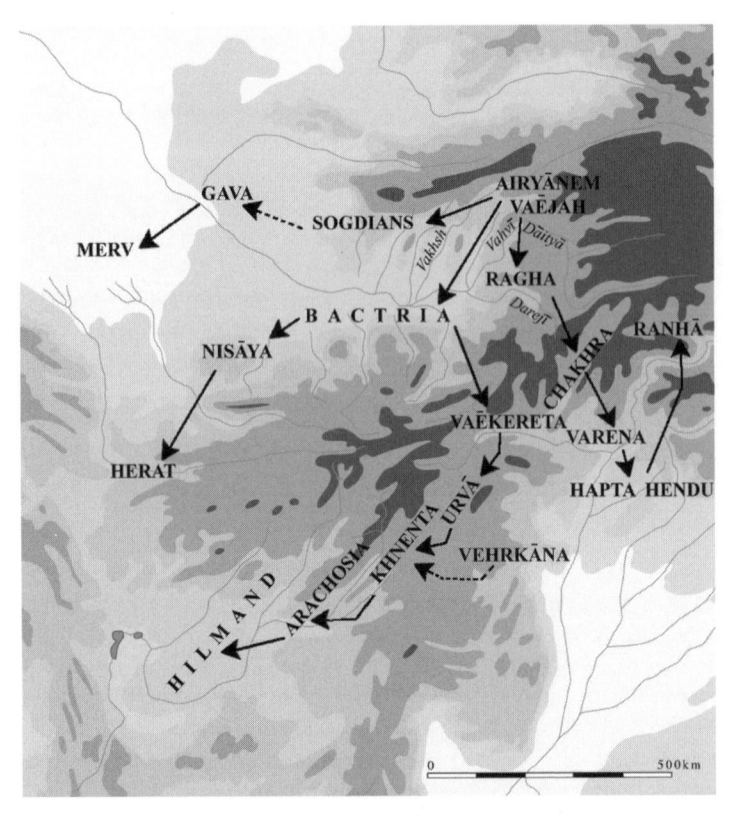

Fig. 5: Map according to the present author

The reception of the Zoroastrian faith by the Medes, then by the first Achaemenids, lay in the future, or maybe it was not a main concern from the viewpoint of those who composed the text. Deioces, Cyrus and Darius were still very much in the wings. It is difficult to imagine that the text was composed anywhere other than in South Afghanistan and later than the middle of the 6th century BCE.

Fig. 6: Aerial photograph of the Hellenic town of Ai Khanum, showing the juncture of four countries on the Vidēvdād list. The river to the right is the Daryā-i Panj (the Vahvī Dāityā), the river to the left is the Kokcha (probably the Darejī). The town may have occupied the western end of Ragha (the Samti ford is 60 kilometres upstream on the Daryā-i Panj). Bactria commences beyond the Kokcha. The mountains on the right bank of the Daryā-i Panj belong to Airyanem Vaējah, those far away to Sogdiana. (Photo ACTED, 2000)

Notes:

1. Gnoli 1989 repeats the same views with an updated bibliography. Skjærvø (1995: 163–5), though less committed in detail, shares the eastern-centred approach.
2. For *skaiti-*, "thorn", see Henning 1947: 52, n. 1.
3. In the case of Arachosia, *ərəδβō.drafšąm* is restituted by Kellens (1999–2000: 739), like *uparō* before *vimanō. hiia-* for Nisāya. In the present article the scientific transcription of Avestan is used only for direct quotations; more familiar transcriptions are used in the text, long vowels being indicated in order to avoid ambiguity.
4. For Kandahar: Helms 1982; McNicoll and Ball 1996 (the 90-hectare walled city dates from the Iron Age). For Bactra: summary and bibliography in Grenet 1989; the long-suspected Achaemenid levels under the 120-hectare citadel were discovered in 2004 (to be published by Roland Besenval and Philippe Marquis). For *ərəδβō.drafša-*, cf. the city Drapsa/Drapsaka; the possibility of its location in the Baghlān plain in southeast Bactria, contemplated in Grenet 1995 (after J. Harmatta and H. Humbach), has now indirectly been confirmed by the identification of Kunduz, the rival claimant, with Warnu, Greek Aornos (Sims-Williams 1997: 16-17, n. 28). Cf. also the festival of the "raising of the standard" still held on *Nowruz* at Mazar-i Sharif near Balkh (Dupree 1980: 105; Vogelsang 2000: 52, n. 20).
5. Gnoli 1980: 84–7.
6. Grenet 1994.
7. K. Hoffmann, *apud* Hintze 1994: 73.
8. Grenet 2002–2003: 154–6.
9. Marquart (1901: 78–9) drew attention to the name Nsai-mianak (**Nisāg ī miyānag*, "The middle Nisa") in the 7th-century *Armenian Geography*, probably to be identified with Maymanah.
10. Main discussion in Humbach 1991: I, 33–6, with reference to earlier articles by him.
11. Steblin-Kamenskii 1978.
12. Witzel 2000: 329–30. According to him, it corresponds to central Hindukush, as it does for Gnoli. Vogelsang put it far in the north, beyond the Syr-darya, according to his conception of a Scythian migration underlying the whole structure. Humbach 1991: I, 36 favours the Pamir region. Kellens 2003 : 104 translates *dāitiiā-* as "suitable" and interprets this epithet as referring to "an appropriate seasonal flow". By the way this is exactly how modern geographers characterise the Daryā-i Panj : "Of all the rivers of the region the Panj is the most regular, as it comes from the highest and most glaciate point"; consequently it always carries a sufficient amount of water, except during winter frosts, and its spring rise is more controllable than that of other rivers, in particular the Vakhsh (Pierre Gentelle, pers. comm.). There is probably a contrasting effect between the name of the Vahvī Dāityā and that of the Vakhsh ("the leaping / surging one").
13. *Apud* Bunsen 1857: V/2, 116.
14. Humbach 1991: I, 45–6, elaborating upon Hoffmann 1979. Witzel (318–19) accepts the western Ragha, while not excluding that "there may also have been two different *Raγas*".
15. As a marginal note to a forthcoming article "Après avoir brisé l'obstacle", where it is demonstrated that the abstract meaning "superior" usually assigned to Avestan *upara-* is not generalised, the word having in certain cases (like in *uparō.vimanah-*)

kept its Indo-Iranian meaning "next, ulterior". I am grateful to Jean Kellens for this information.
16. Tremblay 1999: 45–8 (unpublished PhD); more details in a letter dated 29.1.2004 in which he traces the history of this idea. I express my thanks to him; though agreeing in the main, my views differ from his in some details and he cannot be held responsible for the presentation given here.
17. For Young Avestan *ratu-*, meaning "patron, model", not "master, chief", see Tremblay 1998: 192–6. Cf. Plutarch's obviously well informed translation of Tishtrya's epithet *ratūm paitī.damča:* "guardian and watcher" (*philaka kai prooptēn*) (*De Iside et Osiride* 47 ; see de Jong 1997 : 193-194).
18. Consequently I cannot side with Gnoli's attempt to rescue the Median theological centre at Ray by assuming that *raya zaraθuštri-* is a different place from *raya θrizantu-* (Gnoli 1985).
19. Rightly noticed by Mary Boyce in Boyce and Grenet 1991: 81–2; but she shares Gnoli's view about "holy Raga" (a coined expression by her) being Median Ray, "whose Zoroastrian traditions went back perhaps to the eighth century B.C.".
20. Lastly Humbach 1991: I, 47–9 (and see p. 46 on *'l'k*).
21. From here to the end of this section I summarise and update an earlier article including detailed maps of the sector under discussion (Grenet 2002).
22. Watters 1904–1905: 273. According to Yutaka Yosida (pers.comm.), the reconstructed early middle Chinese form γat-la^h -γə with the normal prothetic γat- before initial r- indicates Rāgh (as assumed by Watters, quoting H. Yule) rather than Rāwan, a district just to the west of the Kokcha river proposed by Marquart [1901: 237–8], who supposed that this name [<*Rāγwan] derived from Rāgh anyway. The form Rāgh instead of the expected *Ragh can be explained, as a *vṛddhi* form generalized from the name of some part of the country, e.g. "plain of Ragha" or "river of Ragha" (both possibilities are suggested by X. Tremblay, pers.comm.). The name Badakhshān, mentioned besides Heluoho by Xuanzang (Boduochuangna) and already attested for the 5th century by the *Weishu* (Futisha), cannot pre-date the Sasanian conquest of Bactria in the 3rd century since it contains the Middle Persian title *bidaxš*, "viceroy, chief minister". The list in Eilers 1954: 300–301 gives the impression that there are more recorded "Rǎgh" toponyms than in reality. The name is actually generic ("plain near a mountain"), but in eastern Iranian countries there are only two clusters, one in western Badakhshān and one in the Toba Kakar range to the southeast of Kandahar. Lur'e 2004: 143–4 adds a few local toponyms scattered in Sogdiana. See also the village Ragh, just north of the town Chitrāl, and the town *Ragau* in Apavarticene to the west of Merv (Isidorus of Charax, 13).
23. For "neighbourhood discords", cf. the formulas a good observer of rural conditions uses about Badakhshān: "ces conflits séculaires qui ensanglantent périodiquement certains des villages de la région – et dont l'origine est à rechercher plutôt dans des vols de troupeaux, des disputes de bornage ou des contentieux sur l'usage des hauts pâturages que dans des différences cultuelles" (Puig 2005: 98; the "différences cultuelles" of today are between Ismailis and Sunni Muslims). The epithet *uparō.vimanah-* can be considered, geographically, as a characteristic of countries where good pasture is scarce or not controlled by a recognised authority, the opposite of *pouru.vāstra-* (characteristic of the country Urvā, see below). Ideologically it appears the opposite to *vouru.gaoiiaoiti-*, "with large pasture rights", epithet of Mithra.
24. It may seem extremely adventurous to propose a date for a text that no longer exists, but there are some indications. In those sections of *Dk.* 7 which are not marked as

quotations from the *zand* of the *Spand Nask*, Wishtāsp is titled either *šāh*, in conformity with the tradition embodied in the Sasanian *Xwadāy-nāmag*, or *dahibed*; in the quotations he is not called *šāh* (which has no corresponding Avestan word) but *Kay Wištāsp*, as everywhere in the subsisting *Avesta*, and in one place (4.86) *dahibed burzāwand Kay Wištāsp*. The underlying Avestan words *daiŋ́hupati-* and *bərəzant-* could echo the Achaemenid royal titles *xšāyaθiya vazraka* ... *xšāyaθiya dahyūnām* (for other sparse indications in Yashts 5 and 19 of a "royalisation" of the Kavis see Kellens 1979: 51, who suggests Achaemenid influence). The central episode of the *Spand Nask* (the revelation from Vohu Manah) was known to Greek philosophers of the Academy and the Peripatos in the 4th or 3rd century BCE, as shown by the remarkable account in Diodorus Siculus 1.94.2: "Thus it is recorded that among the Arians Zathraustes claimed that the Good Spirit gave him his laws, among the people known as the Getae who represent themselves to be immortal Zalmoxis asserted the same of their common goddess Hestia, and among the Jews Moyses referred his laws to the god who is invoked as Iao" (De Jong 1997: 266–7). I tentatively suggested (Boyce and Grenet 1991: 158, n. 26) that this first-hand information (demonstrated by the form *Zathraustes* for Zoroaster) came from Clearchus of Soli, a disciple of Aristotele, known to have visited eastern Bactria in the early 3rd century BCE and to have compared in his works various religious teachings, including those of the Magi and the Jews.

25. See Grenet and Rapin 2001. Recent excavations at Koktepe near Samarkand and at Sangyr-tepe in the Kashka-daryā valley have yielded remains of a fire platform and a fire place with clear indications of a preliminary phase of purification of the ground; these remains, dating probably from the 6th century BCE, give the earliest indications in the eastern Iranian countries of a fire cult organised at community level (Rapin, forthcoming).
26. Gubaev, Koshelenko and Tosi 1998.
27. Rejected by Humbach 1985 in favour of "lord of cattle", but I see no compelling reason for it. The geographical link between Gōbed and the Dāityā provides the best explanation for the choice of the Persepolitan (originally Assyrian) image of the man-headed bull, interpreted as "Gōbedšāh" in the *Mēnōg ī xrad* 62.30–35 (text quoted in Humbach's article), in order to symbolise the god Oxus on the seal of his temple included in the late Achaemenid "Oxus Treasure" (Grenet 2002–2003: 157).
28. Lévi 1925, commenting upon his edition of the *Mahāmāyūrī* (Lévi 1915).
29. P.Ø Skjærvø, letter of 9.4.2004: "Vaēkereta cannot contain Vayu- by regular sound changes, since Vayu only becomes Vaē- before nasal (Vaēm, Acc. of Vayu-) (. . .) The underlying word would be *vikərət-* or *vikərəta-*. This is to my knowledge not attested in Avestan, but it ought to mean 'done apart, removed'."
30. Christensen 1943: 33–4.
31. Gnoli 1980: 26–39.
32. Fussman 1974a: 4, with n. 5.
33. Ultimately Monchi-Zadeh 1975: 119–24.
34. Generally identified as the hedgehog (or porcupine?), a beneficent animal from the Zoroastrian viewpoint, but this particular name is considered depreciative in *Vd.* 13.2, whilst in our list it is mentioned on the positive or neutral side. Witzel 2000: 309, n. 55, suggests another ethnic name.
35. These hypotheses seem compatible with the etymologies proposed in Tremblay 2004, see esp. pp. 125 and 132–5 on Gava and Sogdians.
36. Morgenstierne 1979: 29.

37. Witzel 2000: 318, n. 72–73. In this context the name is "from fém. *vrkī*, 'she-wolf', a strange name for an area, if not taken metaphorically as a tribe 'having sorceresses, witches' ".
38. Vogelsang 2000: 54–5, but his attempt to locate here the people of the Parikanioi (Herodotus 7.68, 86), Elamite *Barrikana*, Aramaic *prkn*, is not tenable because of the initial consonantism *p-* / *b-* instead of *w-*. The Parikanioi should rather be looked for in Gedrosia (Bernard 1972: 172) or in Kermān as ancestors of the Barizān (Bivar 1985: 30–35).
39. Gnoli 1980: 39–42. Ctesias' Barkanioi might in fact be the same people as Herodotus' Parikanioi (cf. Elamite *Barrikana*).
40. *Ibid.*: 27–39.
41. *Pace* Witzel 2000: 308, n. 52, I trust the identification of the Zarenumaitī ("of gold") with the Arghandāb, established by Monchi-Zadeh (1975: 120–23) on the basis of a passage in the *Tārix-e Sīstān*, where it is stated that this river was particularly renowned for its gold.
42. Dupree 1980: 39.
43. Ferdinand 1962: 125 and map p. 127 (reproduced with additions in Dupree: map 9).
44. Witzel 2000: 312, n. 65.
45. Lévi 1915: 71–3, from which Henning (1947: 52–3) drew the inference for Varena of *Vd.*1.17 (adducing also the fortress Aornos captured by Alexander in the region that is today Bunēr).
46. Monchi-Zadeh 1975: 126. "Carx in Khorasan", mentioned by Humbach (1991: I, 34) as an alternative to Chakhr in Lōgar, is in fact Jarγ / Šarγ (*Čarγ?) near Bukhārā, not related etymologically to *Čaxra* (Lur'e 2004: 182, n. 255).
47. Watters 1904–1905: 262–3; Lévi 1915: 73. *Pace* Witzel 2000: 311, Pāṇini's *Varṇu* is Bunēr, not Bannu: see Lévi. There was a third Varena in eastern Bactria: Warnu (see Sims-Williams 1997:16–17 with n. 28). It is Humbach's choice for the country in *Vd.*1 but has not gained support for the same reason that applies to Hapta Hendu: the "untimely menstruations", referring probably to the early puberty of Indian girls (Darmesteter 1892-3: II, 15, n. 43).
48. Gnoli 1980: 65–6.
49. Perhaps the town Bagarda in Ptolemy 6.18.5, if Wardak < *Waγardak? There was actually a Kushan walled town in Wardak (Fussman 1974b). But there is no proof that Wardak is an ancient name. The identification Bagarda – Vaēkereta, suggested by Darmesteter (1892–3: II, 10, n. 22), and more or less upheld by all modern authors except Humbach, is hardly tenable as it would be difficult to account for the loss of -ē- in the first syllable (N. Sims-Williams, pers.comm.).
50. Sims-Williams 1997: 16–18, notes 28 and 34.
51. Schwartz 1990 proposes recognising cult practices similar to those of the Kafirs of the upper Chitrāl valleys (including the spilling of blood in the fire and the cooking of the head in it) in those attributed to the Vyāmburas in *Yt.* 14.54–56.
52. Witzel 2000: 312–16, with various proposals for the translation of the Ohrmazdian and Ahrimanic parts of the description.
53. Most clearly at Naqsh-e Rostam, but demonstrably so in other inscriptions as well, except the one on Darius' statue at Susa where it reflects the centred scheme of the seven parts of the world. I refer in advance to C. Rapin, *Géographie historique et géographie mythique (Génèse des cartes antiques de l'Asie, de l'Afrique et de l'Europe)*, chap. 30 (forthcoming).
54. Witzel 2000: 322. It is also the order of the list of rivers of Sistān in the *Zamyād Yasht*, but they are introduced in a purifying context (*Yt.* 19.68: the Khvarenah they

carry "could sweep away therewith all the [inhabitants of the] non-Aryan lands in one sweep"). In the *Mihr Yasht* the countries are enumerated in clockwise order, a natural option as they are surveyed by the rising Mithra.
55. But Vogelsang's idea that these countries already shared a Scythian aristocratic stratum at the time of the composition of *Vd.* 1 rests on a disputable equation between "Scythians" and "horsemen costumes" such as those depicted at Persepolis. Cf. the reservations in Lyonnet 1997: 118.
56. The recent discovery of potteries of the "Yaz I" type (14th to 10th century BCE) near Peshawar attests to intrusions from regions north of the Hindukush in a period prior to the composition of the Young *Avesta* (Henri-Paul Francfort, pers.comm.).
57. Kellens (1999–2000: 741) interprets some features of Varena and Ranhā as referring to monstrous populations: *čaθru.gaoša-*, "four-eared", *asāra-*, "headless". One can object that *čaθru.gaoša-* is in the Ohrmazdian part of Varena's description, while physical monstrosities are Ahrimanic (cf. the "three mouths" of Azhi Dahāka). The term *čaθru.gaoša-* is more probably "with four corners" and refers to the shape of the country or of its chief fortress. In this context *Cartana oppidum sub Caucaso quod postea Tetragonis dictum* (Pliny, *Hist. Nat.* VI .92) is often mentioned, but it is rather to be looked for in or near Kapisa. Bunēr is roughly rectangular, bound by the Indus, the river of Kābul and the curving Swat; the plain of Bannu is usually described as an "irregular oval", which does not bring to mind "four corners". As for *asāra-* in Ranhā, there are several possible interpretations: see Witzel.
58. Monchi-Zadeh 1975: 114. The name of Urvākhshaya, Keresāspa's brother (*Y.* 9.10; *Yt.* 15.28), has generally been explained as "king of Urvā" since Darmesteter (II: 586, n.18), but see now Kellens 2002: 435–7 for a discussion of the meaning of *xšā* in Avestan. Other etymologies are possible, including from *uruuāxš-*, "joy" (Mayrhofer 1979: No. 321).
59. See Grenet 1994 : 91-92.

Editions of the Avesta and Pahlavi texts

Avesta, die heiligen Bücher der Parsen, ed. Karl F. Geldner, I–III, Stuttgart, 1889–95.
Avesta, die heiligen Bücher der Parsen, translated on the basis of Chr. Bartholomae's *Altiranischem Wörterbuch* by Fritz Wolff, Strassburg, 1910.
Dēnkard (Dk.),VII: Marijan Molé, *La légende de Zoroastre selon les textes pehlevis*, Paris, 1967.
Great Bundahishn: Zand-Ākāsīh, Iranian or Greater Bundahišn, transliteration and translation in English by Behramgore T. Anklesaria, Bombay, 1956.
Pahlavi Vendidād, transliteration and translation in English by Behramgore T. Anklesaria, Bombay, 1949.
Wīzīdagīhā ī Zādspram (WZ): Philippe Gignoux, Ahmad Tafazzoli, *Anthologie de Zādspram*, Paris, 1993 (*Studia Iranica* – Cahier 13).

3

The Achaemenids and the *Avesta*

P.O. Skjærvø (Harvard University)

Introduction

Were the Achaemenids Zoroastrians? This question has been debated by students of Iranian religion throughout the 20th century, and the answer has often been sought in terms of similarities and differences between Zoroastrianism and the religion of the Achaemenid kings, as expressed in their inscriptions. The differences have usually been defined in terms of "omissions and discrepancies" between the two,[1] and it has been argued that the lack of mention of Zarathuštra and key terms such as the six Life-giving Immortals (the *aməša spəṇta*s), which play a prominent role in the *Avesta*, shows that the Achaemenid religion was, at least, not orthodox Zoroastrianism. "Orthodox" would here mean in agreement with the religion expressed in the oldest texts, the *Gāthā*s, but what is today considered to be Zoroastrian "orthodoxy" is largely a construct by Western scholars since the end of the 19th century who have regarded the *Gāthā*s as the teachings of Zarathuštra and expressions of what they believe was his "reformed religion". As the view that Zarathuštra was a historical person, a prophet and a reformer can be shown to rest on shaky, even non-existent foundations,[2] this definition of Zoroastrian "orthodoxy" is equally problematic, and the relationship of the *Avesta* – our only source for the oldest Iranian religion – and the Achaemenid inscriptions to the teachings of Zarathuštra shall not occupy us here.

More importantly, the *Avesta* and the inscriptions are fundamentally different kinds of texts (ritual texts *versus* royal proclamations), as well as in different languages. There is therefore no particular reason to expect any mention in the inscriptions of Zarathuštra or the Life-giving Immortals, who are also absent from the Sasanian inscriptions.

Here I shall compare the Achaemenid inscriptions and the *Avesta*, especially the *Old Avesta*, from a literary point of view. For this purpose, I shall define "Achaemenid religion" loosely as the religion expressed in the various primary and secondary sources at our disposal and "Zoroastrianism" as the religion expressed in the *Avesta*. We shall see that there are so many similarities between Achaemenid religion and Zoroastrianism defined in this manner that it is hard to conclude that the latter was *not* the religion of the Achaemenid kings, at least from Darius onwards.

The original question then has two possible answers. Either the Achaemenids had always been Zoroastrians or, at some time, for some reason, the early Achaemenids became Zoroastrians.[3]

The Elamite texts from Persepolis

The Elamite texts found by the Oriental Institute at Persepolis during the excavations in 1933–1934 led by Ernst Herzfeld and published as the Fortifications tablets (dated 509–494 BCE of the reign of Darius I) and the Treasury tablets (dated 492–458 BCE of the reigns of Darius I, Xerxes and Artaxerxes I) provide a wide range of information about the religious practices of the Achaemenids. Numerous gods are mentioned, as well as several types of priests and several kinds of religious services.[4]

Avestan divinities receiving sacrifices include Ahura Mazdā[5] <d.u-ra-mas-da>, the principal god, who is possibly also referred to by Elamite *napir iršara*, "the Great God"; Išpantāramatiš <d.iš-pan-da-ra-mat-ti-iš>, Av. *spəṇtā ārmaitiš*, "life-giving Humility", deity of the earth, possibly also referred to by Babylonian KI; Irtāna-fruirtiš[6] <d.ir-da-na-pir-ru-ir-ti-iš>, Av. *aṣ̌āunąm frauuaṣ̌i*, "the pre-souls (*fravashis*) of the sustainers of Order", (female) divine beings who assist Ahura Mazdā in his cosmogonic activities;[7] Visai Bagā <d.mi-še-ba-ka, d.mi-ša-a-ba-ka>, "All (the) Gods";[8] Narīsaṇga <d.na-ri-ša-an-ka>, Av. *nairiia saŋha*, "the manly/heroic announcement", the divine messenger.

In addition, divinities of rivers, mountains, places and cities receive sacrifices, with which we can compare the sacrifices to/of the waters in the *Yasna haptaŋhāiti* and the Young Avestan expression *vīspəmca aṣ̌auuanəm gaēθīm yazatəm yazamaide*, "and we sacrifice to every Orderly entity worthy of sacrifice in the world of living beings" (*Yasna* 16.2).

Among religious officials we find the *yašta* <ya-iš-da>, "sacrificer" (Av. *yašta*) and **ātr̥waxša* <ha-tur/tar-ma-ak/ik-šá> (Av. *ātrəuuaxša*); among religious services, we find *dauçam* <da-u-šá-am, tam₅-šá-am, etc.>, "libation service" (Av. *zaoθrəm* "libation") or *dauçiya* <tam₅-ši-ya-um> and *bagadauçiya* <ba-qa-da-u-ši-ya>, "libation service for the god(s)".[9]

The only religious service that seems to have been celebrated on a grand scale, judging from the large quantity of provisions recorded for it, was the *lan* service (Elamite *d.lan*). As Ahura Mazdā himself is only rarely mentioned in these tablets, it is usually assumed that the *lan* service was the official service for the supreme deity and the *lan* service was simply the *yasna*. The most commonly mentioned official is Elamite *šaten*, "priest", who would correspond to the Avestan *zaota*. The *maguš* <*ma-ku-iš*> (OPers. *maguš*) was chiefly involved with the *lan* service.

The Aramaic documents from Egypt

The Aramaic letters found at an Achaemenid military colony on the island of Elephantine in the Nile (mostly from the 5th century BCE) provide further evidence in the personal names, many of which clearly reflect the Avestan religion: e.g. Ṛrtaxwant, "*possessing Order"[10], Ātrfarn, "enjoying the (gifts of) fortune of the fire(?)", Ārma(n)tidāt, "(child) given by (Life-giving) Ārmaiti", Spantdāt, "(child) given by Life-giving (Ārmaiti?)", Miθrdāt, "(child) given by Miθra", Hōmdāt, "(child) given by Hauma", Mazdayazn, "who sacrifices to (Ahura) Mazdā", Miθrayazn, "who sacrifices to Miθra", Žāmāsp, Av. Jāmāspa, epic name.[11]

The Religion of the *Avesta*

The evidence presented briefly above suffices to show that the Achaemenids, at least from Darius on, were Zoroastrian in the sense that their religion, as far as we can tell, agreed with that of the *Avesta*. Before we continue, let me therefore summarise some fundamental notions of the Avestan worldview.

By a primordial sacrifice, Ahura Mazdā established (Avestan, Old Persian verb *dā-*) Order (Avestan *aša*),[12] that is, the *ordered cosmos*. The sun was put in the sky, and the seasons were regulated so as to provide a firm basis for life and fertility on earth and peace and happiness for all living things. The deities of the ordered cosmos and their works are characterised by having "swelling" power (*spənta*), that is, power to produce life.

In the *Old* and *Young Avesta*, this creative activity of Ahura Mazdā is described in several places. A relatively straightforward description is found in the *Yasna haptaŋhāiti*:

Yasna haptaŋhāiti 37.1
iθā āt̰ yazamaidē ahurəm mazdąm yə gąmcā ašəmcā dāt̰
apascā dāt̰ uruuaråscā vaŋͮhīš
raocåscā dāt̰ būmīmcā vīspācā vohū
So, in this way we are sacrificing to Ahura Mazdā, who set (in place) both the cow and Order, (who set in place) both the (good) waters and the good plants,
(who set in place) both the lights and the earth and all good (things in between).

Here, the main items are the heavenly lights and the earth, as well as all things between heaven and earth that provide man with a good life. The description of the cosmogony is usually more esoteric, however, as in the second *Gāthā*, where it is in the form of rhetorical questions about the origins of cosmic phenomena:

Yasna 44.3b-d
kasnā ząθā ptā ašahiiā pauruiiō
kasnā x^vəṇg strə̄mcā dāt̰ aduuānəm
kə̄ yā må uxšiieitī nərəfsaitī θβat̰
Who, I wonder, (is), by (his) engendering, the first father of Order?
Who, I wonder, (first) set (in its place) the road of the sun and of the stars?
Who is he by who(se agency) the moon is first waxing then waning?

Yasna 44.4b-d
kasnā dərətā ząmcā adə̄ nabåscā
auuapastōiš kə̄ apō uruuaråscā
kə̄ vātāi duuąnmaibiiascā yaogət̰ āsū
Who, I wonder, (first) held (up) the earth down below and the clouds (above keeping them) from falling? Who (fashioned) the waters and the plants?
Who yoked the two fleet (coursers) to the wind and the clouds?

The answer to these questions is probably "Ahura Mazdā". After the first cosmic day, however, the forces of darkness assaulted Ahura Mazdā's ordered cosmos, bringing death and destruction upon his creation.

To re-establish the ordered cosmos, Ahura Mazdā needs the help of humans, and the purpose of rituals such as the *Yasna* and the *Vidēvdād* is to heal and regenerate Ahura Mazdā's world. The first human sacrificer, chosen by the gods themselves (*Yasna* 29), was Zarathuštra, who successfully fought the protagonists of evil, including the Evil Spirit himself (Avestan Angra Maniiu) and his minions, the *daēuuas*, the *old* or *other* gods (chasing them underground), and the great cosmic deception, the Lie (Avestan *drug-/druj-*, Old Persian *drauga*), which distorts the truth about Ahura Mazdā's Order. Since then, all human sacrificers perform the work of Zarathuštra.

The relationship between the gods and the human sacrificers is the one obtaining between guest-friends, between whom gifts are given in return for gifts,[13] a process that establishes unbreakable bonds of mutual dependence. In the sacrifice, the sacrificer gives to the gods his thoughts, words and actions. With his thoughts and words he praises the deities, thereby strengthening them, but he scorns the forces of evil, thereby weakening them. The sacrificial offerings, hymns and refreshments are sent up to the gods in a *chariot race* against rival sacrificers.

If his sacrifice is successful, the sacrificer makes the world swell with the juices of life, he becomes a *saošiiaṇt-*, a "revitaliser", and the sacrifice produces the royal *command* (Av. *xšaθra*) for Ahura Mazdā, which enables him to overcome the powers of darkness and evil.

Once *Ahura Mazdā is again in command*, he ensures *peace* (*rāman*) in the cosmos; he vanquishes darkness and death, making light and life reappear. The sun reappears in the sky and rain falls, whereby the earth is warmed and fertilised, making *pasture* (*vāstra*) *grow for the cow*; the world that was desiccated, withered and dead is again *full of the juices of life* (*fraša*);[14] and the sacrificer receives his *fee* (*mīžda*) in exchange for and commensurate in value with (*vasnā*) the services rendered.

The Announcements

The first text that confronts any student of Old Persian is the king's statement, *θātiy dārayavauš xšāyaθiya*, "King Darius announces". The Old Iranian society was an oral one. Writing one's own language, which we take as the norm, was for them unusual. The Old Persian inscriptions are therefore in the oral tradition and are presented as the oral announcements of the kings.

Similarly, the *Old Avesta* contains the sacrificer's oral announcement of his knowledge about the world and its origin, notably of what the god has told him. Among the technical terms for the god's announcements, the most common is the simple word "speak" (Av. *mrao-*, *vac-*), but there is also *sāh-*, "command, instruct, ordain", and *sə̄ŋgha-*, "announce".[15] The Old Persian (etymological) equivalent of *sə̄ŋgha-* is *θaⁿha-*, present *θātiy*, "announces" (from **θaⁿhatiy*, imperfect *aθaⁿha*), the verb that expresses the king's announcements.

Avestan *sə̄ŋgha-* is used about both the sacrificer and Ahura Mazdā. Ahura Mazdā's announcements are by themselves capable of combating the Lie and its evil and so protect all living beings (see *Yasna* 44.14b-c, below p. 71). The sacrificer, by his announcements, praises Ahura Mazdā and his work and scorns those possessed by the Lie (Avestan *drəguuaṇt*). In this manner, he becomes a "revitaliser" (*saošiiaṇt-*), someone who will help bring back dawn and rejuvenate the world (see below, p. 74):

Yasna 48.12
*aṯ tōi aŋhən saošiiaṇtō daxiiunąm
yōi xšnūm vohū manaŋhā hacåṇtē
šiiaoθanāiš ašā θβahiiā mazdā sə̄ŋghahiiā
tōi zī dātā hamaēstārō aēšəm.mahiiā*
Thus, those shall be the the revitalisers of the lands
who with good thought shall pursue your *favour
by the actions of (= according to) your announcement, O Mazdā, according to Order.
For, indeed, they have been established as opponents of Wrath (= the demon of darkness).

If the sacrificer is successful and wins the race against his competitors, he becomes the Life-giving Man and will achieve his goal, which is to put Ahura Mazdā and his supporters back in command for them to produce good things for gods and men, notably "peace and pasture". Note especially the following passage:

Yasna 51.21 (cf. *Yasna*s 34.2, 48.7)
ārmatōiš nā spəṇtō huuō cistī uxδāiš šíiaoθanā
daēnā ašəm spə̄nuuaṯ vohū xšaθrəm manaŋhā
mazdå dadāṯ ahurō tə̄m vaŋʸhīm yāsā ašīm
This one (is now) a life-giving man by the *understanding: "By (my) utterances the works of Ārmaiti (the earth, are produced);
by (my) vision-soul (*daēnā* = thoughts, words, and actions), Order (is again) full of vitality; with (my/his) good thought Mazdā
Ahura establishes (his) command." (So now) I am asking *him* for a good reward.

Similarly, the Achaemenid kings, *in* and so also *by* their statements, express their knowledge of the world, praise Ahura Mazdā and his work, scorn those possessed by the Lie (Old Persian *draujana*) or those siding with the Evil one (*aʰrīka*),[16] re-establish and uphold the Order of the lands and provide peace and "happiness" (*šiyāti*) for his land and subjects.

The King's God And The God's King

In the Achaemenid inscriptions, it is the king who is portrayed as sacrificing to Ahura Mazdā (*auramazdām ayadaiy*, "I sacrificed to Ahura Mazdā", passim), the great god who ordered the cosmos and who bestowed the royal command upon the king, so that he might (re-)establish and maintain order on earth. The purpose of the established order was to provide *happiness* for man:

Darius at Naqsh-e Rostam (DNa 1-8)
baga vazạrka auramazdā	The great god is Ahura Mazdā,
haya imām būmim adā	who established this earth,
haya avam asmānam adā	who established that heaven,
haya martiyam adā	who established man,
haya šiyātim adā martiyahạyā	who established happiness for man
haya dārayavaum xšāyaθiyam akunauš	who made Darius king...

We see that the king fulfils the prerequisites for the sacrificer's success. He *knows* that it was Ahura Mazdā who established the ordered world and happiness for man. He also knows that, although there were other gods, Ahura Mazdā was the greatest (Old Persian *maθišta bagānām*, DH 7, etc).

The cosmogonic "meaning" (the underlying myth) of the sacrifice of the Achaemenid kings was probably no longer exactly that of the sacrifice in the second millennium BCE, and we do not know to what extent the kings or their priests understood the literal meaning of the Old Avestan texts. In the Old Persian texts, however, we see what they *thought* they referred to.

One aspect that remains stable is the relationship between king and god as guest-friends, tied together in mutual dependence:[17]

Darius at Susa (DSk)
manā AM AMha adam
AMm ayadaiy AM-maiy upastām baratuv
Ahura Mazdā is mine, I am Ahura Mazdā's.
I sacrificed to Ahura Mazdā. May Ahura Mazdā bear me aid!

Here the guest-friend relationship between Ahura Mazdā and the king is portrayed as one of *possession* between the god and his sacrificer, in which Ahura Mazdā, in return for sacrifices, assists the king. It is difficult to state more explicitly the function of the sacrifice and the mutual indebtedness of the sacrificer and the divinity.

In the *Old Avesta*, the royal command (*xšaθra*) is generated for Ahura Mazdā by the successful sacrifice. Whether the king was aware of this function of the sacrifice we do not know, nor whether the priests were. To the king, the important thing was that it was the god who had bestowed the royal command (*xšaça*) upon *him* in return for his sacrifices:

Darius at Behistun (DB 1.11-12)
vašnā auramazdāha adam xšāyaθiya a^{h}miy auramazdā xšaçam manā frābara
By the greatness of Ahura Mazdā, I am king. Ahura Mazdā gave me the royal command.

Like Zarathuštra, the king was chosen by Ahura Mazdā, who chose him to perform a specific job: to rule and maintain order in his land:

Darius at Susa (DSf 15-18; cf. DNa 1-8, above)
auramazdām avaθā kāma āha
haruvahạyāyā [BUyā] martiyam [mām] *avạrnavatā *mām XŠyam
  *akunauš *ahạyāyā BUyā
Thus Ahura Mazdā willed it:
He chose me, the (only) man of the whole [earth]. He made [me] king of this earth.

With his royal command, the king rules (*xšaya-*) like Ahura Mazdā and Yima before him (*Yasna* 43.1b [cf. 51.17] *vasō xšaiiąs mazdå dāiiāṯ ahurō*, "Mazdā Ahura, commanding at will, shall give..."; *Yasna* 9.5 *yauuata xšaiiōiṯ... yimō*, "for as long as Yima would rule"). He also fulfils the sacrificers' wish: *Yasna* 8.5 *vasasca tū ahura mazdā uštāca xšaēša hauuanąm dāmanąm*, "and may you, Ahura Mazdā, be in command at will and according to wish of you own creations!", as well as that of the Old Avestan sacrificer: *Yasna* 48.5a *huxšaθrā xšə̄ntąm mā nə̄ dušə.xšaθrā xšə̄ntā*, "let those of good command be in command, let not those of bad command be in command of us!".

Thus the king's sacrifices to Ahura Mazdā ensure the god's status as ruler of the ordered cosmos; in return, the god *gives* support and rewards to the king, ensuring *his* status as ruler of the ordered land, for him to overcome chaos and evil and re-establish and consolidate political order, peace and well-being (in the widest sense). Thus Darius's view of Ahura Mazdā and the sacrificer's functions matches that of the Old Avestan poet, as does his title, *xšāyaθiya*.

The king obviously performs Ahura Mazdā's will on earth, and his achievements in the world of the living parallel and match those of Ahura Mazdā in the world of intangibles. There is no explicit statement to this effect in the inscriptions nor in the artistic representations, but it is implicitly clear. Only in the Sasanian period do we find the idea expressed in the royal reliefs, where the victory over the king's enemy is equal to Ahura Mazdā's victory over the Evil Spirit.[18]

The Poet-Sacrificer's And The King's Self-Presentations

The two principles of Order and the Lie are embryonically present in every man's mind, and he must make a choice (Avestan *var-*) between them that will determine both how his life will be on earth and what will await him in afterlife. Specifically, the sacrificer must prove that he has made the right choice by presenting himself as (1) a competent sacrificer, that is, as another Zarathuštra; (2) a creature of Ahura Mazdā's; and (3) an opponent of the Lie:[19]

Yasna 43.7b-e
hiiat̰ mā vohū pairī.jasat̰ manaŋhā
pərəsat̰cā mā ciš ahī kahiiā ahī
kaθā aiiarə̄. daxšārā fərasaiiāi dīšā
aibī θβāhū gaēθāhū *tanušucā
When one *surrounds me with good thought
and asks me "Who are you? Whose are you?
How would you *submit your daily-*mark-earnings for questioning
*regarding your herds and persons?"—

Yasna 43.8
at̰ hōi aojī zaraθuštrō pauruuīm
haiθiiō duuaēšā̊ hiiat̰ isōiiā drəguuāitē
at̰ ašāunē rafənō xˇiiə̄m aojōŋhuuat̰
hiiat̰ ā būštīš vasasə.xšaθrahiiā diiā
yauuat̰ ā θβā mazdā stāumī ufiiācā
then I declare myself[20] to him first as "Zarathuštra",
the *true* one; (second, that) I wish to command hostilities for the follower of the Lie,
but for the sustainer of Order I wish to be support and strength, (and, third, that,) because I would like to *tie on (your head) the *insignia of one who commands at will,[21]
to the extent that I can, I am praising you, O Mazdā, and weaving (you) into hymns.

Thus the Old Iranian sacrificer has a specific identity, appurtenance and job. What these are depends upon the choice each person makes for himself. Our sacrificer has made his choices.

First, he identifies himself as a/the "real" Zarathuštra. Second, he states that, of the two sides in the universal conflict, he wishes to uphold Ahura Mazdā's cosmic Order. Third, he tries to do his job as sacrificer as best he can by exalting the fame of Ahura Mazdā above everything else through his songs of praise in order to make him the sole ruler.

In the *Young Avesta*, it is stated repeatedly that Zarathuštra was the first to praise Ahura Mazdā's Order but scorn the supporters of evil. The effect of the former is to strengthen, that of the latter to weaken the recipients:

Yašt 17.18 (see below p. 76)
yō paoiriiō mašiiākō	who was the first mortal
staota ašəm yaṯ vahištəm	to praise Order, which is the best,
yazata ahurəm mazdąm	to sacrifice to Ahura Mazdā,
yazata aməšə̄ spəṇtə̄	to sacrifice to the Life-giving Immortals.

Yašt 13.89
yō paoiriiō stōiš astuuaiθiiå	who was the first of the bony existence
staoṯ ašəm nāist daēuuū	to praise Order and scorn the *daēuua*s
fraorənata mazdaiiasnō zaraθuštriš	(and) to choose to sacrifice to Ahura Mazdā as someone in the tradition of Zarathuštra,
vīdaēuuō ahura.ṯkaēšō	to discard the *daēuua*s and follow the *guidance of Ahura (Mazdā).

This, in turn, became the duty of every good Zoroastrian, as expressed in the Zoroastrian "creed", the *Frauuarānē*:

Yasna 11.19-12.1
staomī ašəm ... nāismī daēuuō
frauuarānē mazdaiiasnō zaraθuštriš vīdaēuuō ahura.ṯkaēšō
staotā aməšanąm spəṇtanąm yaštā aməšanąm spəṇtanąm
I praise Order. I scorn the *daēuua*s.
I choose the sacrifice to Ahura Mazdā as someone in the tradition of Zarathuštra, to discard the *daēuua*s, and follow the *guidance of Ahura Mazdā,
to be a praiser of the Life-giving Immortals, a sacrificer to the Life-giving Immortals.

The king's self-presentation is not much different. Thus, the Behistun inscription contains, to put it simply: the king's name and his ancestry; a statement of his appurtenance to Ahura Mazdā, who bestowed the royal command upon him; and statements about the king's activities, which support Ahura Mazdā and combat the forces of the Lie.

1. WHO ARE YOU?

The Old Iranian sacrificer answers the first of the three questions with his name. Similarly the king begins his announcements by stating his name and function: *adam dārayavauš xšāyaθiya vazaṛka* ..., "I am Darius, the great king ...". Conversely, Darius's opponents all present themselves falsely, as, for instance, in the following cases:

Darius at Behistun (DB 1.77-78)
utā I martiya bābiruviya nadi^{n}tabaira nāma *ainairahạyā puça hauv udapatatā bābirauv kāram avaθā adurujiya adam nabukudaracara a^{h}miy haya nabunaitahạyā puça
And a (certain) Babylonian, Nidintu-Bēl, son of Ainaira, rose up in Babylon.
He lied to the army/people: I am Nebuchadrezzar, the son of Nabonidus.

Darius at Behistun (DB 4.80-86)
imaiy martiyā tayaiy adakaiy avadā *āha^{n}tā yātā adam gaumātam tayam magum avājanam haya bạrdiya agaubatā
These are the men who were there at that time until I had killed Gaumāta, the Magian, who declared he was Smerdis.

2. WHOSE ARE YOU? ON WHOSE SIDE ARE YOU?

The obvious way to answer the Gathic question "Whose are you?" would be to give the father's name. This is what Darius does, for instance at the beginning of the Behistun inscription, where he gives his genealogy through five generations. Elsewhere he also states his ethnicity, e.g. DNa 8–15: *haxāmanišiya pārsa pārsahạyā puça ariya ariya ciça*, "an Achaemenid, a Persian, son of a Persian, an Aryan, of Aryan seed".

The Old Avestan sacrificer's answer to this question, however, is to state with whom he sides in the cosmic conflict, and, like Zarathuštra before him, Darius states his appurtenance by asserting that he is on the side of the supporters of Order and against those possessed by the Lie.

The principal threat to the Order established by Ahura Mazdā is the Lie, that is, false statements regarding the true Order. In practice, it is a cosmic principle that acts to confuse gods and men and so cause them to make wrong choices and stray from the straight path.

This theme of *being deceived and bewildered by the Lie* is fundamental both in the *Old Avesta* and in the Achaemenid inscriptions. It happened in the world of the gods, and from there it came to the world of humans. It was, in fact, their wrong choices that apparently demoted the old gods (*daēuua*s) from their Indo-Iranian status as good gods:

Yasna 30.6ab
aiiā̊ nōiṱ ərəš vīśiiātā daēuuācinā hiiaṱ īš dəbaomā pərəsmanə̄ṇg upā.jasaṱ hiiaṱ vərənātā acištəm manō

Especially the *daēuua*s did not discriminate correctly between these two, because deception would come over them as they were discussing (and) because they would prefer the worst thought.

In the Achaemenid inscriptions, it is the absence of the king that produces room for the Lie to deceive and confuse his subjects:

Darius at Behistun (DB 1.34-35)
yaθā ka^mbūjiya mudrāyam ašiyava pasāva kāra a^hrīka abava
[utā] drauga dahyauvā vasiy abava
When Cambyses had gone off to Egypt, then the army/people sided with the Evil one, and the Lie proliferated in the land.

By the domino effect, the originally confused gods then continue to confuse others and turn them away from the straight path:[22]

Yasna 32.4
yāat yūš tā *framīmiθā yā mašiiā acištā dantō
vaxšəntē daēuuō.zuštā vaŋhə̄uš sīždiiamnā manaŋhō
mazdå ahurahiiā xratə̄uš nasiiantō ašāatcā
As much as you shall have *voided (the deals, even) giving, O mortals, what (are) the worst (things)
to the blazing (fire, things) pleasing the *daēuua*s, (so much you are) moving away from good thought,
(and) going astray from the path of the guiding thought of Mazdā Ahura and from Order.

Yasna 32.5
tā dəbənaotā mašīm hujiiātōiš amərətātascā
hiiat vå akā manaŋhā yə̄ŋg daēuuə̄ŋg akascā maniiuš
akā šiiaoθanəm vacaŋhā yā fracinas drəguuantəm xšiiō
Thereby you deceive mortal man, (depriving him) of good living and immortality,
because the bad inspiration, too, (deceives) you (all), whom (we know to be) the *daēuua*s, with bad thought
(and your) action with bad speech, through which (his) lamentation *reveals the one possessed by the Lie.

The scenario is the same in the Achaemenid inscriptions:

Darius at Behistun (DB 4.33-35)
dahyāva imā tayā hamiçiyā abava drauga-diš *hamiçiyā akunauš
taya imaiy kāram adurujiyaša
These lands that became rebellious, the Lie made them rebellious,
so that these (men) lied to the army/people.

In contrast to the king, who is chosen by god:

Darius at Behistun (DB 4.61-65)

avahaya-rādi-maiy auramazdā upastām abara utā aniyāha bagāha tayaiy [ha^{n}tiy]
*yaθā naiy a^{h}rīka āham naiy draujana āham
naiy zūrakara āham naiy adam nai-maiy tau^{h}mā
upariy arštām upariyāyam naiy škauθim naiy tunuva^{n}tam zūra akunavam

For this reason Ahura Mazdā bore me aid, as well as the other gods who are,
because I did not side with the Evil one (and) I was not a liar.
I did nothing crooked, neither I nor my family.
I wandered in straightness. I did nothing crooked, either to the poor or the mighty.

One consequence of being deceived by the Lie is that one no longer knows who the good powers are. The Lie therefore manifests itself in the *sacrifice to the wrong gods*, the *other* gods, the *daivas*, which the kings forcefully oppose, in accordance with the *Frauuarānē*:

Darius at Behistun (DB 5.15-17)

avaiy ūvjiyā [a^{h}rīkā āha] utā-šām auramazdā naiy *ayadiya
auramazdām ayadaiy vašnā auramazdāha [yaθā] mām [kāma] *avaθā-diš akunavam

Those Elamites sided with the Evil one, and Ahura Mazdā received no sacrifice from them.
I sacrificed to Ahura Mazdā. By the greatness of Ahura Mazdā, as was my wish, thus I did to them.

Xerxes at Persepolis (XPh 35-41)

utā a^{n}tar aitā dahạyāva āha yadā-taya paruvam daivā ayadiya
pasāva vašnā auramazdahā adam avam daivadānam viyakanam
utā patiyazbayam daivā mā yadiyaiša
yadāyā paruvam daivā ayadiya avadā adam auramazdām ayadaiy ạrtācā bạrzmaniy

And among these lands, there was (a place) where previously *daivas* received sacrifices.
Then, by the greatness of Ahura Mazdā, I destroyed that den of *daivas*,
and I made a counter-proclamation: The *daivas* are not to receive sacrifices!
Where previously the *daivas* received sacrifices, there *I sacrificed to Ahura Mazdā according to Order in the height.*[23]

Although these expressions are not used by Darius, what Xerxes describes here in words is clearly also what Darius already described in the reliefs on his tomb, where he is shown sacrificing by the altar to the god hovering in the winged disk above.[24]

Moreover, the king's ability to discern between straight and crooked, right and wrong, was obviously part of the mutual dependency relationship between him and his god, to whom this ability clearly belonged:

Darius at Naqsh-e Rostam (DNb 5-12)
*vašnā auramazdāhā avākaram a^{h}miy taya rāstam dauštā a^{h}miy
miθa naiy dauštā a^{h}miy ...
taya rāstam ava mām kāma martiyam draujanam naiy dauštā a^{h}miy*
By the greatness of Ahura Mazdā I am of such a sort that I approve of what is straight,
I do not approve of what is devious/wrong ...
What is straight, that is my wish. I am not one who favours the follower of the Lie ...

Like Zarathuštra, who insists to Ahura Mazdā that he is the/a *true* Zarathuštra (unlike the many, presumably, who only claim to be so), the king takes Ahura Mazdā as his witness(?) that what he says is real and true (*hašiya*) and not a lie said to *deceive* (*duruxta*):

Darius at Behistun (DB 4.43-45; the restoration of the text is problematic)
*auramazdāha *ragam *vạrdiyaiy yaθā ima hašiyam naiy duruxtam
adam *akunavam *hamahạyāyā θarda*
May I ... the ... of Ahura Mazdā if this is true, not a lie said to deceive;
I did (it) in one and the same year.

Thus, behaviour characterising Ahura Mazdā's supporters consists in speaking only what is really true (*hašiya*), behaving with straightness (*ạrštā*), and doing and speaking what is straight (*rāsta*),[25] as opposed to lying (*durujiya-*), leading astray (*vināθaya-*), behaving crookedly (*zūra^h kar-*), deviously or erratically (*miθa^h kar-*). All these are just the wiles of the Enemy, recognisable by their disorderliness, their crookedness and their lack of system, but also by their foul stench (*gasta*). It is therefore the task of the king to try to keep his subjects on the straight path and not mistake what comes from god for the foul impulses of the Evil one:

Darius at Naqsh-e Rostam (DNa 51-60)
*mām auramazdā pātuv hacā gastā utā-maiy viθam utā imām dahạyāum
aita adam auramazdām jadiyāmiy aita-maiy auramazdā dadātuv
martiyā hayā auramazdāhā framānā hauv-taiy gastā mā θadaya
paθīm tayām rāstām mā *ava^{h}ạrda*
Let Ahuramazdā protect me from the evil stench, as well as my house and this land.
This I ask of Ahuramazdā. Let Ahuramazdā give it to me!
O man, let not what is Ahura Mazdā's *forethought seem foul to you.
Do not abandon the straight path!

The *Old Avesta*, too, warns against losing the "straight/straightest paths", which is characteristic of those deceived by the Lie:

Yasna 51.13
*tā drəguuatō marədaitī   daēnā ərəzaoš haiθīm
yehiiā uruuā xraodaitī   cinuuatō pərətaō ākå*

x̮āiš šiiaoθanāiš hizuuascā ašahiiā nąsuuå paθō
Thereby, the vision-soul of the follower of the Lie shall divert the true (...) of the straight (path to the detriment of him)
whose breath-soul will (therefore) make him shudder in fury (when) in view of the Ford of the Accountant,
having, because of its own actions and (the words) of (his) tongue, (for ever) gone astray from the paths of Order.

The straight paths, in fact, lead to Ahura Mazdā's dwelling:

Yasna 43.3 a-d (cf. *Yasna* 32.4-5, cited p. 62, and *Yasna* 33.5c)
aṱ huuō vaŋhə̄uš vahiiō nā aibī.jamiiāṱ
yə̄ nå ərəzūš sauuaŋhō paθō sīšōiṱ
ahiiā aŋhə̄uš astuuatō manaŋhascā
haiθiiə̄ṇg āstīš yə̄ṇg ā šaēitī ahurō
Thus, may that man come to what is better than good
who would teach us the straight paths of life-giving strength
(both) of this world with bones and of that of thought
true (paths and) *drivable, (up) to those with whom the Ahura dwells.

Again, in the *Young Avesta*:

Yasna 68.13
razištahe paθō aēšəmca vaēdəmca   the search for and finding of the straightest path,
yō asti razištō ā ašāṱ   which is the straightest one (and leads) to Order
vahištəmca ahūm ašaonąm   and the best existence of the sustainers of Order.

Miθra punishes the evil kings by diverting them from the straight path, taking away the fortune of their lands and their ability to withstand enemies:

Yašt 10.27
*yō daṅhə̄uš *rąxšaiiqiθiiå*   who carries away the straightest (paths)
para razištå baraiti   of the *rebellious land,
paiti x̮arənå vāraiieiti   (who) *turns the gifts of Fortune away,
apa vərəθraɣnəm baraiti   who carries off their ability to smash the obstructions.

The king's efforts to educate his subjects bring us to the third question asked of the Old Avestan sacrificer.

3. WHAT DO YOU HAVE TO SHOW FOR YOURSELF?

After the good Zoroastrian has declared his side, he has to account for what he has done in the battle between good and evil. Zarathuštra describes his work as a poet and sacrificer whose duty it is to praise Ahura Mazdā, which Darius, also, did.

We have already seen that Darius understood part of his job to be that of an educator, but as king he has to participate in much more concrete fashion, which he does in various ways. The principal purpose of both the sacrificer's efforts and those of the king is to maintain peace for their peoples, the Avestan communities and the king's lands. Only in peace can the land be fertile and its inhabitants prosper from its products. Freedom from human enemies is not the only prerequisite, however; the enemies in the other world are as destructive, especially those who upset the regular natural cycles and send rain at the wrong times and in wrong measure or devastate the fields in other ways. "Darius' prayer" sums up these concerns succinctly:

> Darius at Persepolis (DPd 12-20)
> *manā auramazdā upastām baratuv hadā visaibiš bagaibiš*
> *utā imām dahạyāum auramazdā pātuv hacā haināyā hacā dušiyārā hacā draugā ...*
> *abiy imām dahạyāum mā ājamiyā mā hainā mā dušiyāram ma drauga*
> May Ahura Mazdā bear me aid together with all the gods!
> And may Ahura Mazdā protect this land from the enemy army, from bad seasons, and from the Lie!
> May there not come upon this land an enemy army, bad seasons, or the Lie!

Peace ...

While the sacrificer by his successful sacrifice re-establishes Ahura Mazdā as king of the universe and relies upon him to maintain order in the world, including in the sacrificer's community, the king's work – for which he was chosen by Ahura Mazdā – is that of the soldier who goes into battle in order to uphold the order of his land:

> Darius at Naqsh-e Rostam (DNa 31-36)
> *auramazdā yaθā avaina imām būmim yau[da^{n}tīm] pasāva-dim manā frābara*
> *mām xšāyaθiyam akunauš adam xšāyaθiya a^{h}miy*
> *vašnā auramazdāhā adam-šim gāθavā niyašādayam*
> When Ahura Mazdā saw this earth *being in commotion he gave it to me.
> He made me king. I am king.
> By the greatness of Ahura Mazdā, I set it down in its place.

> Xerxes at Persepolis (XPh 30-35)
> *yaθā taya adam xšāyaθiya abavam astiy a^{n}tar aitā dahạyāva tayaiy upariy nipištā ayauda*
> *pasāva-maiy auramazdā upastām abara*
> *vašnā auramazdahā ava dahạyāvam adam ajanam uta-šim gāθavā nīšādayam*
> There were among these lands which are written above (one that) was in commotion.
> Then Ahura Mazdā brought me support.

> By the greatness of Ahura Mazdā, it was I who smote that land and set it down in its place.

Here, Darius and Xerxes act like the Avestan Miθra and Apąm Napāt, who oversee the political order:

> Yašt 13.95 (to the fravashis)
>
> | | |
> |---|---|
> | *iδa apąm miθrō ... fraδāṯ* | Here, henceforth, Miθra ... shall further |
> | *vīspå fratəmatātō daxʹiiunąm* | all that is foremost of the lands, |
> | *yaozaiṇtīšca rāmaiieiti* | and he pacifies those that are in commotion. |
> | *iδa apąm napå sūrō fraδāṯ* | Here the strong Scion of the Waters shall further |
> | *vīspå fratəmatātō daxʹiiunąm* | all that is foremost of the lands, |
> | *yaozaiṇtīšca niiāsāite* | and he shall restrain those that are in commotion. |

The king must work hard to maintain order in his royal domain to prove himself worthy of Ahura Mazdā's choice:

> Darius at Behistun (DB 1.68-71)
> *adam hamataxšaiy yātā viθam tayām a^{h}māxam gāθavā avāstāyam yaθā paruvamciy*
> *avaθā adam hamataxšaiy vašnā auramazdāha*
> *yaθā gaumāta haya maguš viθam tayām amāxam naiy parābara*
> I exerted myself until I had set in its place the homestead that belonged to us, as it was before.
> In that manner I exerted myself, by the greatness of Ahura Mazdā, so that Gaumāta the Magian did not take away the homestead that belonged to us.

... and pasture

It is the task of both the sacrificer and the king to maintain the peace established for mankind by Ahura Mazdā. To the king this is *šiyāti*, which implies well-being both here and in the hereafter; to the sacrificer it is "peace and pasture". More precisely, Darius strives to maintain the social structures of his subjects within the lands under his command, including their livestock and its pastures:

> Darius at Behistun (DB 1.61-71)
> *adam niyaçārayam kārahayā abicarīš gaiθāmcā māniyamcā*
> *viθbišcā tayā-diš gaumāta haya maguš adīnā*
> *adam kāram gāθavā avāstāyam ... yaθā paruvamciy*
> I restored to the army/people (their) *grazing grounds — (their) herd and (their) household —
> and, throughout the *homesteads that Gaumāta the Magian had taken from them,

I set the army/people down in its place ... as it was before.

Here again, the king does what the Old Avestan sacrificer asks Ahura Mazdā for:

Yasna haptaŋhāiti 35.4 (cf. *Yasna* 47.3b-c)
gauuōi adāiš tāiš šiiaoθanāiš yāiš vahištāiš fraēšiiāmahī
rāmācā vāstrəmcā dazdiiāi
For the sake of the cow, by our *presentations, by/with these actions,
(our) best ones, by which we are (here and now) sending (them) forth
in order for peace and pasture to be established (for her) ...

Yasna 29.10ab
yūžə̄m aēibiiō ahurō aogō dātā ašā xšaθrəmcā
auuat vohū manaŋhā yā hušəitīš rāmąmcā dāt
You all, O Ahura, shall (now) establish for these (men), by (your) Order,
  strength, as well as (for yourself?) yonder
command by (your)/on account of (my) good thought, (a command) by
  which one shall establish good dwellings and peace.

Yasna 48.11a-c (cf. *Yasna* 53.8c)[26]
kadā mazdā ašā mat ārmaitiš
jimat xšaθrā hušəitiš vāstrauuaitī
kōi drəguuō.dəbīš xrūrāiš rāmąm dåntē
When, O Mazdā, will Ārmaiti (the Earth) come
together with Order and command, (she) who gives good settlements and
  pastures?
Who (are those who) will obtain *peace* in spite of the bloody ones possessed
  by the Lie?

Conversely, devastation of the pastures is the work of the forces of evil in the *Old Avesta*:

Yasna 32.10
huuō mā nā srauuå mōrəndat yə̄ acištəm vaēnaŋhē aogədā
gąm ašibiiā huuarəcā yascā dāθə̄ṇg drəguuatō dadāt
yascā vāstrā vīuuāpat yascā vadarə vōiždat ašāunē
That man diverts my songs of fame who (for his part) declares the worst in
  order to see
with (his) evil eyes the cow and the sun, — and who makes (out) the
  followers of the Lie (to be) the ones abiding by the established rules,
and who lays waste the pastures and who holds unyieldingly (his) weapon
  against the sustainer of Order.

We see that Darius' description of how he made order after the disruptions caused by his evil rival to the throne, Gaumāta, matches that of the Old Avestan poet describing the effects of evil rivals, down to the much-discussed OPers. *viθbiš*, which corresponds to OAv. *vīžibiiō*:

Yasna 53.8c
huxšaθrāiš jə̄narą̇m xrūnərą̇mcā rāmą̇mcā āiš dadātū šiieitibiiō vīžibiiō

By those who have good command let them (now) be smashed and bled!
And let (this one?) give peace by these (actions of ours?) to the settled homesteads!

Thus, the simple term *šiyāti* in Darius's inscriptions corresponds closely to OAv. peace and pasture.[27]

God's law – king's law.

To regulate the political and social order there is the king's law, which tells the subjects how to behave:

Darius at Behistun (DB 1.23)
vašnā auramazdāha imā dahạyāva tayanā manā dātā apariyāya
yaθā-šām hacā-ma aθahạya avaθā akunavaya^{n}tā
By the greatness of Ahura Mazdā, these lands which behaved according to my established law;[28]
as was said to them by me, thus they would do.

Darius at Naqsh-e Rostam (DNa 16-22)
vašnā auramazdāha imā dahạyāva tayā adam agạrbāyam apataram hacā pārsā
adam-šām patiyaxšayaiy manā bājim abaraha
taya-šām hacā-ma aθahạya ava akunava dātam taya manā avadiš adāraiya
By the greatness of Ahura Mazdā, these lands which I seized beyond Pārsa, I ruled over them, they bore me tribute.
What was said to them by me, that they did. It was my established law that held them.

Similarly, according to the *Old Avesta*, in order to receive the desired rewards from Ahura Mazdā, man must follow the various rules and regulations (*dāta*, "established law", *uruuāta*, "mutual agreement, deal", *miθra*, "contract") that god established when he first ordered the cosmos:

Yasna 28.10ab
at yə̄ṇg ašāatcā vōistā vaŋhə̄ušcā dāθə̄ṇg manaŋhō
ərəθβə̄ṇg mazdā ahurā aēibiiō pərənā āpanāiš kāmə̄m
Thus, (those) whom you know (to be) both on the side of Order and good thought, following the established rules (*dāta*),
(and so) according to the cosmic models (*ratus*), fill for them, O Mazdā Ahura, with attainments (their) wish!

The king, therefore, like Zarathuštra before him,[29] enshrines Ahura Mazdā's law in his own and fulfils his duties of furthering life and prosperity in his land by making his subjects adhere strictly to his established law. It is this law that governs the king's dealings with his subjects and the way his subjects interact with each other.

The King's Justice

A prerequisite, however, for getting rid of the Lie and maintaining order in the land is to punish those who do its bidding:

> Darius at Behistun (DB 4.37-40)
> *tuvam kā *xšāyaθiya haya aparam āhạy hacā draugā dạršam patipayauvā martiya [haya] *draujana ahatiy avam ufraštam pạrsā yadiy avaθā *maniyāhạy*
> *dahạyāuš-maiy duruvā ahatiy*
> You who are going to be king in the future, guard strongly against the Lie! The man possessed by the Lie, punish him well if you think as follows: May my country be healthy!

> Darius at Behistun (DB 4.67-69)
> *tuvam [kā] xšāyaθiya haya aparam āhạy martiya haya draujana ahatiy haya-vā zūrakara ahatiy avaiy mā dauštā biyā ufrastā-diš pạrsā*
> You who are going to be king hereafter, the man who sides with the Lie or the one who does crooked deeds, favour those not! Punish them well!

It was important, however, that everybody should be treated equally and justly:

> Darius at Behistun (DB1.20-22; cf. DNb 16-24)
> *aⁿtar imā dahạyāva martiya haya *āgariya āha avam ubạrtam abaram haya aʰrīka āha avam ufrastam apạrsam*
> In these lands, any man who *deserved a welcome I treated well. Whoever *sided with the Evil one, him I punished well.[30]

Seizing the evil-doers by one's own hand

Thus the king fulfils his duties to Ahura Mazdā by upholding his law and pursuing and punishing those who do not, who are liars and rebels or foreigners who worship the wrong gods, and his advice to other kings is to behave in the same manner. The king, in fact, participates directly in the punishment of Ahura Mazdā's and his own opponents by seizing them with his hands and mutilating or killing them personally:

> Darius at Behistun (DB 4.33-36)
> *dahạyāva imā tayā hamiçiyā abava drauga-diš *hamiçiyā akunauš taya imaiy kāram adurujiyaša*
> *pasāva-diš *auramazdā manā dastayā akunauš yaθā mām kāma avaθā-diš [akunavam]*
> These lands that became rebellious, *the Lie made them rebellious*, so that these (men) *lied* to the people.
> Then *Ahura Mazdā delivered them into my hands*. As was my wish, thus I treated them ...

Darius at Behistun (DB 1.82-83)
hauv āçina basta ānayatā abiy mām adam-šim avājanam
That Āçina was led bound to me. I killed him.

Darius at Behistun (DB 2.73)
*fravartiš agarbiya ānayatā abiy mām
adam-šaiy utā nāham utā gaušā utā hazānam frājanam utā-šaiy I cašma
   avajam*
Fravarti was seized (and) led to me.
I cut off his nose, ears, and tongue, and I gouged out one eye of his.

Here, too, by seizing (*garbāya-*), binding (*basta*) and leading (*ā-naya-*) the evil-doers, the king is following the example of the Old Avestan sacrificers:

Yasna 30.8
*atcā yadā aēšąm kaēnā jimaitī aēnaŋhąm
at mazdā taibiiō xšaθrəm vohū manaŋhā vōiuuīdaitī
aēibiiō saste ahurā yōi ašāi dadən zastaiiō drujəm*
Thus, also, when the retribution comes for these sins:
then, O Mazdā, he shall constantly present the command to you by (his) good thought
for (you) to announce (it) to these, O Ahura, who shall be placing the Lie in the hands of Order.

Yasna 44.14b-c
*kaθā ašāi drujəm diiąm zastaiiō
nī hīm mərąždiiāi θβahiiā mąθrāiš sə̄nghahiiā*
How might I deliver the Lie into the hands of Order
for (it) to be wiped out by the poetic thoughts of your announcement?

Yasna 31.20 (cf. *Yasna* 46.6)
*yə̄ āiiat ašauuanəm diuuamnəm hōi aparəm xšiiō
darəgə̄m āiiū təmaŋhō duš.x^varəθə̄m auuaētās vacō
tə̄m vå ahūm drəguuaṇtō śiiaoθanāiš x^vāiš daēnā naēšat*
Whoever shall *come to the sustainer of Order, *brilliant fame (will be) his hereafter. Lamentation,
a long lifespan of darkness, bad food, (your only) word the word "woe!"—
to that existence (your) vision-soul will lead you all, O followers of the Lie, on account of your own actions.

Similarly, in the *Young Avesta*, Miθra seizes the evil-doer with his arms:

Yapt 10.105 (cf. *Yašt* 13.41, p. 75)
təmcit miθrā haṇgrəfšəmnō	He is the one whom Miθra wishing to seize
pairi †apaiia bāzuβe	with his arms around him and behind him,
dušx^varənā naštō razišta	the one of bad Fortune, who, having gone astray from the straight (paths),
ašátō asti aŋ^vhaiia	is unhappy in his *innermost being.

And, at the end of the great battle between the Iranians and the Turanians, Haoma seizes the villain Frangrasiian, binds him and leads him bound to Kauui Haosrauuaŋha, who kills him as an act of revenge:[31]

Yašt 9.17-18 (= *Yašt* 17.38)

āaṯ hīm jaiδiiaṯ	Thus he (= Haoma) asked her:
auuaṯ āiiaptəm dazdi mē	Give me yon boon,
vaŋʰhi səuuište druuāspe	O good Druuāspā, most rich in life-giving strength,
yaθa azəm baṇdaiieni	that I may bind
mairīm tūirīm fraŋrasiiānəm	the Turian rogue Fraŋrasiian
uta bastəm vāδaiieni	and (that) I may lead him bound
uta bastəm upanaiieni	and bring him bound
†bastəm kauuōiš haosrauuaŋhahe	(before) Kauui Haosrauuah
janāṯ təm kauua haosrauua...	(so that) Kauui Haosrauuaŋha can slay him ...
puθrō.kaēna siiāuuaršānāi	as revenge for (his) son, Siiāuuaršan,
zūrō.jatahe narahe	the hero killed by crooked (men/deeds).

The two themes are abundantly illustrated in artistic representations, either separately or together,[32] and recur much later in the Sasanian royal inscription. Thus, Shapur I (3rd century CE), recounts how, after the Caesar of Rome had once more "lied" and "sinned" (§9 **druxt* ... *winās kerd*) against Armenia, in a great battle *the king seized the evil-doer by his own hand* (§2 *pad xwēbēh dast dastgraβ kerd*).[33] Here we also note the theme of doing *winās*, "leading astray, sin", the equivalent of OPers. *vināθaya-* and Av. *vīnāsa-*.

In the still later inscription of Narseh, son of Shapur (from the last decade of the 3rd century CE), the evil-doer, who is a liar (*drōzan* < OPers. *draujana*) and a tool of the Evil one and his minions (*ahrimen ud dēwān*, §4), is seized and bound and brought (*grift, bast, ānīd/wāst*) to the court, there to be punished with disgrace (§§58–61).[34]

The late version of the story of Haoma and Frangrasiian in the national Persian epic, the *Book of Kings* by Ferdowsi, preserves the theme using similar formulas (*Šāhnāme*, chap. on "Pādešāhi-e Kay Xosrow"):[35]

The noose he wore instead of a belt, which served him
as the protection of the keeper of the world,
entering the cave, he took it in his hand (*gereft be-dast*).
When he approached, the king jumped up...
Hūm threw him down on the ground and there bound his arms (*bāzu-ye ū be-bast*).
He left, dragging him along ...
Thus Hūm bound the arms of the king and carried him away (*bord*) from his resting place.

The linguistic formulas remain the same throughout this literature:

	Avestan	Old Persian	Middle Persian/Parthian	Modern Persian
"deliver into hands"	zastaiiō dā-	dastayā kar-agạrbiya		
"seize, be seized":	gə̄ruuaiia- haṇ-grəfša-		grift	
"seize by own hands"			(Pa.) pad xwēbēh dast dastgraß kerd	gereft be-dast
"bind, bound"	baṇdaiia-, basta-	basta-	bast	bāzu-ye ū be-bast
"lead"	upa-naiia-vāδaiiaiia-	ā-naya-	ānīd (Pa.) wāst	(bord)

The rewards

The man who behaves well, that is, according to the established law of Ahura Mazdā, will receive a reward both in life and in afterlife. The goal of man is to act in such a way that he becomes happy (*šiyāta*) while alive (which is what Ahura Mazdā intended for him) and at one with Order (*ạrtāvan*) when dead:

> Darius at Behistun (DB 5.18-20)
> *haya auramazdām yadātaiy *yānam [avahạyā] ahatiy utā jīvahạyā utā mạrtahạyā*
> He who sacrifices to Ahura Mazdā will receive a boon both (while) alive and (after he is) dead.

> Xerxes at Persepolis (XPh 46-56)
> *tuva ka haya apara yadi-maniyāiy šiyāta ahaniy jīva utā mạrta ạrtāvā ahaniy*
> *avanā dātā parīdiy taya auramazdā nīyštāya*
> *auramazdām yadaišā ạrtācā bạrzmaniy*
> *martiya haya avanā dātā pariyaita taya auramazdā nīštāya*
> *auramazdām yadataiy ạrtācā bạrzmaniy*
> *hauv utā jīva šiyāta bavatiy utā mạrta ạrtāvā bavatiy*
> You who shall be hereafter, if you think: 'May I be happy while alive and one with Order when dead!'
> behave according to the established law, which Ahura Mazdā has set down.
> You should sacrifice to Ahura Mazdā according to Order in the height!
> The man who behaves according to the established law which Ahura Mazdā has set down,
> (who) sacrifices to Ahura Mazdā according to Order in the height,
> he both becomes happy (while) alive and becomes one with Order (when) dead.

These statements have close lexical and grammatical parallels in *Yasna* 71.15–16.[36]

Yasna 71.15-16

yeiδi zī zaraθuštra	For (these best words), O Zarathustra, if
ustəme uruuaēse gaiiehe framrauuāi	*you say (them) forth at the last turn of (your) life,
pairi tē tanauua azəm yō ahurō mazdå	I, Ahura Mazdā, shall stretch
uruuānəm haca acištāṯ aŋhaoṯ	your soul away from the worst existence ....
yaθa vaši ašāum	As you desire, O Orderly one,
iδa aŋhō ašauua	here you shall be Orderly.
frapāraiiåŋ́he uruuānəm	You shall make (your) soul pass
tarō cinuuatō pərətūm	across the Ford of the Accountant
vahištahe aŋhə̄uš ašauua jasō	up to the best state of existence, arriving Orderly

Compare *Yašt* 10.105 (above, p. 71), in which the unfortunate one has strayed from the straight paths, and note the following correspondences:

	Avestan	Old Persian
(I/you/he) will be(come)	*aŋhō*	*ahaniy, bavatiy*
in life	*iδa* "here"	*jīva*
at one with Order/happy	*ašauua*	*šiyāta*
unhappy	*a-šāta*	
at the end of life/dead	*ustəme uruuaēse gaiiehe*	*mạrta*
at one with Order (in Paradise)	*vahištahe aŋhə̄uš ašauua*	*ạrtāvā*

The King's "Aesthetic" Function

We have seen that the king, like the Old Avestan sacrificers, by his sacrifices acts as a "revitaliser of the lands" by overcoming the powers of chaos by his announcements (*Yasna* 48.12, above, p. 56). Also like the Old Avestan sacrificers, however, the king makes his world Juicy (*fraša-*). The expression has a double meaning: making the world here and now "Juicy" through sacrifice both recreates the original state of the world and anticipates its end, when it will also be permanently "Juicy", as the world returns to the state it was in when first established by Ahura Mazdā. In practice, however, it refers to the return of dawn and the sun and the disappearance of darkness, representative of chaos and the Lie:

Yasna 50.11 (cf. *Yasna*s 34.15 and 50.10)
aṯ və̄ staotā aojāi mazdā aŋhācā
yauuaṯ ašā tauuācā isāicā
dātā aŋhə̄uš arədaṯ vohū manaŋhā
haiθiiā varəštąm hiiaṯ vasnā frašō.təməm

Thus, I shall declare myself your praiser, O Mazdā and you others, and I shall be—
to the extent I by the Order (of my ritual) can and am able—

the (re)establisher of the (first) existence *successfully by (my) good thought!
On account of (my) true (action/utterance) may what is most Juicy in exchange value be produced!

That the sacrificers themselves are important participants in this process of remaking and rejuvenation is clear also from *Yasna* 30.9a: *aṯcā tōi vaēm x̌iiāmā yōi īm fəraš̌əm kərənaon ahūm*, "Thus, also: may *we* be ([the men of?] those) who shall make it Juicy, (this) world!".

Darius, however, interpreted "making *fraša*" to mean making amazing work on earth (DSf 55–57): *çūšāyā paruv frašam framātam paruv frašam kar[tam]*, "in Susa *much *wonderful* (work) had been ordered, *much *wonderful* (work) *has been made*". We do not, however, know exactly what Darius had in mind when he said *fraša*. In Akkadian, the word is rendered as *būnu*, "good", which is also how Xerxes understood it, who used *naiba* (Akk. *tabbanû*) instead of *fraša*:

Xerxes at Persepolis (XPg 3-5)
*vašnā auramazdāha vasiy taya naibam akunauš
utā frāmāyatā dārayavauš xšāyaθiya haya manā pitā*
By the greatness of Ahura Mazdā (there was) much good
that Darius the king, my father, did and ordered.

This shift in meaning had probably already taken place by Young Avestan:

Yašt 19.10
yaθa dāmąn daθaṯ ahurō mazdå   when Ahura Mazdā made his creations
pouruca vohuca pouruca srīraca   many and good, plentiful and beautiful
pouruca abdaca pouruca frašaca   plentiful and marvellous, many and
                                    Perfect ...

In this light we must also, no doubt, see the constructions of "paradises", that is, royal gardens imitating and anticipating the heavenly existence awaiting the followers of Order after death.[37] Note especially that one name of a paradise known from the Persepolis tablets is Vispašiyātiš, All Happiness,[38] containing the word *šiyāti*, which is the happiness established for man on earth corresponding to the heavenly bliss after death.

The King And Zarathuštra

In the *Old Avesta*, the sacrificer has to prove himself competent before he can have any hope of performing a successful ritual. His competence consists in being the equal of Zarathuštra in knowledge and efficiency. In practice, he *becomes* Zarathuštra for the duration of the ritual.[39] In fact, in the *Young Avesta* it is said that for the sacrificer to succeed he should sacrifice like Zarathuštra, model or prototype of sacrificers:

Yašt 13.41 (cf. *Yašt* 10.105, above, p. 71)
dāθrīš ahmāi vohu x͏ʸarənō   (... the fravashis,) who give good Fortune to

	the one
yō hīš aθa frāiiazāite	who sacrifices to them in the manner
yaθa hīš hō nā yazata	in which that Man sacrificed to them,
yō ašauua zaraθuštrō	the Orderly Zarathuštra.

According to the *Frauuarānē* (see above, p.54), every good Zoroastrian has to make his choices as befits a follower of Zarathuštra, and, like every good Zoroastrian, the Achaemenid king acts accordingly: he has chosen to sacrifice to Ahura Mazdā (in the tradition of Zarathuštra); he scorns the *daiva*s and follows the guidance of Ahura Mazdā. In addition, like the Old Avestan sacrificer, he proves himself competent in order to obtain the royal command. After this, he is then chosen by Ahura Mazdā and endowed with the command by the god himself. But there is more.

In the *Young Avesta*, Zarathuštra was the first to be invested with the three main social functions:

Yašt 13.89 (see above, p. 60)
yō paoiriiō āθrauua	who as the first priest,
yō paoiriiō raθaēštå	who as the first charioteer,
yō paoiriiō vāstriiō fšuiiąs ...	who as the first husbandman ...

Similarly the king, whom we have already seen sacrificing, is, of course, a supreme charioteer and fighter, but he also pays attention to the well-being of his subjects and his land. Like Zarathuštra, the first *vāstriia fšuiiant*, that is, the first to take care of the tasks of farming and cattle-raising, the king cares for his herds (*gaiθā*, DB 1.61–71, above, p. 68) like Zarathuštra (see *Yasna* 43.7, above, p. 59) and strives to ensure that his lands do not suffer damage to farming from evil powers in this world (enemy armies) or the other world (bad seasons, the Lie).

The Chariot Race

The Old Avestan sacrificer fulfils the task of behaving like Zarathuštra, "the first charioteer", by sending his sacrifice up to the gods in a chariot race against the rivals. This ritual chariot race from earth to heaven probably also provides the model for the chariot of the sun, which, while the ritual race is run, will start its own race across the sky, with Miθra and his helpers clearing a straight path for it.[40] One of the requirements for its success is therefore that the charioteer has *strong legs*, since otherwise he would be thrown off the chariot. The theme of strong legs is mentioned several times in the *Old Avesta*, where the stability needed is through the ritual fire, which (apparently) provides its model. The reference to chariot racing is also clear:

Yasna 31.19c (similarly *Yasna* 43.12)
θβā āθrā suxrā mazdā vaŋhāu vīdātā rąnaiiå
(you) who, through your glowing fire, O Mazdā, provide a firm stance to the two legs in (the race for) good (renown).[41]

Yasna 47.6ab
tā då spəṇtā maniiū mazdā ahurā
āθrā vaŋhāu vīdāitīm rānōibiiā
Through that (your) life-giving inspiration, O Mazdā Ahura, you (now) make
through (your) fire a firm stance for the two legs in (the race for) good (renown) ...

Darius, too, boasts of his physical fitness. Artistic representations show the king standing upright in his chariot pulling his bow against wild animals, and his personal inscription on his tomb describes him in detail:

Darius at Naqsh-e Rostam (DNb 36-37, 40-45, see also below, p. 78)
ima pati-maiy aruvastam taya-maiy tanūš tāvayatiy...
yāu^hmainiš a^hmiy utā dastaibiyā utā pādaibiyā
asabāra uv 'asabāra a^hmiy
θanuvaniya uθanuvaniya a^hmiy utā pastiš utā asabāra
arštika a^hmiy uv 'arštika utā pastiš utā asabāra
And this, too, is my agility of which my body is capable ...
I am *coordinated[42] in both hands and feet.
As a horseman, I am a good horseman.
As an archer, I am a good archer both on foot and on horse,
as a spearman, I am a good spearman both on foot and on horse.

Note that *aruvastam*, "agility", is from **aruvant-*, Av. *auruuaṇt-*, "fleet", typically said of horses.

In the *Avesta*, one of the punishments of the enemies of Order is exactly the weakening or incapacitating of the legs and hands:

Yašt 10.48
āat̰ yat̰ miθrō frauuazaite   So when Miθra flies forth
auui *haēnå yå xruuišiieitiš ...   against the bloody armies ...
aθra narąm miθrō.drująm   there he chains the evil hands
apąš gauuō darəzaiieiti   of the contract-belying men in the back,
para daēma vāraiieiti   he turns their eyes away,
apa gaoša taošaiieiti   he deafens their ears.
nōit̰ pāda vīδāraiieiti   (This man) can no longer keep his feet apart,
nōit̰ paiti.tauuå bauuaiti   he has no capacity to withstand ...

Yasna 9.28-29
yō cišca ahmi nmāne yō aṅhe vīsi   In this home or in this house
yō ahmi zaṇtuuō yō aṅhe daṅhuuō   or in this tribe or in this land—
aēnaṅ^v hå asti mašiiō   whatever mortal is sinful,
gəuruuaiia hē pāδauue zāuuarə   take the strength away from his feet,
pairi šē uši vərənūiδi   cover his (hearing) senses,
skəṇdəm šē manō kərənūiδi   make his thought impotent.—
mā zbaraθaēibiia fratuiiå   "May you not be capable (of going)

	forth with your crooked legs,
mā gauuaēibiia aiβi.tūtuiiā ...	may you not be capable (of grasping) with your evil hands!" ...
yō aēnaŋhaiti nō manō	he who sins against our thought,
yō aēnaŋhaiti nō kəhrpəm	who sins against our body!

The senses or abilities that are removed from the evil men in these passages are those possessed in full by Darius:

> Darius at Naqsh-e Rostam (DNb 13-15, 33-40, 45-49)
> *ya-ci-maiy *pạrtanayā bavatiy dạršam dārayāmiy manahā
> uvaipašiyahạyā dạršam xšayamna a^{h}miy ...
> Whatever in me is in conflict I hold strongly (= have a firm grip on) by my mind.
> I am strongly in command of myself...
>
> aita-maiy aruvastam upariy manašcā ušīcā
> ima pati-maiy aruvastam taya-maiy tanūš tāvayatiy...
> hakaram-maiy ušīyā gāθavā hištataiy ya-ciy vaināmiy hamiçiyam ya-ciy naiy vaināmiy
> utā ušībiyā utā framānāyā
> adakaiy fratara maniyaiy afuvāyā yadiy vaināmiy hamiçiyam yaθā yadiy naiy vaināmiy
> This is my agility in both thought and (hearing) senses.
> And this, too, is my agility of which my body is capable ...
> Once it stands in place in my (hearing) senses whatever I see (as) rebellious and whatever I see as not rebellious,
> both with my (hearing) senses and my *forethought.
> I think myself more above fear at the time I see something hostile than when I do not.
>
> imā uvnarā tayā auramazdā *upariy mām niyasaya utā-diš atāvayam bartanaiy
> vašnā auramzdāhā taya-maiy kạrtam imaibiš uvnaraibiš akunavam tayā mām auramazdā upariy niyasaya
> These (are) the manly talents that Ahura Mazdā bestowed upon me. And I was capable of carrying them.
> By the greatness of Ahura Mazdā, what I have done, (that) I did with these manly talents that Ahura Mazdā bestowed upon me.

Finally, being like a god himself, the king, like the gods, may punish evil-doers by removing their senses, their ability to see, hear and speak, before killing them (see DB 2.73, p. 71, above).

Conclusion

It is also the above three functions of the king, I believe, replicating those of Zarathuštra, that we should see in artistic representations showing the king standing upright in his chariot pulling his bow against wild animals, with Ahura Mazdā in the sun disk hovering above and date palms symbolising the fertility of the earth framing the tableau. Indeed, in his function as mediator between the gods and men and as royal sacrificer, he, like the Old Avestan sacrificer, becomes, as it were, Zarathuštra, not only for the duration of the ritual but permanently.[43]

Marijan Molé denied that the king has the function of *zaotar*, "libator, sacrificer", stressing that the king's prototype is Yima, the first to celebrate the New Year festival, at which the kings of the whole world would assemble at the court, in the same way that the kings would assemble at Persepolis.[44] The king *does*, however, sacrifice to (*yad-*), not simply (vaguely) worship, Ahura Mazdā.

Darius, in fact, unites in one and the same person the functions of supreme king, prototype Yima (who kept expanding the earth to accommodate its growing population), and supreme sacrificer, prototype Zarathuštra. In the later, Sasanian literature of the Sasanian period, this constellation is said to introduce the end of time, when the world will again be made *fraša*, which, as we have seen, Darius has already done:

Dēnkard 3.129 [45]

hād ān ī ganāg mēnōy kōšišn padiš škefttar ēk abar xwarrah ī xwadāyīh ud weh-dēn pad ēk tan abartar zōrīha ō ham madan abesīhišn ī-š az ēn hamīh rāy.

čē agar pad ǰam abāg ān abartar-zōrīhā xwarrah ī xwadāyīh abartar-zōrīg-iz xwarrah ī weh-dēn ayāb pad zarduxšt abāg abartar-zōrīg xwarrah ī weh-dēn xwarrah-iz ī abartar-zōrīha čiyōn pad ǰam būd ō ham mad hē tēz ganāg mēnōy abesīhišn dām az ēbgad bōxtagīh ud fraškerd pad kāmag andar axwān dahišn būd hē

- The following: The one thing the Foul Spirit labours against more violently than anything else is the coming together in the strongest degree of the fortunes of kingship and the good religion in one person, because then he will be destroyed by this combination.
- For, if the fortune of superiour strength of the good religion had come together with the fortune of kingship in the strongest degree in Jam(shid), or if the superior strength of kingship as it was in Jam(shid) had come together with the fortune of the good religion in the strongest degree in Zarathuštra, then the destruction of the Foul Spirit, the deliverance of the creation from the Assault, and the establishment of the Perfectioning (*fraškerd*) in the (two) worlds (of thought and of living beings) would have quickly come about.

In this light, it seems clear that, in making his world *fraša*, the king also acts like the final Revitaliser, the Saošiiaṇt *par excellence*, the last of Zarathuštra's three eschatological sons, who will perform the final "Juicy-making" of the world (*ahūm frašəm kar-/dā-*):

Yašt 19.89 (to the earth and the divine Fortune)

yaṯ upaŋhacaṯ saošiiaṇtəm	which *will follow the obstructions-
vərəθrājanəm	smashing Revitaliser.
uta aniiå̄sciṯ haxaiiō	and the others, (his) companions,
yaṯ kərənauuāṯ frašəm ahūm ...	when he shall make the existence Perfect ...
daθaite frašəm vasna aŋhuš	(and) make the existence Perfect in exchange value.

Thus the Achaemenid king fits into a long line of Iranian kings who may have expected the end of the world, its Juicy-making or Perfectioning (Av. *frašō.kərəiti-*, Pahlavi *fraškerd*), to be, as it were, around the corner.[46]

The Persians Guardians Of The *Old Avesta*?

How do we explain these Avestan, especially the Old Avestan, parallels – one might say "quotations" (or, at least, "interpretations" of the *Avesta*) – in the Achaemenid inscriptions? Are they the result of the Achaemenid kings converting to Zoroastrianism: that is, were they introduced to the *Avesta* and its version of Iranian religion relatively recently? Or were the ancestors of Darius always Zoroastrians: that is, was the *Avesta*, or at least the *Old Avesta*, part of their religious heritage?

Let us for a moment consider the possibility that the Old Avestan religion was that of the king and that his holy text was the *Old Avesta*. Based on the chronology of the *Avesta* and the historical data about the migrations of the Persians, we may then imagine the following scenario:

1500–1000	The *Old Avesta* has already been crystallised and perhaps canonised as a sacred and closed corpus in Central Asia by speakers of (early) Young Avestan and other Iranian languages.
± 1000	The Persian tribe migrates onto the Plateau, somehow making its way into western and southwestern Iran by the 9th–8th centuries, bringing with it the *Old Avesta*.[47]
	The "Young Avestan" tribe migrates into Arachosia/Sistān, where the *Young Avesta* is composed, incorporating all or some of the *Old Avesta*.[48]
	Other tribes migrate onto the central Plateau, among them the Medes.
6th cent.	Darius, (conveniently?) convinced that he is Ahura Mazdā's chosen, stages his coup and founds his dynasty on the principles of the *Old Avesta*.
5th cent.?	The establishment of protected trade routes to eastern Iran opens up the way for the *Young Avesta*, which finds it way into the Achaemenid ritual and finally replaces the *Old Avesta* as the ritual text, which however it incorporates. Miθra and Anāhitā start being worshipped.

The advantage of such a scenario is that it would explain Darius's single-minded insistence upon Ahura Mazdā, as opposed to the later inclusion of the names of Miθra and Anāhitā in the inscriptions. There are too many holes, however, in our present knowledge to argue for or against it with any degree of confidence.

Notes:

1. See, e.g., Duchesne-Guillemin 1962: 165–8; Herrenschmidt 1980; and, most recently, Kellens 2002.
2. See, for instance, Skjærvø, 1997.
3. Mary Boyce (1982: 7–9, also p. 39, conclusion) argues for the first solution by simply pointing out that there are no indications in our sources that there was any kind of religious reform at that time. Other scenarios can also be imagined, however. If, for instance, the religion was brought by Persian conquerors, there would be no reform, just the superimposition of their religion upon that of the conquered.
4. Cameron 1948; Hallock 1969.
5. For the sake of simplicity, I shall use the form Ahura Mazdā throughout, although it is spelled Auramazdā in the Old Persian inscriptions.
6. Remarkably, Irtāna is like the form Artana, the name of the first month in the Achaemenid calendar of Cappadocia (see Panaino 1990).
7. See Koch 1977: 81–100. I am indebted to Shahrokh Razmjou for drawing my attention to Išpantāramatiš and Irtāna-fruirtip in Hallock's transliterated, but unpublished texts. See also Razmjou 2001. On non-Iranian gods, see Koch 1977: 101–112.
8. Cf. DPd 13–15 *manā Auramazdā upastām baratuv hadā visaibiš bagaibiš*, "let Ahura Mazdā bear me aid together with all the (other) gods (or All the Gods)!".
9. See Koch 1977: 129–40, 154–70. In addition, Aramaic inscriptions on ritual implements show that the *hauma* played an important part in the ritual: see Bowman 1970.
10. Perhaps for *ṛtāwan (Avestan *ašauuanəm*, OPers. *ạrtāvanam) by analogy with *farnaxwant, "endowed with good fortune", and similar forms.
11. There are numerous publications, for instance, the recent translation of the Aramaic texts by Bezalel Porten: see Porten 1996.
12. For a discussion of the meaning of this word, see Skjærvø 2003.
13. For a recent discussion of mutual gift-giving in the *Old Avesta*, see Hintze 2004.
14. The etymology and exact meaning of *fraša* have been and still are debated. The traditional connection is with Rigvedic *pṛkṣ*, *pṛkṣa*, *prakṣa*, and the verb *pṛc-*, all of which seem to have to do with abundance of liquid foodstuffs. Here, I render it as "Juicy" in Old Avestan but as "Perfect" in later texts. See also p. 75-76, above, on the king's "aesthetic" function.
15. On this archaic term (cf. Latin *censeo*), see Benveniste 1969: vol. 2, 143–8.
16. This interpretation of <a-ra-i-k> was first (?) proposed by Roland G. Kent (Kent 1953: 170: *ahra- + -ika-) and is, I think, the correct one. It would be an adjective formed from *ahriyā-, OAv. *aŋriiā-*, "*evilness", in *Yasna* 48.10 (on which see Skjærvø, 2004: 255-70) and refer to a servant of *Ahra-manyu.
17. This relationship also obtains between the king and his supporters, his *ba^{n}daka*s, "bondsmen", who are obviously "bound" to him by oaths of loyalty, etc.
18. See, e.g., Ardashir I's investiture relief at Naqsh-e Rostam in Schmidt 1970: 122–3 and plate 81.
19. See, e.g., Skjærvø 2002: 9-31, (esp. pp. 32–6); also Skjærvø 2003.
20. The verb *aog-/aoj-* is used here in the sense of "present oneself as, boast of oneself as", similar to that of the etymologically related Greek *eukhomai* and that of OPers. *agaubatā* in DB 4.80–86 (see p. 61).

21. Cf. the expression *dēdēm sar bast*, "bound the diadem on the head of ...", in the inscription of Narseh at Paikuli (see Humbach and Skjærvø 1983: 26–7).
22. These notions are common in Indo-European literature (cf. *Rigveda* 9.73.6 *ápānakṣā́so badhirā́ ahāsata r̥tásya pánthāṃ ná taranti duṣkŕ̥taḥ*, "The blind (and) deaf have gone astray and fallen behind. The evil-doers cannot traverse the path of Order"), but also in Mesopotamia, where we read in the *Code of Hammurapi* (1792–1750 BCE), col. 5: "When Marduk commanded me to direct the people along the right path ..." and col. 48: "Lord Hammurabi ... has pleased Marduk, his lord, and secured the permanent welfare of the people and led the land along the right path".
23. On this expression, see Skjærvø 1999.
24. The meaning of the winged disk and the identity of the male figure in it have been much discussed. Among recent contributions are those of A. Shapur Shahbazi (1980), who argued that the winged disk represents the *farnah* or royal "glory" (as commonly translated, whatever it means), and Bruno Jacobs (1991), who concluded (p. 65) that the winged disk represents the sun and the figure Ahura Mazdā, as has long been maintained (see also Briant 1996: 260, 928, with Shahbazi's remarks in his review of this work in *Nāme-ye Irān-e Bāstān. The International Journal of Ancient Iranian Studies* 3/2 [2003–2004]: 77–8, which convince me as little as his earlier article). – The modern interpretation of the figure as a *fravashi*, commonly, but erroneously, interpreted as a "guardian spirit" (or "guardian angel"!), is impossible, if for no other reason than because the *fravashis* are female warriors.
25. Zarathuštra is the straight, upright person *par excellence* (Avestan *ərəzu*; cf. *Yasna* 33.6a), and the portraits of the king, if anything, show us a person sitting or standing *straight*.
26. See Skjærvø 2004: 278.
27. First seen by Clarisse Herrenschmidt (Herrenschmidt 1991). The objections by Gherardo Gnoli (review of Kellens 1991 [ed.], *La religion iranienne*, in *East and West* 42 [1992]: 528) and Andrea Piras ("A proposito di antico-persiano *šiyāti*", *Studi Orientali e Linguistici* 5 [1994–5]: 91–5) target aspects of the terminology different from mine.
28. Cf. Old Persian *apariyāya*, "went around", with Middle Persian *pahrist* < **pairi-haiza-*, "move around", in the similar expression in Kerdīr §16: *pad dēn mazdēsn ... nē pad wizār pahrist*, "who did not behave according to the Mazdayasnian religion *correctly" (MacKenzie 1989: 55, 59).
29. The "law discarding the *daēuua*s" is that of Zarathuštra (*Yasna* 2.13 *dātəm vīdōiiūm dātəm zaraθuštri*), as is, in general, any other instruction in the *Avesta*, since it was he who received them from Ahura Mazdā and passed them on to humanity.
30. Cf. *Yasna* 0.4 = *Yasna* 11.17 *aibigairiiā daiθe vīspā humatācā hūxtācā huuarštācā paitiriciiā daiθe vīspā dušmatācā dužūxtācā dužuuarštācā*, "I regard as worthy of welcome all (thoughts) well thought, (words) well spoken, (acts) well done. I regard as worthy of being left out all (thoughts) badly thought, (words) badly spoken, (acts) badly done".
31. In the beyond, it is the demon Drag-off (Vizaresh) who performs the same action (*Vidēvdād* 19.29): *vīzaršō daēuuō nąma spitama zaraθuštra uruuānəm bastəm vāδaiieiti druuatąm daēuuaiiasnanąm*, "the demon Drag-off, O Zarathuštra Spitama, leads bound the soul of those possessed by the Lie, who sacrifice to *daēuua*s".
32. The verbal formula is, in fact, at least Indo-Iranian, cf. *Rigveda* 10.34.04 (the gambler) *pitā́ mātā́ bhrā́tara enam āhur ná jānīmo náyatā baddhám etám*, "His father, mother and brothers say: We do not know this one. Lead him away bound!"
33. See Huyse 1999: 28, 37 (= Corpus Inscriptionum Iranicarum III/1, Texts 1).

34. See Humbach and Skjærvø 1983: 28–9, 54–5.
35. Mohl 1838–68: vol. 4, pp. 198–9, lines 2284–5, 2286–7, 2291.
36. See Skjærvø 1999: 46-7.
37. See, e.g., Briant 1996: 244–50.
38. See Skjærvø 2002.
39. See also Herrenschmidt 1995–6 and 1996.
40. According to Greek historians, the king drives his chariot into battle, as well as those of Ahura Mazdā and the sun. See Briant 1996: 262.
41. On this use of the (elliptic) locative, cf. *Yasna* 30.10 *yōi zazənti vaŋhāu srauuahī*, "who shall leave (the competitors) behind in (the race for) good renown", and see Hoffmann 1968.
42. The interpretation of this word is problematic, as it is spelled variously as *yāumainiš* and *yāumaniš* (XPl 44-45). I tend to believe it is a vriddhi formation **yāuxmani-* of **yauxman-*, "harnessing".
43. I first suggested this interpretation of the Achaemenid king's religious function in a lecture given at the École Normale des Hautes Études of the Sorbonne, Paris, in May 1997, only to find that Clarisse Herrenschmidt had just made the same connection: see above, note 39.
44. Molé 1963: 35–6.
45. Ed. Madan 1911: 129–30. See Molé 1963: 37–9, with additional texts. Molé assumes that the combination is only valid for the end of time, however. See also Menasce 1973: 133.
46. See Boyce 1987: 872.
47. See Waters 1999; cf. also the problems with this scenario discussed by Young 1967.
48. See especially Gnoli 1980.

4

The Contribution of the Magi

Albert de Jong (University of Leiden)

In the year 158 or 159 CE, the North African author Apuleius of Madaura stood trial in the city of Sabrata, not too far from the ancient city of Oea, present-day Tripoli in Libya. Apuleius had been accused of using magic to win the love of his wife, a wealthy, upper-class widow named Pudentilla. Not surprisingly, her more distant relatives frowned upon the marriage of a young upstart to a much older woman who possessed considerable wealth. We only know about this case from the defence speech of Apuleius himself, which he turned into a long text that counts as one of the important sources on the subject of magic in antiquity and as a masterpiece of Latin literature. The text is known nowadays mainly as the *Apology*, but its earlier title was simply *On Magic*.[1] From the fact that it was published at all, scholars have deduced that Apuleius won his case and was acquitted.[2] It is almost certain, moreover, that the case revolved more around matters of inheritance and property than magic itself, but since the accusation of "magic" became the legal ground for the case, Apuleius devoted most of his text to a discussion of that problematic subject.[3] In order to do so, he provided his audience with a number of definitions of "magic". One of these, which served as an important starting point for his defence, referred back to Plato and to Iran. Apuleius writes the following:

> What is a sorcerer? I have read in many books that *magus* is the same thing in Persian as priest in our language. What crime is there in being a priest and in having accurate knowledge, a science, a technique of traditional ritual, sacred rites and traditional law, if magic consists of what Plato interprets as the "cult of the gods" when he talks of the disciplines taught to the crown prince in Persia? I remember the very words of that divine man [Plato]. Let me recall them to you, Maximus:

> *When the young prince has reached the age of fourteen, he is handed over to the royal tutors. There are four of them, chosen as the most outstanding among the Persian elders. One is the wisest, one the most just, one the most restrained, one the bravest. One of them teaches [the crown prince] the 'magic' of Zoroaster, the son of Oromazes, which is the worship of the gods. He also teaches him the art of being king.*

Listen to this, you who rashly slander magic! It is an art acceptable to the immortal gods, an art which includes the knowledge of how to worship them and pay them homage. It is a religious tradition dealing with things divine, and it has been distinguished ever since it was founded by Zoroaster and Oromazes, the high priests of the gods. In fact, it is considered one of the chief elements of royal instruction, and in Persia no one is allowed lightly to be a *magus* any more than they would let him be king.[4]

The text that Apuleius quotes here is taken from Plato's *Greater Alcibiades*,[5] which in antiquity was considered one of the most important of Plato's writings, although many modern scholars believe it was not written by Plato himself but originated in the Platonic Academy.[6] However one wants to settle this matter of authorship, there is no doubt that the ideas on the Magi in the *Alcibiades* reflect the opinions of a cultured group of people in Athens in the 4th century BCE. In fact, the passage from the *Alcibiades* is quoted in a surprisingly large number of classical passages.[7] This shows that a more or less correct idea of what Magi were, Zoroastrian priests, was available for the better part of antiquity. This notion of what the Magi were, however, had to compete with a very different notion of these men.

For most Greeks and Romans, the word *magus*[8] conjured up the image of magic as it is popularly understood even in our own days: private, non-social types of ritual activity, often with sinister overtones, harnessing unseen powers to reach concrete goals.[9] In fact, most dictionaries of Greek and Latin will give two basic meanings for the word *magos/magus*: a Zoroastrian priest and a sorcerer.[10] When a word can be used with such different meanings, one would expect mutual interference and there is, indeed, much evidence to suggest this. This is where the real problems begin for historical research.

This can be illustrated briefly with a problematic example, taken from one of the most important sources for the history of the wars between Persia and the Greeks: the *Histories* of Herodotus.[11] In his description of the expedition of Xerxes against the Greeks, in Book VII of the *Histories*, Herodotus briefly describes a detour taken by the Persian army, on the wish of Xerxes himself, to visit the plain of Troy, in the year 480 BCE.[12] In the *Histories*, the Trojan War pops up regularly as a sort of prototype for the Persian wars: this is, to be sure, a reinterpretation of the narratives of the Trojan War in terms of a conflict between "East" and "West" that is not evident from the *Iliad* itself.[13] From several other Greek texts, including fairly recently discovered fragments by the poet Simonides,[14] we know that this reinterpretation was current among Greeks since the Persian wars. Herodotus, however, attributes this interpretation of the Trojan War to Persian historians (*logioi*).[15] Several modern scholars have followed his judgement in this respect, but there appears to be room for more than a little scepticism.[16]

What Herodotus describes is the following: Xerxes' armies are suffering from a shortage of water, since the river Scamander has all but dried up.[17] He makes the detour to the plain of Troy, shows his interest in the remains there and offers a sacrifice of 1,000 oxen to Ilian Athena the goddess of Troy. The

Magi pour out libations for the heroes who died at Troy. That same night, terror struck the camp.

There are reasons to doubt the veracity of the story and especially to distrust its details. One would, for example, require evidence from a source other than Herodotus to believe that the Persian king would exploit Greek literature for purposes of propaganda. Herodotus himself shows too great an impact of Homer to count as a reliable source. Besides, as mentioned earlier, there is the problem of the interpretation of the Trojan narratives in terms of a conflict between Asia and Europe, which may well have been produced during Xerxes' expeditions against Greece, in which case the propaganda value in his own time may have been rather limited.[18]

Attempts have been made, nonetheless, to dispel all such doubts by giving a wholly Iranian interpretation of the passage: the sacrifice to Ilian Athena would be a "mask" for a sacrifice to Anāhitā, the goddess of waters, invoked here because of the water shortage. The libations for the deceased of Troy would not be that at all, but rather a sacrifice to the *fravashis* or guardian spirits; it would have almost nothing to do with the fact that the rituals took place in the plain of Troy.[19]

The same passage has been used, on the other hand, with almost the reverse interpretation. It has been suggested that the Magi, in bringing their libations, called up the ghosts of the Trojan warriors and that this would explain the terror that struck the camp.[20] This interpretation, elegant enough, is largely framed by the conviction that there is some truth behind the Greek idea that the Magi were especially good at raising ghosts. This idea, in which the spirit of the deceased Darius makes such a dramatic appearance, is indeed one that has been with the Greeks from Aeschylus' *Persians*, onwards.[21]

This particular passage thus suitably illustrates the difficulties caused by the semantic polyvalence of the word *magos*: one modern authority sees in the Magi at Troy nothing but Persian Zoroastrian priests, willing to serve their king; another scholar sees in them the prototype of religious specialists conjuring up the spirits of the dead. The present author considers both interpretations untenable and sees Herodotus' story as an intriguing piece of literary fiction. If there is going to be a remedy for the difficulties caused by this semantic plurality, it surely must be sought in the Iranian traditions concerning these priests. If this sounds like a thoroughly old-fashioned quest for facts, to the neglect of the extremely important questions raised by the image of the Magi in Greek literature, so be it. We shall, eventually, come back to the Greeks, but only after a long detour through the fragmentary world of ancient Iran.[22]

There is only one fact on which everyone agrees. The Greek word *magos* is a loan-word from the Old Persian word *magu-*. The Old Persian word *magu-*, however, is of uncertain etymology and of uncertain meaning. Its Avestan counterpart is found only once in the *Avesta* in a difficult passage (Y. 65.7), where it supposedly means "member of the tribe".[23] It has been suggested that this is, in fact, the original meaning of the word and that it came to be used, in

Western Iran, to mean "member of *the* (that is the priestly) tribe" and hence "priest", but this is uncertain.[24] Our knowledge of the social organisation of the Avestan people is at best rudimentary and, although we all use such terms as "tribe" lightly, we really do not know to what type of social grouping it would refer. This is equally true for the word "priest", which has caused a number of problems in interpretation, as we shall see. The only thing we know is that the word was apparently not a term used for any religious specialist by the Eastern Iranian Zoroastrians, who were responsible for the composition of the *Avesta*.

The word *magu-* is well attested in Western Iran from the Achaemenian period onwards. It is found in the Old Persian inscriptions and in administrative documents in Elamite found in Persepolis.[25] It is also very well attested in contemporary non-Iranian sources, chiefly in Greek.[26] Although we have, therefore, a wide range of sources, it is very difficult to specify what these religious specialists really were or did.

In the royal inscriptions of the Achaemenian kings, the word is only used in the context of Darius' accession to power, which revolved around his struggle against the usurper Gaumata, who is consistently described as a *magus*.[27] The relevance of the fact that he is always called the magus is less than clear. This is as true of Darius' own words as it is of the (largely identical) version of the events given by Greek authors. The struggle between Darius and Gaumata, of which we only have Darius' own version, has long been a source of learned speculation. Since Gaumata is always referred to as "the *magus*", the problem of the religion of the Achaemenians has been drawn into this discussion and some things must be said on the subject.

The question of the religion of the Achaemenian kings has most often been phrased in relatively simple terms: were they Zoroastrians or not? This matter was and continues to be passionately debated. Many scholars would agree nowadays that this is not the real question. The real question is what we *mean* when we say a certain king was a Zoroastrian. There can be no doubt that the religion of the Achaemenians is part of the history of Zoroastrianism.[28] The alternative, to believe that there was a Western Iranian, non-Zoroastrian religion almost entirely identical to Zoroastrianism, is difficult to conceive.[29] If one reviews the history of scholarship on this matter, however, it emerges that many scholars felt sufficiently confident to write that it was "all but certain" that the Achaemenian kings were not Zoroastrians.[30]

Nowadays, we are facing the alarming situation that the Persian inscriptions are in fact considered so very Zoroastrian that they are said to contain and exploit imagery or even texts from the *Avesta*.[31] In that case, serious reflection of how we conceive of Zoroastrianism in early Iranian history becomes urgent. In his recent article on the Achaemenian royal ideology, J. Kellens has suggested two very different things: first, by analysing the genealogy of the kings of Persia in the inscription of Darius at Behistun and comparing it with the genealogy of the *kavis* or leaders of the Iranians in *Yašt* 19, the hymn to the divine Glory,[32] he finds nine persons in both lists: the Avestan list ends with Vištāspa, the patron of Zarathuštra, the Old Persian list ends with Darius. That there would be nine persons in both lists cannot be a coincidence, according to Kellens, and he uses the parallel to claim that Darius, in making up his own genealogy, used his knowledge of the Avestan list to proclaim himself the new Vištāspa: in other words, that he exploited Zoroastrian traditions as his private propaganda.[33] The second thing he wants to explain is the fight against the *magus* Gaumata. Here, he suggests we can perceive a double conflict: a national conflict and a religious conflict. The national conflict would be evident from the fact that the Magi were a Median tribe, to which we shall return, but the religious conflict is much more difficult to outline. Since Darius presents himself as a restorer of divine order and the Magi remain in office as religious specialists, the conflict between Darius and Gaumata is not one between two religions: Darius does not found a new religion, nor does he abolish the group of the Magi. Kellens suggests, therefore, that Darius' struggle against the *magus* Gaumata was his attempt to establish himself as the supreme religious authority, in other words, as the *zaraθuštrōtema*.[34]

None of this will stand up to closer scrutiny. It is true that there are many gaps in our knowledge and in our sources. It is also true that the Old Persian inscriptions and the *Avesta* can be studied in connection to each other, chiefly in the interest of historical linguistics: they are the only documents we have for the Old Iranian languages and there are sometimes remarkable correspondences between the two corpora. Both of them, for example, reserve a special place for the god Ahura Mazdā, creator of heaven and earth. It seems unwise to consider that accidental. The fact that virtually all Old Persian royal inscriptions open with a brief theological statement, consisting of the affirmation that Ahura Mazdā is the creator of heaven and earth, sharply distinguishes these inscriptions from the vast corpus of royal inscriptions from the ancient Near East, which only use such opening lines when the inscription actually refers to religious activities (such as dedicating a divine statue or [re-]opening a temple).[35]

What we do not know is *what* the *Avesta* was in Western Iran in any period before the (late) Sasanian Empire. The Magi play a crucial role here, for we can reasonably assume that they were the ones who memorised the texts.[36] We can probably all accept the idea of Avestan texts as the special domain of trained priests; it is likely that the corpus of Avestan literature was very large and that some specialisation existed, with certain groups memorising parts of the text.[37] We shall come back to these questions shortly. We do not know, however, whether Avestan texts were anything other than sacred texts or formulas, mantras if one likes, in the heads of religious specialists, and used in the rituals they were trained to perform. The idea that the *Avesta* would be in any sense comparable to the Bible in Hellenistic Judaism or in Christianity, that is, a source of inspiration and stories for everyone to exploit, as a sacred book, is surely misleading.[38] First of all, we cannot know which parts of the *Avesta* were known in Western Iran at any time before, perhaps, the late Sasanian period. We can assume several things, but we can rarely confidently identify specific texts as having been there.[39] There are no direct quotations from the *Avesta* in any text from the period,[40] perhaps because it was not considered a "text" that one would apply to ordinary circumstances. If Darius wanted to present himself effectively as the new Vištāspa, which was, of course, the name of his father, we would have to believe that everyone for whom the inscriptions were intended would immediately recognise a pattern from *Yašt* 19, which must be considered extremely tenuous.

The other matter, that of Darius' struggle against the *magus*, is equally difficult to accept. There is no evidence at all to suggest that the Persian kings were in any way interested in possessing authority in religious matters, whatever that is supposed to mean. There seems to be another factor that could explain why Gaumata was consistently referred to as a *magus*; it is the opposite of what Kellens tries to prove, but it also requires a certain willingness to accept speculation. The Iranian organisation of society as we know it appears to have been rather strict, dividing human society into several distinct classes.[41] This has been greatly exaggerated, because many scholars have attempted to translate the "ideal" ways of organising society that we find in religious literature into real, fixed, social structures. This has produced the notorious image of Iran as a wholly static society and this image is contradicted by almost all the evidence we have.[42] Still, we would not go far wrong if we assumed that, ideally, the classes of priests, warriors and agriculturalists were kept separate at certain levels. If we want to look for more evidence for this type of social structure, the fact that Gaumata is always accompanied by his class title, *magus*, and is in some sources only known as "the *magus*", sends the powerful message that he had no right whatsoever to usurp a position that was not for his class. Just as warriors were unsuited to officiate as priests, so priests had no business ruling the land. That is why Darius chose wisely to put as much emphasis on Gaumata's background as he did.

The final element to discuss on what has gone wrong in our perception of the Magi for the moment is their supposed Median background. This rests on two tiny pieces of evidence. The first, negligible, one is the fact that in the Babylonian version of Darius' inscription at Behistun, a word that can possibly be read as "Median" has been inserted near the name of Gaumata.[43] Hardly anyone has ever paid much attention to this and seemingly for good reasons, for Darius would never have failed to mention the fact that Gaumata had been a Mede and he does not. In *Histories* 1.101, Herodotus lists the six tribes or families of the Medes: he gives us six names. We cannot really understand these names, although some of them sound genuine, but among them is the name *Magoi*.[44] The evidence of Greek ways of transcribing Iranian words and names shows that this could still be interpreted in several ways, but it seems no one has ever even attempted to do this. It has generally been accepted that one of the tribes of the Medes were called "Magi". This has subsequently been reversed, without good reason, into the statement that the Magi were one of the tribes of the Medes. This, in turn, has led to the idea that the Magi were "originally" one of the tribes of the Medes, who developed into a priestly class.

This is a trick that has been played on us and its consequences have been dramatic. It has opened the floodgates for a large number of speculations, most of which attribute many of the aspects of Zoroastrianism that seemed difficult to understand to the pernicious influence of these Median Magi.[45] By following this path, many scholars, and among them some of the greatest scholars of Zoroastrianism of the 20th century, shaped for themselves the image of a pristine Zoroastrian theology, going back to the prophet Zarathuštra himself, which had been perverted by later generations and especially by the Median Magi.[46] Let us consider two further pieces of information given by Herodotus. He notices two things among the Magi (*Histories* 1.140). The first is that they are dedicated to killing various types of animals: "the Magi slay with their own hands all animals except a dog and a man, and they make this an object of rivalry, slaying alike ants and snakes and other reptiles and birds".[47] The second thing he mentions, in the same passage, is this:

> This much I can say about the Persians from exact knowledge. Other things are talked of as secrets and not openly, with regard to the dead – how that the corpse of a Persian is not buried before it has been torn by bird or dog. Now I know that the Magi do this, for they do it without concealment; but the Persians cover the corpse with wax and bury it in the earth.[48]

One does not have to know much about Zoroastrianism in antiquity to realise that these two things, the killing of noxious creatures (*xrafstras*) and exposing corpses to be eaten by dogs and birds, are typically Zoroastrian institutions.[49] Many scholars have therefore assumed, in the present author's view correctly, that this qualifies the Magi as Zoroastrians, but others have used exactly the same information to suggest that these elements of later Zoroastrianism were brought into the religion by the non-Zoroastrian Magi because they would not let go of their cherished practices. It is not necessary to go into detail here, for it does not seem that there is anyone left who would subscribe to the latter view. Nevertheless, the idea that the Magi were originally a Median tribe appears almost ineradicable and we have to rid ourselves of it.[50]

In the works of Herodotus and Xenophon, devoted chiefly to the (military) conflicts between Persians and Greeks, the Magi appear quite often, in a large variety of different functions. They accompany the Persian armies, performing libations and sacrifices;[51] their presence is required for every sacrifice, because they are the only ones who can recite the texts necessary for a valid sacrifice;[52] they interpret signs, dreams and portents;[53] and they also have functions that seem to be entirely unconnected with their religious core business, functioning as court officials, in administrative and legal positions.

Many of these aspects appear time and time again in Greek literature on the Magi. A few generations after Herodotus, in the 4th century BCE, two important extra functions came to be attached to the Magi: their role in Persian education and their role as theologians who spread and interpret the ideas of Zoroaster.[54] The evidence from the large number of Greek sources available has been shown to be fully compatible with what we can reconstruct of priestly duties from Iranian sources.

For the Achaemenian period, the most important evidence comes from the Elamite Persepolis tablets. These are chiefly administrative documents, recording the transfer of amounts of wine, grain and other foodstuffs for services rendered. The Magi occur several times in these texts, along with other types of priest, as specialists in ritual (for a large number of gods) and in other, not clearly religious functions. This situation is similar to the evidence from the Greek sources and is, in fact, typical for the later history of Zoroastrian priests.

Most of our evidence for that later history comes from the Sasanian period (224–642 CE). In post-Sasanian Zoroastrian sources, the Pahlavi books, the word *mogh* (*mgw*), the Middle Persian descendant of Old Persian *magu-*, is hardly ever attested. Instead of this generic word, more specific titles are always given; where a generic word is necessary, the word *mard*, "man", is used.[55] Since many reconstructions of Sasanian history are based on sources from later periods, the existence of the word in Sasanian Iran has sometimes been obscured. It is, however, not only frequently found in non-Iranian Sasanian sources (in Aramaic, Syriac and Greek), but it is also very well attested in the most reliable Iranian sources from the period itself, namely personal seals.[56] In fact, the word *mogh* is a very common word on Sasanian seals and *bullae*. The word had a long and distinguished career in Islamic Persian poetry (*pīr-e moghān* etc),[57] which shows that it had not disappeared from the common speech of the Persians. The question therefore arises why the Zoroastrians, who formulated their tradition in the 9th century, wanted to get rid of it, but so far no reasonable hypothesis has been suggested for this problem. The only suggestion one can think of that makes sense is the fact that the Aramaic word *magūšā* and the Arabic *majūs* were used not just to refer to Persian priests, but to Zoroastrians in general, and that the term came to be felt to be misleading for those who wanted to distinguish themselves as members of the priestly class.

The duties of Zoroastrian priests in the Sasanian period were varied: apart from ritual and theology, Magi also occupied themselves with administrative work in general, and legal affairs in particular.[58] They can be found at court, as advisers to the king, and interpreters of signs and dreams.[59] Evidence for priests in all these functions comes from seals, legal texts, literary texts and also in significant quantities from Christian literature, chiefly in Syriac and Armenian, where the Magi are always represented as the chief imperial force attempting to stem the tide of conversion to Christianity by trying and executing Zoroastrian apostates.[60]

The core of priestly duties evidently consisted of ritual, theology and the transmission of Zoroastrian literature. Since the latter function is critical for the first two, we should discuss it in some detail.[61] Almost all Zoroastrian literature from the pre-modern period that has survived is priestly literature. This consists of several distinct collections: the *Avesta*, in its own language, chiefly consists of ritual texts. Most non-ritual texts in Avestan have been lost, but there is some information on their contents from summaries in Middle Persian.[62] The second important part of Zoroastrian literature consists of exegetical translations of the Avestan texts. These are collectively known as *Zand* ("knowledge"). Far from being only a translation of Avestan texts, the *Zand* texts are interspersed with explanatory notes and exegetical discussions.[63] The third part of Zoroastrian literature consists of theological, historical and other works that are based on the *Zand*.[64] The fourth part, finally, are priestly *compendia* and answers to questions posed by members of the community.[65]

The latter two categories are clearly part of the priestly tradition from a period when writing had come to be accepted for the purpose of transmitting priestly knowledge: they are written compositions. This is not the case with the first two collections. For a variety of reasons, we can show that writing came to be used for the transmission of religious texts and of literary works only late in the development of Zoroastrianism. The evidence is strongest for the *Avesta* itself, for a special alphabet was designed for it, covering all the nuances of priestly pronunciation of the holy texts in ritual. This alphabet cannot have been designed before the 4th or even the 5th century CE. Even after the invention of the alphabet, it seems that the oral transmission of the holy texts and of their commentaries continued as the normal procedure. To use a practical argument: since priests need to use both hands in the rituals they perform, they could not hold a book and had no use for it in most rituals.[66]

Before the 4th century CE, the transmission of religious knowledge was an exclusively oral process. Since the *Avesta* was transmitted in an Eastern Iranian language but has been preserved among Western Iranian priests, it is likely that the texts of the *Avesta* were memorised word-by-word by these Western Iranian priests, the Magi, from a very early period onwards. How early, we cannot say, but many scholars believe firmly in the 6th or 5th century BCE.[67] To facilitate comprehension of these texts, they were provided with a translation in the local language, which was transmitted alongside the Avestan texts. This translation grew considerably in size over time with the addition of explanations and learned comments. The amount of texts that were thus orally transmitted was very large and there are clear signs of specialisation to make this oral transmission possible. First of all, the texts were divided between numerous specialists, who memorised part of the sacred literature. A further development, evident from later sources, divided the priesthood into two different classes: those whose chief responsibility was the performance of rituals and those whose responsibility lay in education and theology. Ritual priests would memorise the Avestan texts with their accompanying rituals and teacher-priests would memorise the Avestan texts with their commentaries. As usual, we only find out about this system once it began to disintegrate. Teacher-priests were unsuited for the performance of many rituals and, in the first few centuries after the Arab conquests, it seems that there were too many priests for the dwindling communities and teacher-priests tried to make a living by performing rituals, which raised all sorts of questions.[68] They were, at any rate, responsible for the development of Zoroastrian theology, and this will lead us back to the Magi in the Achaemenian period.

The oral system of transmission appears to have been highly successful, but it has considerable disadvantages for modern scholars. Since we depend on the written texts that survive, all we have is the final outcome of well over a thousand years of oral traditions. This final outcome, the Pahlavi books, reflects first and foremost priestly knowledge of the early Islamic period and one cannot use these texts to shed much light on the realities of the Achaemenian period.

Fortunately, we have the evidence of Greek literature to help us out here. Greek literature shows much earlier traces of recognisable Zoroastrian theologies, attributed to Zoroaster and the Magi.[69] Since the majority of Avestan texts have been lost and our main evidence for Zoroastrian theology is late, we cannot reach a firm chronology of the development of Zoroastrian ideas. There are many different versions of the crucial Zoroastrian narrative on the creation of the world and the mixture of good and evil in it, and also of ideas about how history will come to an end in the perfection of creation and the separation of evil from good. These are, however, by and large variations on a fixed pattern.[70] This pattern is only partly evident from the *Avesta*, a collection of ritual texts not known for their systematic explorations of philosophy or theology.

In the works of several Greek authors, chiefly those associated with the schools of Plato and Aristotle, we find many traces of an active interest taken in the theology of the Magi.[71] It is not so much a matter of direct influence, but the dualist position taken in Zoroastrian theology that assigns two primal beings as the cause of everything is seriously taken up for discussion, and much effort was evidently put into a quest for further information. This information was sought among Persian Magi and the interest taken in the 4th century BCE in Zoroastrian theology, of which fragments have survived in Greek, shows that what one could call a priestly synthesis had been reached by that period.[72] In fact, we can probably push back that date considerably, since evidence survives, for instance, of speculations on the division of time, in the shape of millenary schemes, from the 5th century BCE.[73] There is no doubt that this particular division of time, which is governed by astronomical observations on the course of stars and planets, was vastly influenced by Mesopotamian ideas,[74] but the interesting thing is that the application of this millenary scheme to Zoroastrian religious ideas only makes sense in the context of the whole story of the creation and perfection of the world.[75] It is precisely on this subject that Peter Kingsley has convincingly reconstructed elements of real Persian propaganda in the context of the wars with the Greeks: the fact that, in the oldest passage we have, Xerxes' crossing of the Hellespont is said to have taken place 6,000 years after Zoroaster's birth would place Xerxes' crossing at the turning-point of history, the beginning of the final victory of good.[76] Such propaganda would only work, of course, if the notion of the arrival of that final period, phrased in a definite measurable period of time, was widely known. It is not to be found in the *Avesta*, but it takes up and strings together numerous ideas to be found in Avestan texts; it has certainly been influenced by Babylonian speculations and must therefore be connected with Western Iran. It had a lasting impact on the development of Zoroastrianism, for it was only developed further and was never dropped from the tradition. It is, in a few words, the most important contribution the Magi made to Iranian civilisation.[77] That the Magi were specialists in ritual has always been known, that they were experts at raising ghosts has frequently been assumed, but their talents for theology have only rarely been acknowledged. Far from perverting the development of a noble religion with outlandish tricks, they enriched it with successful systematic views on the realities of the past, the present and the time to come.

Notes:

1. For the text, see Hunink 1997.
2. The legal aspects of the trial are the subject of Amarelli 1988.
3. For this aspect of the case, see Graf 1996: 61–82.
4. Apuleius of Madaura, *Apology* 25–26, quoted here in the translation of G. Luck (Luck 1985: 110–111), with a few changes.
5. (Pseudo-)Plato, *Alcibiades* I.121E–122A.
6. The most recent edition of the text, with a substantial defence of the authenticity of its attribution to Plato, is Denyer 2001.
7. De Jong 1997: 213, with n. 29; see also De Jong 2003: 169.
8. The Greek word is *magos*, which was borrowed into Latin as *magus* (pl. *magi*).
9. Not a single modern academic work on magic would, of course, endorse such a definition. In fact, the status of "magic" as a concept in the study of religion is the subject of a lively and important debate, with the majority of scholars favouring all attempts at getting rid of it. For introductions consult, e.g., Versnel 1991, Smith 1995, Johnston 2004.
10. See also De Jong 1997: 387–94.
11. The literature on Herodotus is immense. General introductions (but not particularly good with regard to Iranian questions) are available in Bakker, De Jong and van Wees 2002.
12. Herodotus, *Histories* 7.43.
13. It is clear that the two warring sides in the *Iliad* are not distinguished as divided by their culture, language or religon. See the remarks by E. Hall (1989: 13–17).
14. See West 1993; Flower 2000. Simonides of Keos lived from approximately 556 to approximately 468 BCE.
15. Herodotus, *Histories* 1.1–5. For these Persian *logioi*, see in particular in Evans 1991 the essay "Oral tradition in Herodotus" (89–146), esp. p. 98.
16. An attempt at reconciling the conflicting interpretations can be found in Georges 1994: 51–66.
17. For water shortage in Herodotus and the *topos* of "drinking the rivers dry", see Burn 1984: 328–9.
18. See also De Jong 1997: 353; Georges (1994: 58–66) tries to make the most of this passage and is good in showing the later history of the story, which is also indicated briefly by Briant (1996: 718).
19. Gnoli 1998.
20. Ogden 2001: 130.
21. An excellent discussion of the fruitless efforts of many scholars to find in Aeschylus' *Persians* evidence for Persian religion in general, and necromancy in particular, is found in Hall 1989: 86–93.
22. The following remarks expand upon the entry "Magi" written by the present author for the forthcoming second edition of *The Encyclopedia of Religion*.
23. Benveniste 1938: 5–17.
24. See Boyce 1989: 10–11 for a discussion.
25. For these Elamite texts, see Cameron 1948: 5–9; Hallock 1969: e.g. PF 757; 772. For an interpretation of the data, see Koch 1977: 156–7; Razmjou 2004.
26. For an overview, see De Jong 1997: 387–403.
27. For this episode see, for example, Briant 1996: 109–118.

28. As argued by De Jong (1997: 39, with n. 1); for a similar opinion, see Shaked 2005: 188–9.
29. Such an unlikely construct is still offered as fact by Lecoq (1997: 154–64).
30. This sentiment is expressed with admirable clarity by Widengren (1965: 142–9), especially on p. 149: "If one surveys the discussion, one sees immediately that on the side of those who deny the Zoroastrianism of the Achaemenians, reference is made to facts, whereas those who defend the opposite point of view cannot base themselves on a single fact – with the exception of the name of the god Ahura Mazdā – cannot name a single truly Zoroastrian characteristic, but have to rely on indirect conclusions and vague assumptions. Until new real facts are brought to light that speak in favour of a Zoroastrianism of the Great Kings, it remains all but absolutely certain that the Achaemenians were not Zoroastrians" (trl. AJ).
31. For a pioneering effort at discovering possible echoes of Avestan texts and *topoi* in the Old Persian inscriptions, see Skjaervø 1999.
32. For this hymn, see Hintze 1994.
33. Kellens 2002: 417–34.
34. For this office, which represents the notion of an ideal (but imaginary) leader of the Zoroastrians who has memorised the whole tradition, see Kreyenbroek 1994.
35. A large selection of such monumental inscriptions is available in Hallo *et al.* 2000.
36. See Kreyenbroek 1996.
37. That this was so can only be established from much later sources and from comparative materials. See, for example, the "evidence" from Ibn Hazm discussed by S. Pines (1990: 41–9).
38. See, for instance, Stausberg 1998.
39. An exception must be made, probably, for the *Yasna*, for it is difficult to imagine Zoroastrianism without it. The history of the *Yasna* itself, however, (both ritual and text) is obscure. For a promising perspective on that history, see Hintze 2004.
40. Several "parallels" however have been suggested, especially by Skjaervø (1999).
41. Benveniste 1932.
42. See De Jong 2004.
43. For the text, see von Voigtlander 1978: 14 (BD Bab. line 15). See also Lecoq 1997: 190 (Lecoq uses it to support the Median connection of the Magi).
44. Schmitt 1967, by far the most reliable guide in these matters, lists all names of the Median tribes (with the exception of the Magi) as of uncertain etymology and meaning.
45. See especially Moulton 1913: 182–253. Moulton is the best example of the trend sketched here, but we should record that he found the "Magian" practices so utterly abhorrent that he could not even consider them Median; he thought the Magi were "aboriginal" (i.e. non-Aryan and non-Semitic, but coming from the North) and managed to make themselves indispensible to the Medes: "We may safely regard them as an aboriginal folk, who retained under the influence of religion usages which were generated in a low state of culture. They gained, it would seem, a reputation for occult powers among tribes more advanced than themselves; and the retention of their characteristic customs was bound up with this reputation and the profitable results of it. That an inferior race may enjoy such privileges as powerful shamans, can be shown from parallels elsewhere." (Moulton 1913: 193). Similar sentiments appear to underly Bickerman and Tadmor 1978.
46. A critical discussion of this trend in scholarly literature, on the basis of a discussion of animal sacrifice, is De Jong 2002.
47. Herodotus, *Histories* 1.140 (translated by Moulton, 1913: 398).

48. Herodotus, *Histories* 1.140 (translated by Moulton, *ibid.*).
49. For the killing of the *xrafstras* (noxious creatures), see De Jong 1997: 338–42; for the Zoroastrian rites of exposure, see *ibid.*: 440–444; and see now Huff 2004.
50. For a recent example of this idea, see, for instance, Handley-Schachler 1998.
51. Herodotus, *Histories* 7.113; 7.191; Xenophon, *Cyropaedia* 4.5.14; 7.5.57.
52. Herodotus, *Histories* 1.132.
53. De Jong 1997: 397–9.
54. For their role in education, see the evidence of the *Greater Alcibiades* referred to above, also De Jong 1997: 446–51; for the development of Zoroastrian theology, see Plutarch, *De Iside et Osiride* 46–47 (and see below).
55. The evidence for this usage comes chiefly from the *Nērangestān* (e.g. *Nērangestān* 7.5, 10.14, etc), for which see Kotwal and Kreyenbroek 1995 and 2003.
56. See, for example, Gyselen 1995.
57. Melikian-Chirvani (1987) gives a very speculative interpretation of the theme of the *pīr-e moghān*.
58. See Shaked 1990.
59. These functions are especially clear from narrative sources such as the *Book of Deeds of Ardašīr son of Pābag*, edited recently by F. Grenet (Grenet 2003).
60. The Armenian evidence has been surveyed by J.R. Russell (Russell 1987); in spite of their evident importance, the materials from Syriac literature have not yet been assembled or studied systematically. For a quick survey, see Gillman and Klimheit 1999: 109–127; for an in-depth study of the kind of materials available, see Jullien and Jullien 2002.
61. For the process of transmission, see Bailey 1971: 149–94. There is, surprisingly, no good recent introduction to the *Avesta*, although there have been several attempts at outlining the history of the transmission of Avestan texts: Hoffmann and Narten 1989; Kreyenbroek 1996; Kellens 1998. An overview of Pahlavi literature is given in Cereti 2001.
62. The chief evidence can be found in books 8 and 9 of the *Dēnkard*.
63. For a discussion of this literature, see Shaked 1996; Shapira 1998; Cantera 2004.
64. A good example of this type of literature is the seventh book of the *Dēnkard*, which contains a history of the Zoroastrian religion from the prophets before Zarathushtra to the end of time. This text was studied by M. Molé (1993), with a marked focus on the pieces of *Zand* that can be reconstructed from the text. For the context of *Dēnkard* 7, see Josephson 2003 and (briefly) De Jong 2005: 203–204.
65. This includes the so-called *Rivāyat* literature (including the *Šāyest nē-šāyest*) and its later elaborations in the New Persian *Sad dar* texts.
66. Boyce and Grenet 1991: 237–8.
67. See Kreyenbroek 1996.
68. This is described in two articles by P.G. Kreyenbroek: see Kreyenbroek 1987a and 1987b.
69. See De Jong 1997 for an overview.
70. This subject is elaborated in Shaked 1994: 5–51.
71. See especially Kingsley 1995.
72. The crucial evidence is to be found in the works of Plutarch (*De Iside et Osiride* 46-47) and Diogenes Laertius 1.6–9. See De Jong 1997: 157–228.
73. Kingsley 1990 and 1995 (and see below).
74. Boyce (1982: 234–6) and Kingsley (1990) give clear evidence for these Mesopotamian influences but regard them chiefly as evidence for a particular variety of Zoroastrianism, which sees the two spirits as the children of Zurvan, the god of

Time. We need not go into the thorny subject of "Zurvanism", however, because the doctrine of the millennia is a fixed part of all Zoroastrian theologies from the Achaemenian period onwards. See, for instance, Kreyenbroek 2002.
75. The fact that this element of Zoroastrian theology – the interdependence of creation and the end of time – goes back to the earliest layers of the religion has consistently been elaborated in Shaked 2005.
76. Kingsley 1995: 191–5.
77. It should be noted here that it now seems likely that the Zoroastrian calendar is also a product of the Achaemenian period and therefore presumably of the Magi. See Boyce 2003 (in reference to M. Boyce, "Jašn-hā-ye īrānīyān", in K. Mazdāpūr [ed.], *Sorūš-e pīr-e moghān. Yādnāme-ye Jamšīd Sorūšīyān*, Tehran 1381/2002: 889–919). The earliest attestation of the use of the Zoroastrian calendar appears on a recently discovered Aramaic document from Bactria: see Shaked 2004: 42–5.

5

The History of the Idea of Iran

A. Shapur Shahbazi (Eastern Oregon University)

My purpose today is to argue that the idea of Iran as a national entity – that is, a country with linguistic, political and ethnic identity – had originated in the Avestan period and continued an unofficial existence until Ardašīr Pāpakān gave it official sanction as a measure of fostering his claim to the ancient Iranian throne. As you know, this was the traditional view until vigorously challenged by Professor Gherardo Gnoli.[1] He concluded that, in the 3rd century AD, eight hundred years after Hellas and Rome had become national concepts, the founder of the Sāsānian empire *invented* the idea of Iran as a national state to serve his religion-based agenda. This revisionist thesis is primarily based on the fact that the available evidence seems to indicate that the Achaemenid and Arsacid states did not bear the official designation "Iran" but were called "Persian" or "Parthian" empires respectively. It will be seen that this *argumentum ex silentio* is quite untenable and that a closer examination of our sources reveals a much greater antiquity for the idea of "Iran" as a national state.

Let me start by noting that Professor Gnoli's view is not novel, as his readers are disposed to conclude. It originated with Paulus Cassel some 120 years ago. Early European scholars followed the biblical and Classical tradition of referring to Iran as Le Perse, Persien and Persia. Travellers, however, repeatedly remarked that Iranians themselves had from remotest antiquity consistently called their country "Iran".[2] Gradually, a number of 19th century Orientalists took notice and came to call the country "Iran" and its people "Iranians". This was exemplified by the appearance in 1873 of the first volume of Friederich Spiegel's *Eranische Altertumskunde,* a monumental work about "Iranian" antiquity from the Avestan period to the Arab conquest. The choice of title was criticised by Paulus Cassel, who pointed out that the name "Iran" was not attested as the designation of the entire Achaemenid empire in Classical or Hebrew sources. If "Iran" had been the official name of the Median or Persian state, he argued, we would "unquestionably" (*ohne Zweifel*) have heard of it in such works. Even Strabo's *Ariana* referred to a *province* [in eastern Iran], not to the entire empire.[3]

The proverbial traditionalism of Iranians and the claim of Ardašīr, son of Pāpak, to have *revived* the ancient Iranian empire that Alexander of Macedon had destroyed[4] shelved Cassel's opinion until it was presented in a new form and with impressive documentary support by Professor Gnoli.[5] He noted[6] that the Achaemenid inscriptions "are completely lacking in any name that could define, in a geographical or ethnic sense, the State or 'kingdom', *xšaça-*". This was not surprising, he remarked, for such terms would have limited the extent of the royal authority claimed by the Great King. Gnoli explained the attestations in the Assyrian[7] and Achaemenid[8] texts of the name *Ariya* as well as references in Herodotus and classical authors[9] as ethnic or possibly religious, not political. Nor did he see any evidence that Zoroaster viewed the term *Ariya* as an indication of nationality.[10] Accepting a widely held view that after Zoroaster "Zarathuštric priests" assimilated "different religious trends" in the so-called Great *Yašts* of the *Avesta*, Gnoli asserted that in the process these priests invented "the myth and legends of *airyå daiŋhāvō*".[11] In Gnoli's view, in these texts *Airya* is mainly used "as a description of the airya lands or peoples" and of their *X^{v}arenah-*, or God-given Fortune; it distinguishes the lands and peoples who are Zoroastrians from those who are not. Because they wanted to place their prophet in the centre of the world, these priests "invented" the concept of an ancestral homeland as the cradle of mankind and called it "*Airyanem vaējō*" (Ērān-vēž).[12] Thus, even here the term Airya was essentially religiously based.[13] It does not recur in its original Avestan sense until Ardašīr, son of Pāpak, revives it in order to legitimise his claim to the old Kayānid throne and dominion. With him at last the term Airya/Arya assumes a political sense and provides an official name for what was *simultaneously the empire of the Iranians and the realm of Zoroastrians*. In other words, Ardašīr *coined* the idea of an "Iranian empire" (*Ērānšahr*) in order to substantiate his claim that he had in fact *resurrected* what had once been a *national Mazdayasnian state*.[14]

This thesis was hailed by some eminent scholars as a novel and entirely acceptable interpretation and the opinion was repeatedly voiced that, since the idea of Iran was not old, to insist on the use of the name *Iran* rather than the more familiar *Persia* was a sign of folly. One eager writer jumped on to the bandwagon by claiming that "Der Terminus 'Iran' bezeichnete *im Laufe der Geschichte* [emphasis mine] keineswegs durchgehend ein politisch und administrative konzipiertes Territorium",[15] and that[16] with the fall of the Sasanians their "arbitrarily invented [*willkürlich geschaffene*]" ideological terminology was abandoned until the Mongols revived it.[17] Worse still, relief-seeking idle poets and amateur writers found a fertile ground to belittle Iranian nationalism in general by dismissing the idea of Iran as an invention of western scholars and their foolish ultra-nationalist Iranian students. The title of a book betrays the political agenda that the author pursued. Published in 1993 by Paragon House, it is called *Iran as Imagined Nation: The Construction of National Identity*. It sees the modern, unified Iran as an arbitrary creation that marginalises religious minorities (Jews, Buddhists, Christians and Babis) and asserts that the imagined Iranian history anachronistically ignores speakers of non-Iranian languages. Such inadvertent consequences of Gnoli's thesis make a serious critique of it not only a scholarly necessity but also a political urgency.

Let us first examine the basis of Gnoli's interpretation of the Avestan evidence.[18] He claims that the idea of "Iran" evolved when "Zarathuštric priests" restricted the appellative Airya to themselves and the realm they had converted. However, in the *Frawardīn Yašt* (143–44), one of the oldest and most authentic Avestan texts, the *fravašis* (departed souls of the ancestors) of *five nations*, namely Airya, Tūirya, Dāha, Sairima and Sāinu-, are venerated. Clearly not *all* of these nations were Zoroasterians, and clearly here "Airya" does not mean "Zoroastrian". Gnoli's discussion of the identity of the Avestan Airyas begins with a foregone conclusion: "We must," he writes, "make it clear first of all that these Avestan Airyas never had – at least as far as we may deduce from the few available sources – a State political organization of a centralized, or, even less, an 'imperial' type, as the Medes and the Persians had later on".[19] From the Avestan evidence (particularly *Mihr Yašt* 13–14) and *Vidēvdād* (I, 1–8), the extent of the "Aryan lands" – usually called *airyå daiŋhāvō* and occasionally referred to as *airyō.šayanəm* – may be given as the area west of the Indus and east of Kirman.[20] The list of the lands in the *Vidēvdād* is as follows: Gava (Sogdian), Mourv (Merv), Bāxδi (Bactria), Nisāya (around modern Ashkabad), Harōiva (Herat), Vaēkereta (Gandhara), Urvā (probably the district of Ghazna), Xnenta (Jurjaniya of Islamic geographers), Haraxuvaitī (Arachosia), Haētumant (the Hermand basin, Seistan), Ragha (in east Iran), Čaxra (Charkh, between Ghazna and Kabul), Varena (Bunēr), Hapta Hendu (eastern Punjab) and Rangha (a region watered by a river, probably the Jaxartes). The Choresmians are not mentioned here and on another occasion I shall bring forth evidence suggesting that, at this early stage, the Choresmians were not yet in the land bearing their name but further to the south, around Nisāya.

Now, the Avestan hymn to Mithra (*Mihr Yašt*) mirrors (17–18, 87) a *five-fold* organisation that is not only ethnic but also, as the late Ilia Gershevitch demonstrated,[21] *socio-political*. Vertically, it started from *nmāna-*, "house" headed by a patriarch (*nmānō-paiti-*), and proceeded to *vīs-*, "clan" presided over by a "clan-lord" (*vīspaiti-*), *zantu-*, "tribe" under a "tribal chief" (*zantupaiti-*), and *daḣyu-*, "country" ruled by a "ruler" (*daiŋhupaiti-*). The fifth division is called *daiŋhusasti-*. As Ilia Gershevitch explained, the *daiŋhu-* in this compound, though singular, conveys the meaning of a vast region, like the Latin *imperium*: "the context of st[anza] 87 does suggest that *daiŋhusasti-* is used in the sense of 'empire'".[22] In fact this last socio-political division was dominated by a *daḣyunam fratemaδāō*, "council of premiers of countries, that is, a Council of State".[23] As James Darmesteter[24] and Gershevitch[25] have argued, this proves that there was already a sense that an *empire* had been created.[26] The sense of unity, of belonging to one nation, or – as we say today – of *nationalism*, shared by those knowing themselves as *Airya-*, is indicated by the fact that they called their home *airyå daiŋhāvō* or *airyō.šayanəm-*, "Aryan Countries"; and so exclusive was this term that they referred to the realm of unrelated people as *anairya daiŋhāvō*, "Un-Aryan Countries".[27] Now, among the rulers of these countries some bore the title *Kavi* (>*Kay*), which originally meant inspired seer/hero.[28] One family of the Kavis in particular came to dominate Iranian traditional history as *the* Kavi (*Kayān*)[29] dynasty, the paragon of rulership, heroism and national splendour. This was due to the support its last member, Kavi Vištāspa (<Kay Goštāsp), gave to Zoroaster, resulting in the Avestan celebration of this house in sacred hymns.[30] The most famous member of the Kavi dynasty was Kavi Haosrava (>Kay Khosrow), who flourished a few generations before Zoroaster. The *Avesta* calls him *arša airiyanąm daiŋhunąm xšaθrāi hankeremō,* "Hero of the Aryan countries and consolidator of the empire" (*Yt* 15.32). Now, all the Avestan evidence is assembled and learnedly discussed by Professor Gnoli but, surprisingly, given a wrong interpretation by appealing to a *four-fold* organisation (*"a pattern that we must reconstruct"*[31] – emphasis mine). However, the title of Kavi Haosrava alone is sufficient proof of the existence of a *nation,* created when *political unity* had been achieved by many "countries" all sharing in a common Aryan heritage. This was a nation which under a unifier had gained the status of a federation. In other words, it was an *empire,* and here we do have the very term that the Iranians were to employ for their *state,* namely *xšaθra,* and this was the term that later came into Iranian political ideology as *Aryānšatra* > *Ērānšahr* > *Iran.* Even in the Avestan period one readily spoke of *vispe aire razuraya,* "Pan-Aryan Razura Forest" (*Yt* 15.32), or *nāfō airyanąm daŋyunąm čiθrem airyanąm daŋyunąm,* "the kindred of the Aryan countries, the origins of Aryan lands" (*ibid.*). The national identity was so distinctly felt and conceptualised that, as with Rome and Hellenistic states at a much later period, it was hypostatised by a divine force, the Aryan Fortune/Glory (*Airyanem x^{v}arenō* > *Ērān Xurrah, Xurra Ērānšhar* > *Farr-e Iran*),[32] which, as the *Avesta* specifies, "Belongs to the Aryan lands, to the born and unborn" (*yat asti airyanąm daŋyunąm azatanamča* [i.e. was *not* restricted to Zoroastrians!]); it smote the Evil and its emissaries, protected the Aryans and bestowed on them great wealth, wisdom and welfare.[33] The implication of this concept has not been sufficiently taken into account. It is self-evident that the idea *presupposes* an Aryan nation. For a political union of the Aryan people and lands must have existed before the conception of a protecting national force of divine origin – the "(God-given) Aryan Fortune" – could come about. In other words, when the "Aryan Fortune/Glory" was mentioned, the "Aryan nation" was understood as a solid, rooted reality. This is the meaning of the prayer of Darius III on the eve of his last battle with the Macedonian invaders: "O ye gods of my race" with "and kingdom," above all things else grant me that I may leave the Tyche of the Persians re-established in the prosperity wherein I found it' (Plutarch: *Alexander* 30.12). Here by "my race" Darius means Aryan and by the Persian Tyche the *Airyanem x^{v}aren.*[34]

We next turn to the alleged lack of attestation of the idea of Iran in the Median and Persian periods. As for the Medes, Herodotus (VII. 62) testifies that at first everyone called them Aryans. When they created a large state, which included western Iran, parts of Asia Minor and northern Mesopotamia, they naturally could not call it "Aryan". Even then one of their major tribes distinguished itself by retaining the name Arizantoi, "Aryan Tribe" (Herodotus I. 101). Similarly with the Persians. These cousins of the Medes, too, called themselves *Arya čiça*, "Aryan by origin/race".[35] During the second half of the 6th century BCE they expanded far and wide and settled in many non-Aryan lands, creating an empire "from the Scythians beyond Sogdian to Ethiopia, and from Sind to Sardis".[36] This state, which Heinrich Schaeder rightly called a "*world empire*",[37] was *two-thirds un-Iranian*. It was *dahyūnām vispazanām*, "the lands of all nations",[38] and the jewel in the crown of the Achaemenid empire, Persepolis, demonstrates the concept clearly. As one ascends the majestic staircase leading to the palace area, one first enters the Gate House of Xerxes. In the cuneiform inscriptions carved upon its doorway pillars, the building –the entrance to Persepolis – is called *Duvarθim visadahyum*, "The Gate of All Nations".[39] The pivotal policy of this empire was tolerance.[40] Within this vast empire, every subject nation was allowed to maintain its national identity by keeping its religion, language, traditions and lifestyle. Although the Iranians were mainly Mazdā-worshippers (Mazdayasnians) and the Achaemenid kings were *personally* devoted to Ahura Mazdā, in contrast to earlier civilisations of the Near East they considered religion a private matter and usually did not allow theirs to play a part in politics.[41] When necessary, the Achaemenid court actively supported priests of all religions: Babylonian,[42] Elamite,[43] Jewish,[44] Egyptian[45] and Hellenic.[46] Furthermore, the Persian empire was politically and culturally influenced by ancient Near Eastern nations. It employed Elamite, Babylonian and Aramaic scribes to run its complex chancellery and record its documents in their own languages.[47] It was *these scribes* who called the empire *Persia* after its ruling class, a designation which the Jews and Greeks used and transferred to the Islamic and Western worlds. The Persians themselves referred to it in vague terms such as "Asia"[48] or "this Empire" (*ima xšassam*),[49] in the sense of *the Empire*,[50] exactly as a German used to say "das Reich", a Russian referred to his state as "the Soviet Union", or an Englishman still refers to his country as "the United Kingdom".

In spite of their imperial policy, the Persians showed a strong concept of national identity. They called themselves "Aryan by origin/race" (*Ariya čiça*), as we saw, and what they understood by it is clear from the following facts: they referred to Ahura Mazdā as "God of the Aryans",[51] implying a *national* God; Darius proclaimed that he was a Persian by birth but an Aryan by ethnic identity; and his language, which we term Old Persian and which was undoubtedly understood by the Medes and many other Iranians, was named "Aryan", that is "Iranian".[52] The taxation list in Herodotus (III, 89–118) shows that the truly Aryan (Iranian) subjects of the Achaemenids paid much lower taxes than did non-Iranian subjects. Persepolitan carvings and other sources show that they were given prominence in military affairs and accorded honoured positions in court ceremonial and administration. It was no coincidence that Alexander easily subjugated the non-Iranian provinces of the Persian empire, even though the Great King was still in power. However, he met staunch resistance in east Iran in a sort of patriotic war even though the central authority had disintegrated.[53] Similarly, the invader's memory was honoured in lands west of the Zagros but reviled in countries to the east.

The most important testimony to the ideology of the Achaemenid state is borne by the façade of the tomb of Darius the Great at Naqsh-e Rostam in Fārs.[54] There his empire is symbolised by thirty throne-bearers who represent his subject peoples. Trilingual cuneiform inscriptions identify each figure, and all are further enumerated in the accompanying longer texts which serve as the testament of the king. There we read that these figures represented Persia, Media, etc. The naming and sculptural arrangement of the subject peoples follow the geographical division of the empire into seven regions.[55] It is self-evident that such a vast empire could not be called the "Aryan empire", but the lack of such a designation does not exclude the existence of that term during the Persian period. It would have been the designation of a *specific part* of the Persian empire. Now, if we look closely, we see that the third division of this empire comprised the truly Iranian lands/peoples of Parthia, Aria, Bactria, Sogdia, Choresmia and Drangiana. The inhabitants of the "Aryan countries" are thus grouped together as a unit, similar to the Avestan evidence, in a *single* region between the Indus and Kirman. From the Behistun inscription and Classical sources we know that a large region in the Persian empire was called *xšaça-* (Avestan *xšaθra-*). The logical inference would be that the third division just noted would be called a *xšaça-*, that is, it would be the **Aryānām xšaça*.[56] This is not an idle supposition. It is substantiated by a fact recognised by Herzfeld in one of his sounder conclusions[57], but denied by Gnoli[58], on arbitrary grounds. This region was actually called Ariane in the early Hellenistic period (Strabo, *Geography* XV. 2, 1–8, from Eratosthenes), a term which was revived in 1851 with the publication of H.H. Wilson's *Ariana Antiqua*.[59] It is usually forgotten that Eratosthenes' long description of Ariana as quoted by Strabo (which we will discuss below) starts with these words: "After India one comes to Ariana, the first portion of the country *subject to the Persians* after [i.e. to the west of] the Indus". In Eratosthenes' time, that is, the 3rd century BC, there was *no Persian rule* over this area. The "Persians" here are undoubtedly the Achaemenid Persians, not the Iranians of the Hellenistic period. Eratosthenes' ultimate source was thus *contemporary* with Persian rule over eastern Iran, and Ariana was already the recognised name of the region, or *xšaçam-*, of East Iran under the Achaemenids. It is clear that this geographical term could not have been coined by the Greeks of the post-Achaemenid period had there been no Iranian antecedent. Only an Iranian **Aryānām xšaθram*, which was already implicit in the epithet of Kavi Hausrava (see above), could have given rise to the concept of a single region of Aryan dominion west of the Indus all the way to parts of Persis and Media.

That the idea of Iran was known to the Achaemenids is inferred from other observations. Firstly as H. Hübschmann[60] and J. Marquart[61] pointed out long ago, the Parthian form *Ariyān* and Middle Persian spelling *Airyān* – attested first in the trilingual inscription of Ardašīr I at Naqsh-e Rostam – point to a time when the suffix *-ya* was not yet obsolete, i.e. the Achaemenid period. In fact, as Kent formulated it, often in Old Persian "the ethnic is formed from province name by the -*ya* suffix".[62] The following examples suffice:[63] Armina > Arminya, Asagarta > Asagartiya, Sparda > Spardiya, Hinduš > Hinduya, Maka > Mačiya, Bābiruš > Bābirwiya, Uvja > Uvjiya, U'ārazmiš > U'ārazmiya. Secondly, the traditional usage of calling a region after its inhabitants or a people after its home means that the Hellenistic Ariane and Arianoi went back to an Iranian ethnic name that had a suffix -*ya*, that is *Ariya,* gen. pl. *Ariyānām.* Thirdly, as Hübschmann has explained,[64] Classical Armenian has two terms for Iran. The Armenians had borrowed the word *ari-* in a very remote time when the Persians still pronounced it *ariya-*, and they had preserved it well into the late Sasanian period,[65] when the Old Persian genitive plural *Ariyānām* (= *Arianun* in Ardašīr I's Greek inscription at Naqsh-e Rostam) had developed through *aryān, airyān* ... into *Ērān* so that Łazar 187 [66] still spoke of *dprpet Areac*, [Middle] Persian *Ērān *dibīrbaδ* (Pahlavi *Airān *dipīrpat*),[67] the Secretary of Iran, the Imperial Secretary. When Ardašīr founded the second Persian empire and officially called it *Airyānšatra > Ērānšahr*,[68] the Armenians borrowed this term directly, rendering it as Ašxarhn Areac'.[69]

Let us now consider the Hellenistic and Parthian periods. Once the Persian world empire collapsed, the Graeco-Macedonian rule did not permit the continuation of a term such as **Aryānām xšaθram*, just as the Islamic conquest was to force out *Ērānšahr/Ērān* from *official* records. Hence, only the plain **Aryānām*, which by then had evolved into Middle Iranian *Ariyān,* remained in use and when, following Alexander's conquest, Hellenistic authors became familiar with the area between the Indus and the Hāmūn lake, they called it *Ariane/Ariana* and their inhabitants *Arianoi*. The geographic term renders an early Middle Iranian *Ariyān,* derived from Old Persian *Ariyānām,* "of the Aryans/Iranians". The genitive plural presupposes an ethnic compound. Indeed, Eratosthenes in the late 3rd century BCE "defined" Ariana "as of a single ethnical group" (*άv ένος έθνους* Strabo II. 1, 31) in a *single region* which he described in detail and located between the Indus and Kirman (*ibid*. XV 2, 1– 8). He reported that "the name of Ariana is further extended to a part of Persis and of Media, as also to the Bactrians and Sogdians, for they speak approximately the same language, with but slight variations" (*ibid*. XV 2, 8). This evidence is now partially substantiated by the recently discovered Rabātak inscription of Kanishka the Great, who states that he issued an edict in Greek "and then put it into Aryan" (l. 3), by which he meant Bactrian.[70] That the Greeks understood Ariane to be a political term is clear from the report by Diodorus (I. 94,2; cf. II. 37, 6, based on older sources) that peoples who bordered India [of the Mauryans] were, from north to south, Scythians, Bactrians (that is, Graeco-Bactrians) and Arianoi. In the same sense, Eratosthenes (cited by Strabo I, 4, 9) criticised the traditional division of mankind into Greeks and Barbarians and pointed out that "not only are many of the Greeks bad, but many of the Barbarians are refined – Indians and Arianoi, for example", as well as the Romans and Carthaginians. Here there is a reference to the Arianoi (Iranians) who had a place in history on a par with the Romans, Carthaginians and Mauryan Indians. We are dealing with a clearly defined nation, not merely a linguistic or ethnic group.

As for the Parthian period, there is evidence that the Parthians continued to use the name *Ērānšahr* for their original country and its surroundings. For the province of Nišāpūr, with its capital at Abaršahr,[71] was occasionally called *Ērānšahr*.[72] Moqaddasīi reports[73] that some even counted Seistan as a part of this *Ērānšahr*;[74] and he describes its beauty and prosperity[75] in terms recalling the Avestan description of the *Airyanem vaējō* (Ērān-vēž), and counts nearly a dozen of its towns, including Rēvand and Sabzavār. Yāqūt quotes Balāδūrī as writing "*Ērānšahr* is Nišāpūr, Qohestān, the two Tabases, Herāt, Pūšang, Bādγeys and Tus also called Tāberān".[76] I hardly need to point out here that *Ērānšahr* is not a corruption of Abaršahr (which is solidly attested for the city of Nišāpūr), and the statement of Balāδūrī just quoted demonstrates that geographically it corresponded to the Parthian state before its expansion into Kirman, Persis and Media. Once this state became an empire by incorporating those provinces as well as Mesopotamia, thereby subjugating *many non-Iranians*, then the Arsacids, like the Achaemenids before them, could not *officially* designate their state as *"the Empire of the Iranians"*. Nevertheless, that *Ērānšahr* persisted in oral tradition as the logical historic development of an earlier, Achaemenid **Aryānām xšaçam* – even if it is not attested in the *surviving* records of the time – is proved, as Hübschmann noted, by the Armenians borrowing the word *ari-* in a very remote time when the Persians still pronounced it *ariya-* (see above, p. 100).

Finally, we come to the *Ērānšahr* of Ardašīr Pāpakān. The career of this dynasty founder is well illustrated by his coinage.[77] The first series showed him as a local ruler called simply "King Ardašīr, son of King Pāpak", and the father is also portrayed on the coin (on the reverse). Writing to "petty kings" of various provinces of the Parthian empire, Ardašīr claimed that he had risen *to unite the countries (bilād)* once belonging to his royal ancestors, the "Persian" (i.e. Achaemenid) sovereigns (Tabari I: 813). He expanded his state first eastward. His coins reveal that he had assumed the role of the resurrector of the old Iranian empire (the empires of Darius and Mithridates II), for he had now instituted a royal fire (an Achaemenid tradition on the accession of a Great King). The fire was represented on an altar placed on a throne imitating the throne of Darius the Great on his tomb façade. He put on the royal tiara of Mithridates II and called himself "King of Iran" (*MLK' 'yr'n*). Only after killing the last Parthian King of Kings, Ardavān, did Ardašīr assume the title "King of kings of Iranians" (*MLK'n MLK' 'yr'n*). The choice was clear. Ardašīr needed to exchange the name Pahlav, which had become a familiar designation of the Parthian empire, for one that could unify Iranians while indicating his claim to their ancestral empire. Pārsa/Pārs could not do, *Ērānšahr* could. It was not a political use of the equation of "Zoroastrians" with "Iranians," it was the conscious re-employment of an ethnicon which was also political and meant to satisfy the national pride of the Parthians, Persians,

Sakastanians, Aturpatakanians, Heratians and other Iranians, even many Armenians. As long as the Sasanian empire remained mainly Iranian, the designation "King of Kings of Iranians" remained, but when Shapur's conquest brought large numbers of non-Iranians under his sway, the title had to be altered to "King of kings of Iranians and Un-Iranians".

A curious fact needs to be mentioned here as a warning to those who reach conclusions based on the absence of data. The Sasanian official name *Ērānšahr* could not eclipse the use of "Persia" by tradition-orientated bureaucrats. The Manichaeans who created the most literate society of the pre-Islamic Iran knew perfectly well that the *official designation* of the Sasanian empire was *Ērānšahr*. Yet, as the late David Neil MacKenzie noted, in no "Manichaean Parthian or Persian [text] has the term *Ērānšahr* been met".[78] If we had only the Manichaean evidence, some of us would have insisted that the Sasanians had never called their state *Ērānšahr*!

Let me conclude with another warning: one should not ignore the fact that, once established, a *national identity* keeps its ideological conception even when *the name* is eclipsed by a different political appellation. "Official names" of empires are often arbitrary and transitory, coined out of political expediency and usually vague enough to satisfy a large number of subject people. They exist side-by-side with older, national names that they try to eclipse. When the "British Empire" evolved as a universalist state, *England* was still unofficially the name of the country and *English* its language. The official name "Soviet Union" did not eclipse *Russia,* and when that world empire was in danger during the Second World War it was *Mother Russia* that was invoked to wage the "Great Patriotic War". Similarly, the collapse of the Sasanian *Ērānšahr* in AD 650 did not end Iranians' *national* idea. The name "Iran" disappeared from official records of the Saffarids, Samanids, Byuids, Saljuqs and their successors. But one still *unofficially* used the name Iran, *Ērānšahr* and similar national designations, particularly *Mamalek-e Iran* or "Iranian Lands", which exactly translated the old Avestan term *Airyanąm daiŋunąm*. On the other hand, when the Safavids (not Reza Shah, as is popularly assumed) revived a national state *officially* known as *Iran,* bureaucratic usages in the Ottoman empire and even in Iran itself could still refer to it by other descriptive and traditional appellations.

Notes:

1. Gnoli 1989. Although Professor Gnoli has written repeatedly on the subject since the late 1960s (for references see *ibid.*: 196–7), this is his most detailed exposition and will suffice for our consideration.
2. In his letter dated January 1808, M. Tancoigne, a member of Napoleon's embassy to Tehran, emphasised: "Iran is the true name of Persia amongst the Orientals. & It would be unintelligible to them to term it Persia"; and he explained that "Persia which the Europeans have adopted is only the name of the province of Fārs [ancient Persis]": see *A Narrative of a Journey into Persia and Residence at Tehran* (London 1820): 147. Similarly, see Kinneir 1813: 2; Ouseley 1819–23: xii; cf. Shoberel 1828: 136 and Nöldeke 1887: 147–9.
3. Cassel 1886: 1–3.
4. On this, see in detail Shahbazi 2001.
5. Unaware of Cassel's thesis, Gnoli was evidently spurred on by O. Klima's "coherent and logical conclusion" that "although it seems to be impossible, the Achaemenian empire had no official names (…) as the official titles of modern states are used at present" (Gnoli 1989: 6, quoting Klima 1967: 146–7, esp. p. 144f.).
6. Gnoli 1989: 6.
7. *Ibid.*: 8–11.
8. *Ibid.*: 7–8, 13–25.
9. *Ibid.*: 11–13, 103–118.
10. *Ibid.*: 32ff. and *passim*.
11. *Ibid.*: 35. Cf. p. 51 and *passim*.
12. *Ibid.*: 34. Cf. p. 40ff.
13. *Ibid.*: 68ff.
14. *Ibid.*: 129ff.
15. Franger 1999: 365–76, esp. p. 370.
16. *Ibid.*: 371.
17. For a refutation of such bombastic claims, see the many references to "Iran" as a political concept used by Iranians in the Samanid, Ghaznavid, Saljuq and Khwarazmshahid periods collected by J. Matīnī *seven years before* Fragner's publication: Matīnī 1992: 243–68, esp. 255–61.
18. Discussed in detail by Professor Gnoli (1989: 32–70), making it unnecessary to go into detailed references and documentation here.
19. *Ibid.*: 67–8.
20. For what follows, see *ibid.*: 42–68.
21. Gershevitch 1959: 296–9.
22. *Ibid.*: 297.
23. *Ibid.*: 298.
24. Darmesteter 1892: I, 388, n. 20; II, 465.
25. Gershevitch 1959: 296–8.
26. Ernst Herzfeld recognised that the Avestan text referred to an organised state, but since he had dated Zoroaster to the late 6th century BCE and made him a courtier at the imperial court of Media and Persia, he was forced to write that the last division implies "the union of many satrapies in one empire, not as a hope, but as a projection of the worldly facts [Median and Persian Empires] into myth" (Herzfeld 1948: 445, quoted and commented on by Gershevitch, *op. cit.*: 296).
27. See Bailey, "Arya" 1987: 681–3.

28. For details see Geiger 1882: 425–38; Gershevitch 1959: 296–9; Boyce: I, 5, 13; Schwartz 1985: 648–50.
29. Bailey, *op.cit*: 681. For the terms see Bartholomae, *AiWb*, cols. 120, 198.
30. See Christensen 1933; Yarshater 1983: 365, 374–7, 436–40, 445–53, 461–70; Shahbazi 2002.
31. Gnoli 1989: 16.
32. Bailey 1943: 23. For symbolic depiction of it in Achaemenid art as a winged circle, see Shahbazi 1974 and 1980; Calmeyer 1981 and 1987; Ahn 1992: 99–217. A detailed refutation of P. Lecoque's "restatement" of the old Ahura Mazdā hypothesis is in the press. I now subscribe to the derivation of the noun $X^v arenah$ from *hvar* "sun": see Duchesne-Guillemin 1963: 19–31, endorsed by Boyce 1982: 17, n. 23.
33. *Yt* 18.63 with Bailey, *op.cit*.: 27.
34. Shahbazi 1980: 129.
35. Darius, Naqsh-e Rostam *b*. inscription, ll. 4–8 (= Kent, *Old Persian:* 1953: 136–7); Darius, Susa *e* , ll. 12–14 (Kent: 141*);* Xerxes, Persepolis *h* inscription, ll. 12–13 (=Kent 1953: 151), wrongly interpreted by Briant (2002: 182): "we get the impression that here [to with: *Ariya čiça*] the word *Arya* refers narrowly to the Persians or even the royal family".
36. Darius, Persepolis *h* inscription, ll. 4–8 (= Kent 1953: 136–7).
37. See Schaeder 1941.
38. Darius, Naqsh-e Rostam *a* inscription, ll, 10–11 (= Kent 1953: 137). Detailed discussion and documentary evidence of the terms used for the Persian empire is found in Herrenschmidt 1976.
39. Xerxes, Persepolis inscription e, l. 12 (= Kent 1953: 148) with Schmidt 1953: 65–8.
40. See Meyer 1980: vol. 6, 20–26; Schaeder, *op.cit.:* 17–34; Toynbee 1954: 178–9, 580ff.; Hinz 1979: 189–202.
41. Meyer, *op.cit.*: 157–64; Schaeder, *op.cit.*: 22, 34.
42. See Oppenheim1985.
43. See Hallock 1985.
44. Schaeder, *op.cit*.: 25; Widengren 1977.
45. See Posener 1963; see also Bresciani 1985.
46. Meyer, *op.cit*.: 89; Boyce 1982: 47–8, 255–97.
47. Meyer, *op.cit.:* 39ff.; Hinz 1979: 79–121.
48. Herodotus I. 5, 130; VII, II; IX. 116, 122; Q. Curtius III. 3.3–4. The idea was already Median: Herodotus I. 108.
49. Darius, Behistun [Old Persian] inscription col. I, ll. 25, 26 (= Kent, *op. cit*.: 117); Darius, Persepolis *h* inscription , l. 4 (= Kent: 136).
50. For this and other designations see Herrenschmidt 1976: 37–8.
51. Darius, Behistun inscription, Elamite version, III, l. 77; Schmitt 1991b.
52. Darius, Behistun Old Persian inscription, IV, l. 89 (= Kent: 130, and now Schmitt 1991a: 45, 73); see also Meyer, *op.cit.:* 24, n. 1. The difference between Median and Persian was dialectical, while Strabo testifies (*Geography* XV. 2, 8, from Eratosthenes) that "the name Ariana is further extended to a part of Persis and of Media, as also the Bactrians and Sogdians on the north, for these speak approximately the same language, but with slight variations".
53. For Alexander's eastern campaigns see Badian 1985.
54. See Schmidt 1970: pp. 79ff.
55. Shahbazi 1983 (ignored by Gnoli in his discussion of the evidence: 1989: 19–23).
56. See in particular Herrenschmidt 1976: 52–65 and 1979; see also Calmeyer 1982: XV, 135–9, 164; and 1983: XVI, 157–60, 220–221.

57. Herzfeld 1948: 699.
58. Gnoli 1989: 2ff.
59. Wilson 1851; the subtitle reads *A Descriptive Account of Antiquities and Coins of Afghanistan*. In Chapter III (119–214), Wilson collected and analysed all ancient sources on "Ancient Ariana: the country between Persia and India". It is still useful. It was this book which a century later gave "nationalist" Afghans a tool to fabricate a glorious past and brand the Achaemenids and Sasanians as usurpers and invaders (on such pseudo-scholarship see Matīnī 1990: 3–31 and 1992: 247–8).
60. Hübschmann 1894–5.
61. Marquart 1895.
62. Kent, *op.cit.*: 56.
63. *Ibid.*: 56–7.
64. Hübschmann: *loc.cit.*
65. See also Lamberterie 1989 and Schmitt 1991b.
66. See *The History of Łazar P'arpec'i*, tr. Robert W. Thomson (Atlanta, Georgia, 1991): 106.
67. For the attested forms of this title see Huyse 1999: II, 140–41.
68. See Huyse 1999: II, 9–11.
69. Hübschmann 1897: 26.
70. See Sims-Williams and Cribb 1995-96, esp. 78, 83.
71. For which see H. Gaube, "Abaršahr", *EIr* I 1982: 67.
72. A number of notables originating from this place are known, the most famous being the $3^{rd}/9^{th}$ century scholar several times quoted by Bērūnī, *Ketāb Qānūn al-Mas'ūdī* (Heydarabad, India), II, 1375: 632, 870.
73. Moqaddasīi, *Ahsan al-taqāsīm fi al-ma'rifat al-'qālīm*, ed. M.J. de Geoje (Leiden 1877): 299.
74. *Ibid.*: 299–300, 314–16.
75. *Ibid.*: 50, 300.
76. Yāqūt, *Mu'jam al-buldān*, ed. F. Wüstenfeld, 6 vols (Leipzig 1866–73), I: 418.
77. For which see more recently Alram 1999: 67–76 (with varying interpretation).
78. "*Ērān, Ērānšahr*", *EncIr* VIII, 1998: 535.

6

Iron Age Iran and the Transition to the Achaemenid Period

John Curtis (The British Museum)

Contributors to this series were asked to consider some aspect of the "Idea of Iran", but it is mainly with the Achaemenid period that this concept becomes meaningful.[1] Thus on his tomb at Naqsh-e Rostam, Darius proudly proclaims:-

"I am Darius, the great king, king of kings, king of the counties containing all races, king on this great earth even far off, the son of Hystaspes, an Achaemenid, a Persian, the son of a Persian, an Aryan, of Aryan lineage".[2]

Here, then, through the reference to Aryans, we have some allusion to the "Idea of Iran". However, as the Iranian or Iranian-speaking peoples of pre-Achaemenid date have left no contemporary written records, we know little about how they perceived themselves or the country which they inhabited.[3] In other words, the concept of Iran as defined in linguistic, ethnic and geopolitical terms becomes more difficult to deal with the further back one goes into history, especially into periods when there are no written records, or at least no written records of the Iranian people themselves. As it is impossible to consider the "Idea of Iran" in the pre-Achaemenid period, I intend instead to consider some aspects of Western Iran in the Iron Age, and consider where the main cultural influences came from in that period. Then we will examine the transition to the Achaemenid period. This will give us an opportunity to consider how much continuity there is between the pre-Achaemenid and Achaemenid periods, and assess to what extent Achaemenid material culture is a product of pre-Achaemenid traditions or whether some of the features are borrowed from other contemporary cultures.

For the record, the commonly held view is that people speaking Indo-Iranian languages started to arrive on the Iranian plateau some time after 2000 BCE, first attested at sites such as Tureng Tepe.[4] They are thought to have come down the east side of the Caspian Sea, from a putative homeland or homelands somewhere in the Eurasian Steppes. The arrival of these new peoples gathered momentum during the Iron Age I period, that is from about 1450 BCE onwards, and is characterised by the introduction of new pottery types in the form of monochrome red or grey-black burnished wares. Also, the dead were now buried in cemeteries outside settlements. This whole theory is appealing but is almost certainly an oversimplification. To start with, the association between the innovations noted in the material culture record and the arrival of new peoples speaking Indo-Iranian languages, remains hypothetical. And, even if there was a link between the changes in the archaeological record and these supposed Indo-European migrations, the numbers of peoples involved, and the extent to which the existing population was displaced, are unknown factors. In south-western Iran it is known that the Elamites, who had inhabited the region from at least 3000 BCE onwards, continued to flourish down to the Achaemenid period, and it is possible that other indigenous groups did likewise. To return to the Iranian-speaking peoples, the Medes[5] and possibly the Persians[6] are first mentioned in contemporary Assyrian texts of the 9th century BCE. At this date, however, it is very difficult to identify these peoples in the archaeological record, and although in the Early Iron Age we can note new features in the material culture but we cannot responsibly link them with language and ethnicity.

One of the sites at which the distinctive red and grey ware pottery has been found is Marlik in Gilan, in the lush area between the Alburz Mountains and the Caspian Sea. Here, the pioneering Iranian archaeologist Professor Ezat O. Negahban opened more than fifty tombs in 1961-2.[7] The rich finds from these graves included large pottery figurines, both of human and animals. Vessels in the form of hump-backed bulls, with pouring spouts and wearing gold earrings, were particularly popular (Fig.1).

Fig. 1. Pottery vessel in the form of a humped-backed bull from tomb 18 at Marlik, National Museum of Iran. Photograph J.E. Curtis.

They occur in both grey ware and red ware pottery. Gold and silver beakers with concave sides are particularly diagnostic of Marlik: they have cable-pattern borders at top and bottom, and geometric rosettes on the base. The embossed designs on the sides often show winged bulls and other mythical beasts. There are also many beakers of this kind from unofficial excavations, presumably at Marlik or in the vicinity. These graves at Marlik, dating mainly between c.1400 and 1000 BCE, provide evidence of a rich and flourishing culture that is essentially local in character. However, there are some tie-ups with the contemporary Middle Assyrian civilisation in Northern Mesopotamia, to the west, particularly through some of the cylinder seals and jewellery. The stamp seals, on the other hand, are of a distinctive local type.

A key site for our knowledge of the late second and early first millennium BCE in Western Iran is Hasanlu, a large mound in the Solduz Valley to the south-west of Lake Urmia.[8] The Early Iron Age or Iron I period, c.1450-1250 BCE, is represented at Hasanlu by the remains of buildings known as Hasanlu period V. Also dating from this time are large quantities of burnished pottery, chiefly in grey but also in red. In the next period (Iron II) there was a series of buildings arranged around courtyards which were twice destroyed by fire. Already we can see the columned buildings that are the prototype of the later "apadana" plan. They have central columned halls, porticoes around the sides which may or may not have columns, and corner towers. The Hasanlu IV settlement was finally destroyed probably by the Urartians around 800 BCE,[9] although this date is disputed and it might have been a bit later.[10] In the destruction debris were found both the bodies of humans who had been overcome while trying to escape from the fire and as many as 7000 artefacts (Figs. 2-3), many of which remain unpublished.[11]

Fig.2. Horse's breastplate from Hasanlu, National Musem of Iran. Photograph J.E.Curtis.

Fig. 3. Bronze drinking-cup in the form of a ram's head from Hasanlu, National Museum of Iran. Photograph J. E. Curtis.

Outstanding amongst them is a gold bowl with a complex scene that is probably mythological. It may well be of local inspiration. Alongside objects showing both local and North Syrian influence, there was also much "Assyrian related material".[12] For example, there are at least twenty-one cylinder seals in Neo-Assyrian style, of which six may be actual Assyrian imports[13] and there are Assyrian-style ivories.[14] A glazed wall-tile[15] is comparable with ninth-century examples found at Nimrud and Balawat in Assyria.[16]

Of course, we should not be surprised by some evidence of Assyrian influence. It is well-known that most of the Late Assyrian kings campaigned in the Zagros Mountains or other parts of Western Iran. They may even have approached modern Tehran if the Mount Bikni of the texts is correctly identified as Mount Damavend, the tallest peak in the Elburz range.[17] These campaigns in both the Iron II and Iron III periods are described in the inscriptions of various kings including Ashurnasirpal II, Shalmaneser III, Tiglath-pileser III, Sargon II and Ashurbanipal. They are also illustrated on Assyrian reliefs, where for example Iranian fortresses are shown.[18] In Iran itself, there are memorials left behind by the Assyrian kings. These are sometimes in the form of stelae carved on rock faces, as at Shikaft-i Gulgul in Luristan probably from the time of Ashurbanipal[19] and at Tang-i Var (Urumanat) in Kurdistan, dating from the reign of Tiglath-pileser III or Sargon II.[20] Also known are free-standing stelae, notably at Najafabad near Kangavar, dated to the reign of Sargon II.[21] Another stela of Tiglath-pileser III is unprovenanced, but is believed to derive from Luristan.[22]

What is *surprising* is the alleged absence of Assyrian or Assyrianising material in Hasanlu IIIB,[23] which in the excavators' view lasted *c.*750-600

BCE. After the destruction of Level IVB there was a squatter occupation (IVA), followed, after a period of abandonment, by the construction of a massive fortification wall around the top of the mound (IIIB). Associated with this occupation level were "sherds of polished red ware of Urartian type".[24]

Although there is apparently no Assyrian-related material at Hasanlu in the Iron III period, it can be found at a few other sites in Western Iran. Thus, at Tepe Giyan near Nahavand, Ghirshman found "an imposing structure with door-hinges in the pure Assyrian style of the eighth century" (Ghirshman 1954: 88).[25] The published plan is scrappy,[26] but there is no mistaking the door-socket capstones ("crapaudines") which are being referred to. These are stone slabs with stepped decoration whose purpose is to hide the pivot-stones at the bottom of the doorposts. They are a distinctive feature of Assyrian buildings, where they are often incorporated into threshold slabs, and as noted by Reade[27] they are attested at many Assyrian sites. This Assyrian style building at Tepe Giyan was above a destruction level, suggesting that it was constructed under Assyrian influence after the previous settlement at Giyan had been destroyed.

Then we have the fortified site of Haidar-Khan (Qalaichi), 8 km east of Bukan.[28] Wolfram Kleiss noted here a circular fortress with rectangular buttresses, and he found on the surface Iron Age III and Parthian-period pottery. In 1985 Mr Ismail Yaghmayi and Mr Bahman Kargar of the Iranian Archaeological Service undertook rescue excavations here. They found traces of a building decorated with polychrome glazed tiles and bricks and an Aramaic inscription.[29] Unfortunately, the site had already been extensively plundered, but between 500 and 600 bricks were retrieved,[30] some of which are now in the National Museum in Tehran. The painted designs include concentric circles, rosettes, lotus and bud motifs, fragments of winged disc, and some figural decoration. In addition to the bricks now in Tehran, there are many tiles on the art market that are believed to come from Qalaichi. Altogether there are well over 100 tiles in circulation. They are painted in blue, black, brown, yellow, and white, and a few of them were published by Ali Mousavi in 1994. The range of designs includes human-headed winged bulls, winged lions and winged horses, all with horns of divinity, kneeling human figures with wings, composite creatures, bulls, lions, ibexes, birds of prey, and floral motifs. The Assyrian influence here is unmistakable, particularly with the human-headed winged figures, but there are sufficient differences to show these tiles were painted under Assyrian influence rather than by Assyrian artists. Probably the tiles date from around the reign of Sargon (721-705 BCE). The stela found at Qalaichi has a 13-line Aramaic inscription that has been dated to the 8th century BCE.[31] Unfortunately the beginning of the inscription (and the top of the stela) are missing, but the remainder contains curses directed against anybody who removes or tampers with the stela. It is not clear who erected the stela and for what purpose.

By contrast, a different situation prevailed at Ziwiye near Saqqiz in Iranian Kurdistan. This site is problematic in that a bronze coffin containing a very rich burial was allegedly found here in the 1940s,[32] but doubts surround the discovery and much material has been considered as being from Ziwiye that clearly does not come from.[33] However, Iranian excavations from the 1970s onwards have confirmed that Ziwiye was an important site in the Iron III period, and ivories of local inspiration and other objects of great interest have been found here (Figs. 4-5).[34]

Figs. 4-5. Dish in "Egyptian blue" with bird's head on rim, from excavations at Ziwiyeh in 1977, National Museum of Iran. Photograph J. E. Curtis.

To return to the burial, it was allegedly in a bronze coffin of a type which is probably Assyrian of the late 8th century BCE.[35] These coffins have straight sides, rounded at one end and squared off at the other, a flat ledge-shaped rim, and a pair of handles at each end. There are examples from Nimrud, Ur and Zincirli. The Ziwiyeh coffin had incised vertical strips on the sides and incised decoration around the rim showing a beardless Assyrian dignitary attended by officials and servants, and foreign tributaries wearing floppy hats, spotted robes and shoes with upturned toes. The objects that were allegedly inside the coffin, however, have nothing to do with Assyria. A gold belt, of which there are pieces now scattered around the world, shows a network pattern and alternating rows of recumbent stags and ibexes.[36] The network pattern with frontal lions' heads is possibly Urartian in origin, but the animals are distinctively Scythian in influence, or at least belonging to the northern animal style tradition of the steppes. The same is true of a strip of gold showing lions and along the edges opposed birds' heads.[37]

In Luristan in the Iran III period the distinctive local cultures that are a hallmark of earlier periods continue to flourish. On the whole, Assyrian influence in Luristan seems to have been very limited,[38] but there are occasional examples of artefacts of Assyrian type, showing at least Assyrian influence even if they were not actual Assyrian imports. For example, there is a polychrome glazed jar and some seals from War Kabud[39] and a bronze bucket and bowl with Assyrian designs from Chamahzi Mumah.[40]

We now move onto the vexed question of the Medes and Median material culture. The Medes first appear on the historical scene in the 9th century BCE, when they are mentioned in contemporary Assyrian texts. They were an Indo-European people who, like the related Persians, spoke an Iranian language. We do not know exactly when the Medes entered Iran, but from the 9th century BCE onwards they were well established in western Iran and frequently clashed with the Assyrians, their powerful neighbours to the west. Herodotus includes an account of the Medes in his *Histories*, in which he provides a great deal of information, but certainly for the early periods of Median history his account is unreliable. We are therefore fortunate that an independent record can be found in Assyrian sources, both textual and pictorial. Representations of campaigns against the Medes, notably during the reigns of Tiglath-pileser III (744-727 BCE) and Sargon (721-705 BCE), appear on Assyrian reliefs, and Median fortresses are shown with towers and crenellated battlements. From the reign of the Assyrian king Esarhaddon (680-669 BCE) are vassal treaties in which the Medes promise to recognize the succession to the Assyrian throne. During the early stages of their history the Medes were probably little more than a loose confederation of tribes, but by the seventh century BCE they are thought to have controlled an extensive area around their main city of Ecbatana (modern Hamadan), while the subject Persians were settled in Fars. By 612 BCE the Medes, under their king Cyaxares, were strong enough to overthrow, in alliance with the Babylonians, the ailing Assyrian state. In spite of all this, modern scholarship has tended to be sceptical about the existence of a united Median "kingdom" or "state", at least for most of the 7th century BCE. Thus, David Stronach has recently written that "there are, quite simply, no sound grounds for postulating the existence of a vigorous, separate and united Median kingdom at any date substantially before 615 BC".[41]

We know a little, then, of Median history, but very little of their art. In the past various scholars, particularly the late R.D. Barnett, have attempted to define Median art, and amongst the items they have pointed to are the gold swords from Kelermes and Chertomlyk.[42] This was clearly overstating the case, but in redressing the balance, the existence of any sort of Median art has been denied.[43] The result has been that during the last 25 years the subject has been effectively closed for academic discussion. Only now are some young scholars reconsidering the question. One possible way into it will be through the artefacts and other items of material culture that are shown on the Persepolis reliefs in association with people wearing Median costumes.[44] In any investigation, the finds from the frozen tombs at Pazyryk in the Altai Mountains will clearly be crucial.[45] These tombs are of Iranian people closely related to the Medes and the Persians, and although of 5th century date they show clearly what the earlier tradition might have been, based largely on felts, textiles and woodwork that in an Iranian archaeological context would not have survived. But such an investigation has yet to be undertaken.

In the meantime, we can do little more than look at material from the three or four sites that might loosely be termed "Median". These are Nush-i Jan, Godin Tepe, perhaps Baba Jan and now Tepe Ozbaki, about 75 km north-west of Tehran, excavated by Youssef Majidzadeh.[46] Ozbaki[47] is of considerable interest in that there are a number of similarities with Nush-i Jan. David Stronach has noted various points of comparison including the following:- a building with long rectangular magazines like the fort at Nush-i Jan; a square columned hall with wooden columns supported on undressed stones; the probable existence of a central "shrine"; arched and square wall-niches; and the pottery forms, which are certainly similar between the two sites.[48] In view of these many shared features, it seems reasonable to assume that both sites are products of the same cultural milieu, and if that is indeed "Median" (and there is still a question-mark over this) then the Median cultural sphere can be extended from the Hamadan region to the north-east towards Qazvin and Tehran.

With regard to the small objects from these "Median" sites, there are few finds from Iron III contexts at Baba Jan and Godin Tepe, and the Ozbaki material is not yet available, so I shall concentrate on Nush-i Jan. The most notable find at Nush-i Jan is the silver hoard packed in a bronze bowl that was discovered in the Fort in a corner of the ascending ramp (Room 24). It had been hidden beneath an incomplete brick that had been placed on the floor. Stronach comments: "Such a hiding place could never have been chosen unless the fort had fallen out of use and we may assume that the brick itself was selected from the debris that had already begun to collect on the floor".[49] Amongst the 231 silver items in the hoard were bar-ingots, scraps of silver, spiral rings, an earring, 2 finger-rings and a bracelet, and double-spiral pendants and quadruple-spiral beads. On the basis of numerous parallels from around the

Ancient Near East I have argued that the double-spiral pendants and the quadruple-spiral beads must date from the late 3rd to the early 2nd millennium BCE, in which case they would have been of considerable antiquity when they were hidden at Nush-i Jan.[50] This is not particularly surprising, however, as what we have here is clearly a currency hoard, including pieces of silver gathered together and kept for their intrinsic value. The pendants and beads may have been found in a grave, or during digging in an ancient site. These items, then, can tell us nothing about the material culture of Nush-i Jan in the Iron III period.

Many of the objects found in Iron III contexts at Nush-i Jan, such as tools, weapons, beads and fibulae, belong to types that can be found at sites across the Ancient Near East at this time and are not diagnostic of any particular culture. But some other finds demonstrate clear Assyrian connections (Fig. 6).

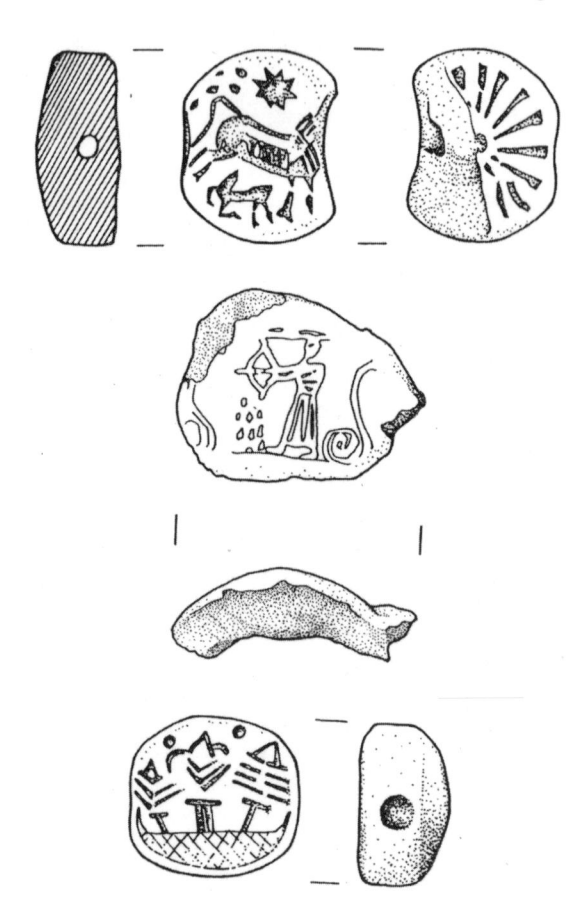

Fig. 6. Drawings of seals and a sealing from Tepe Nush-i Jan.

These are a bronze pendant of the Mesopotamian demon Pazuzu;[51] a black stone stamp seal showing a cow and calf with a star and four or five dots above,[52] a scene that is popular in Assyria and is found on seals from Nimrud;[53] and a cylinder seal impression showing an archer shooting at a snake.[54] This is related to a group of Late Assyrian faience seals with similar scenes, examples of which are known from Ashur, Khorsabad and Tell Halaf. Then we have a seal and sealings that although not of Assyrian origin are types that are widespread in the Assyrian empire. First there is a faience stamp seal showing a boat with upturned prow and stern, a stylised tree and an offering-stand.[55] The association here is with Syro-Phoenician seals showing Isis in the solar barque, but although not Assyrian, this seal is certainly of a type that might have been current in the Assyrian Empire. Next we have seal impressions from the "upper Median floor" of the western temple. The running spiral design[56] is probably of Egyptian origin and it may be significant that archaic Egyptian designs are found amongst the seals and seal impressions in the 7th century contexts at Nimrud.[57] The other design, possibly an animal's head[58] may be compared with Nimrud sealings or with seals engraved with Urartian hieroglyphs.[59]

The Assyrian or Assyrianising nature of some of these finds cannot be disputed. In the publication of the small finds from Nush-i Jan, I suggested that they were "local copies of Assyrian originals",[60] but as pointed out by Roger Moorey (1986) "they are (just) as likely to be imported originals manufactured anywhere in the broad zone from the Euphrates to the Zagros foothills that fell under the Assyrian Empire for most of the seventh century BC". This is of course quite true, but in any event, whether the objects are local imitations or whether they are imported, they are still testimony to Assyrian influence.

At some stage, Nush-i Jan was formally abandoned. The Central Temple was filled with shale, and much of the surrounding area was packed with mudbricks. After that, there was some secondary occupation on the site, by people who used the shelter of the surviving buildings to eke out a miserable existence. When this formal abandonment happened is of some considerable significance, as we shall see shortly. David Stronach has suggested that the site was abandoned in the period 650-600 BCE, and that the so-called "squatter" occupation lasted for several generations after that.[61] A re-examination of the small finds from the squatter levels, however, suggests that the later occupation may have lasted well into the Achaemenid period, i.e. after 550 BCE.[62] In particular, there are two objects from the squatter occupation that seem to be of Achaemenid date (Fig. 7):-

(1) A fragment of a bone cheekpiece in the form of a horse's leg and hoof.[63] Parallels in bronze may be noted from Achaemenid contexts at Persepolis and Deve Hüyük, and the type is also shown on the Persepolis reliefs. This piece was found in the squatter deposits in the Columned Hall.

(2) A castellated bronze kohl-stick[64] that has parallels in Achaemenid contexts at Pasargadae, Kamid el-Loz, Deve Hüyük, Al Mina, Tell

Jigan in the Eski Mosul project, and Nimrud. At Nimrud three of these kohl-sticks were found, one in a grave with two "Late Babylonian" seals. The Nush-i Jan pin was found in a disturbed context just above the top of a wall in the Columned Hall.

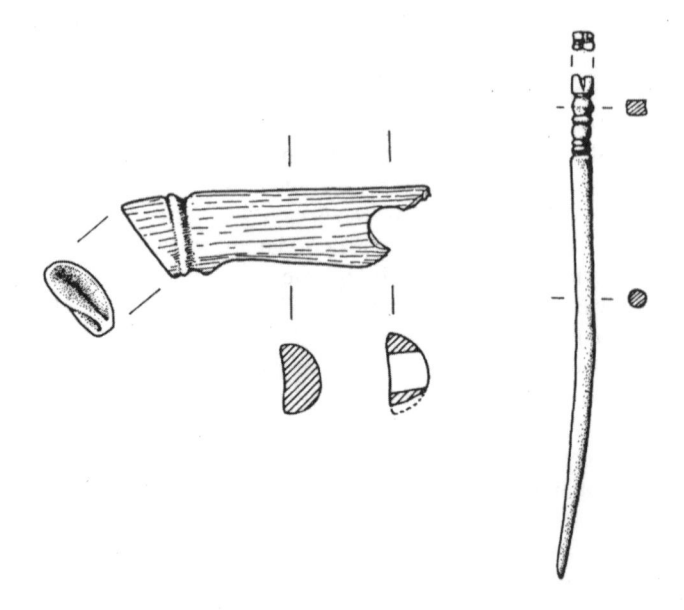

Fig. 7. Drawings of possible Achaemenid period material from Tepe Nush-i Jan.

In addition, there is other material from Nush-i Jan that one might suspect is of Achaemenid date, including two glass eye-beads.[65] There is a powerful case, then, for suggesting that the 'squatter levels' at Nush-i Jan continued into the Achaemenid period.

To consider what implications this might have for the end-dating of the main occupation at Nush-i Jan, we need to review the circumstances surrounding the abandonment. Why the Central Temple was filled with shale and the surrounding area packed with mud-bricks is not clear. Stronach and Roaf "favour the hypothesis that it was intended as a foundation or substructure for a new and more impressive building which was never built".[66] It seems to me that if this was the intention, then the building would have been knocked down to create a level platform. Rather, I would suggest, the temple was filled in for religious reasons. This project must have been enormously expensive and would have required considerable planning. The implications to my mind are that the temple was greatly venerated, but was no longer needed for the same kind of worship. Perhaps there was the introduction of new and slightly different religious practices at this time. The temple, then, was no longer to be used, but out of respect for its past history, it was to be safeguarded by filling it with clean shale.

When did all this happen? The obvious moment would be when power was transferred from the Medes to the Persians in *c.* 550 BCE, resulting almost certainly in the introduction of some slightly different religious practices. A possible scenario, then, is that the site was formally closed down in *c.* 550 BCE, and squatter occupation lasted until *c.* 500 BCE. Distinctive Achaemenid ceramics, which are absent at Nush-i Jan, would probably be later than this.

The implication of this new dating is that Tepe Nush-i Jan (and perhaps other Iron III sites) were formally occupied right down to the start of the Achaemenid period. If this is the case, then there would be no hiatus in the occupation of Median sites, as suggested by some scholars, implying a breakdown of central authority in the period 600-550 BCE.[67]

Having talked about the Medes, we should now consider what was happening in Elam. In a pitched battle at Tell Tuba on the River Ulai in 653 BCE the Elamites were defeated by the Assyrian king Ashurbanipal and their king Teumman killed.[68] These events are graphically depicted in a series of stone reliefs decorating the North Palace of Ashurbanipal at Nineveh.[69] On this occasion the Assyrians apparently withdrew without devastating the country, but a few years later, the Assyrians returned and sacked Susa in 646 BCE. It is often thought that after this Elam ceased to exist as a significant power, but this is unlikely to have been the case. For example, there is some evidence to suggest that Elamites may have been involved in the sack of the Assyrian palaces in 612 BCE. If we look carefully at the Assyrian reliefs showing the defeat of Elam, we can see that the faces of the Assyrian soldiers killing Teumman and the crown prince have been disfigured, almost certainly by Elamite soldiers as others would mot have understood the complicated narrative.[70]

Thus, in addition to Medes and Babylonians who according to the ancient chronicles were involved in the overthrow of Assyria, there may also have been Elamites.

Also dating from this period is an important Elamite tomb discovered by chance in 1982 at Arjan near Behbehan in Khuzistan, about 250 km south-east of Susa.[71] The body was buried in a bronze coffin with straight sides, rounded at one end and squared-off at the other, and with a pair of handles at either end. This is the same type of coffin that we referred to above in connection with Ziwiyeh, and which I have argued is an Assyrian type that should date not earlier than the late 8th century BCE.[72] Associated with the burial was a heavy gold bracelet or armlet with flat terminals decorated with antithetical winged lions standing on either side of a palmette. These winged lions have inevitably been compared with the antithetical griffins on the scabbard of the king's weapon bearer at Persepolis, and the inference drawn that the Arjan ring must be late, perhaps even Achaemenid period, but this need not necessarily be so. The design is in fact not so far removed from that on a bronze openwork plaque from Nimrud, probably of 8th century BCE date.[73] This furniture plaque shows winged griffins, with heads turned backwards, on either side of a sacred tree. A date earlier than the Achaemenid period for the Arjan ring is, therefore, clearly permissible. A bronze stand, *c.* 75 cm high (Figs. 8-9), has at the bottom a combination of bull protomes, rampant lions and Atlas figures with upstretched arms. These figures support a column which is surmounted by a bowl held up by lions.

Figs. 8-9. The base and the top part of a bronze stand found in an Elamite tomb at Arjan, National Museum of Iran. Photograph J. E. Curtis.

There is here a curious mixture of styles. The Atlas figures are Assyrian in inspiration. They wear Assyrian dress, and have Assyrian hairstyles and beards. They recall the supporting figures that are shown on Assyrian reliefs of the 8th century BCE in association with furniture. However, the twisted pose of the lions and the tear-shaped folds on the sides of their face suggest a later date, not far removed from the Achaemenid period. Similarly, the bull protomes with front legs folded beneath them seem to anticipate the bull protome capitals of the Achaemenid period. There were also in the tomb gold clothing ornaments, a dagger with an iron blade, a silver rod, a silver jar and a number of bronze vessels. Amongst the latter was a large bronze bowl, 43.5 cm in diameter, with intricate incised decoration in five registers surrounding a central rosette.[74] These show scenes of banqueting, presentation, hunting and date-harvesting. As noted by various scholars there are a host of Elamite features here, shown in the distinctive architecture, the way the ruler is seated on his throne, later found at Persepolis, and so on. Javier Alvarez-Mon has undertaken a detailed analysis of the decoration on this bowl and come to the interesting conclusion that it represents a *complete* view of the world ("imago mundi") centred around the life of a ruler.[75] Both the bowl and the gold bracelet bear an Elamite inscription recording the name of "Kidin-Hutran, son of Kurlush". François Vallat has argued that this Kidin-Hutran must have reigned in the period between 646 BCE and 539 or 520 BCE.[76] Given this date-range, and the above observations on the objects, we can agree with David Stronach that the Arjan tomb should be assigned to the Elamite IIIb period, that is 605-539 BCE.[77]

Next I would like to consider a highly controversial group of material that might be of similar date or even later. This is the hoard of silver vessels allegedly found in a cave at Kalmakareh, near Pol-i Dokhtar close to the boundary between Elam and Luristan.[78] Unfortunately, none of these silver vessels was recovered in a proper archaeological excavation, and when the Iranian authorities did eventually inspect the cave it was found to be empty. Sadly, many of the vessels were illegally exported from Iran, but some were confiscated at the Iranian border and are now in the National Museum in Tehran or in the local museum at Khorramabad. I have seen the pieces, mostly fragments, in Tehran. There are very many vessels in circulation, and there are suggestions that some of them are faked. It is clear that the whole group must be handled with extreme caution. In the hoard are many fantastic creations, such as a silver rhyton in Tehran,[79] and a figural group in the round showing a lion with its prey, now in Khorramabad.[80] Many of the pieces, particularly the vessels, have Neo-Elamite inscriptions around the rim generally mentioning a king called Ampirish, king of Samati, and often giving the names of other members of his dynasty. These inscriptions would imply a date in the late 7th or early 6th century BCE, which some commentators have seized upon as being consistent with the style of the objects. Such a pre-Achaemenid date is possibly supported by the fact that some of the objects also bear Assyrian cuneiform inscriptions giving the names of Esarhaddon and Ashurbanipal. On the other hand, some of the objects would appear to be Achaemenid in style (if they are not faked). For example, there is a silver bowl with lotus-and-bud decoration and gadroons and a horn-shaped silver rhyton ending in a lion's head.[81] These lions have the pear-shaped folds on the side of the face that are a hallmark of the Achaemenid period. If some of the objects are genuine (and this is a major assumption) a possible scenario is that the hoard spans the pre-Achaemenid and early Achaemenid periods. If part of the hoard does indeed date from the early Achaemenid period, how can we explain the existence in the Zagros Mountains of an apparently autonomous dynasty at this time? A possible explanation might be that there was not so much centralisation in the reigns of Cyrus and Cambyses as is often thought, and that it was not until at least the reign of Darius that all the petty kings were brought to heel. It must be stressed again, however, that none of this material is provenanced, and it cannot be used to construct historical models.

As is well known, in 550 BCE Cyrus the Great established himself as king over the now-united Medes and Persians, and it is from this date that the Achaemenid period is generally reckoned to start. With the capture of Babylon in 539 BCE the former Neo-Babylonian empire came under Persian control, and Cyrus' son Cambyses extended Persian domination into Egypt. This expansion was consolidated in the reign of Darius, and from then until it was overthrown by Alexander in 330 BCE, the Achaemenid dynasty controlled a vast area extending from the River Indus to North Africa and from Central Asia to the Persian Gulf. The art of this period is best represented at the capital cities of Persepolis, Pasargadae and Susa, all in Iran. There has been much discussion about the nature of this art, and most scholars agree that it was eclectic, that is, it inherited or borrowed inspiration and motifs from different cultures and welded them together to form the homogeneous style that we call Achaemenid. Being now in control of the largest empire the world had seen up until that time, for promotional and propaganda purposes the Achaemenid kings were in need of an official or 'court' art style that was instantly recognisable as Achaemenid. At Pasargadae we find early attempts to create such a style, which already by the reigns of Darius and Xerxes was fully-fledged at Persepolis.

In the context of this lecture, the most important question for us is to what extent there was continuity from the pre-Achaemenid to the Achaemenid periods, and the degree to which features apparent in the pre-Achaemenid cultures of Iran, such as we have been discussing above, reappear in Achaemenid art and architecture. Ironically, it is the contributions of the Medes, Persians and Elamites that are most difficult to assess. Much has been made of the "foreign" contributions to Achaemenid art and architecture, and scholars have focused on the Ionian, Lydian, Greek, Egyptian, Babylonian and other influences, sometimes at the expense of indigenous influences. For the purposes of the present investigation, I would like to consider which features already noticed in the pre-Achaemenid cultures of Iran can be identified in the Achaemenid period.

At Persepolis, we can see straightaway that there are on the terrace a number of columned halls all built according to the so-called "apadana" plan, with a central columned hall, corner towers and porticoes on at least three sides. Most of the major buildings at Persepolis are designed in this way. This "apadana" plan is also to be found at other major centres, for example at Susa. Here the Palace of Darius was first uncovered by W.K. Loftus in the middle of the nineteenth century. Then at Pasargadae we have two palaces, Palace P and Palace S, situated in the plain surrounded by gardens. There are also two small pavilions, again built on the "apadana" plan. As I have already explained, this "apadana" plan is distinctively Iranian or Persian, and can be traced back at least to Hasanlu in the Iron Age. Also Iranian in inspiration and style are the column capitals which are in the form of bull protomes, human-headed bulls, griffins ("homa" birds) and lions. We have already observed that an echo of the bull capitals is to be found in the bulls of the bronze stand from Arjan, and it would be unwise to underestimate the extent of Elamite influence in Achaemenid art. Elamite influences, together with Persian and Median, can all be clearly seen on the Persepolis reliefs, particularly in the dress, costumes and some of the artefact types.

In the course of this lecture we have remarked on the amount of Assyrian influence that can be observed in the pre-Achaemenid cultures of Western Iran, and this also filters through into the Achaemenid period proper. Thus at Pasargadae, in sculptures dating from the time of Cyrus, the gateways of Palace P are decorated with figures which are copied almost directly from Assyrian originals, including a bull-man and a figure dressed in a fish-cloak. At Persepolis, we may point to the Gate of All Nations, built by Xerxes. The gateway is flanked by human-headed bulls, and while these are different from the Assyrian prototypes, having curled wings and only four legs instead of five, there is no doubt that the form was copied from an Assyrian original. There are various other points of contact. Thus, Michael Roaf compares the stone relief from the Apadana at Persepolis showing the enthroned king with a wall painting from Til Barsip.[82] In general terms, many scholars have compared the decorative scheme at Persepolis with Assyrian wall reliefs, but there are substantial differences. While the tradition of stone bas-reliefs is well-known in Assyria, it finds a completely different sort of expression at Persepolis. The reliefs are on the outside of buildings, rather than the inside, and the composition is exclusively Persian. In fact, the Persepolis reliefs are no more Assyrian than are Greek. I am referring here to the absurd claim that a Greek sculptor called Telephanes was the "grand master of the Persepolis frieze." On the contrary, there is much more likely to have been Persian influence in Greece, and some modern scholars have seen an element of Persian influence in the Parthenon friezes.

In conclusion, the Achaemenid kings drew inspiration and ideas from many different sources, including their own traditions, and blended them together to form a style that was distinctively Achaemenid Persian.

Notes:

1. This lecture was delivered on 18th May 2004 under the title of 'The Iron Age in Western Iran'. This text is a modified form of the lecture.
2. Schmitt 2000: DNa
3. Although some scholars have drawn inferences from the *Avesta* – see Shahbazi in this volume.
4. But see Young 1985 for some cautionary remarks on this subject.
5. See Radner 2003.
6. It used to be thought that the Parsua first mentioned in Assyrian texts in 844 BCE could be equated with the Persians, but this now seems unlikely. See Stronach 2003: 251 and Young 2003.
7. Negahban 1996.
8. Dyson and Voigt 1989. For a summary of the Early Iron Age in Western Iran, see Mousavi 2005.
9. Dyson and Muscarella 1989.
10. Medvedskaya 1988; 1991
11. Dyson and Muscarella 1989: 1, 19-20.
    In view of the fact that so much material from Hasanlu remains unpublished, it may be of interest to list here the material from Hasanlu that is now (July 2005) on exhibition in the National Museum in Tehran:-

    Burnt ivory handle, 8847.
    Two fragments of burnt ivory plaque, 25850.
    Burnt ivory face, 8854.
    Ivory kohl pot, 14187.
    Fragment of burnt ivory plaque with wing, 8861.
    32 bone spindle whorls, many with ring-and-dot decoration, 12 burnt and 20 not burnt, 5052.
    Bone arrowhead with barbs, 14265.
    Fragments of stone vessel, 25739.
    Bone handle ending in animal head, not burnt, 3151.
    Bone handle with ring-and-dot decoration, not burnt, 5240.
    3 fragments of vessel in Egyptian Blue, 25747.
    Fragment of vessel in lapis lazuli (?) showing rampant ibex to side of tree, 4513.
    2 bronze lions with iron pins, 6776.
    Bronze lion (smaller) with iron pin, 10092.
    Bronze handle/fitting ending in lion's head, 14220.
    Bronze ladle with animal head at end of handle, 11530.
    Bronze cauldron handle with bird, 10591.
    Bronze human figure, 14186.
    Black stone macehead, 25764.
    Bronze macehead with spikes, 6760.
    Stone macehead, 25753.
    Bronze spearhead, 10625.
    Bronze sword, 12288.
    Necklace, 3162.
    Painted pottery vessel, 6842.
    Black stone tripod vessel with ram's heads above the legs, 11200.
    Stone vessel (half of shallow pyxis with ring-and-dot decoration), 25770.

Triple pottery vessel, grey ware, 6754.
Black pottery 'teapot', 10598
Red pottery vessel in form of 2 boots with curled toes, 10106.
Footed pottery bowl with 2 handles, grey ware, 10101.
Pottery vase with handle on neck, grey ware, 6255.
Pottery strainer vessel with twisted handle, grey ware, 10100.
Small square-sectioned pot on 4 feet, glazed?, 3107.
Small pottery jar with x-hatched decoration, 14196.
Pottery bowl on 3 feet with elaborate animal handle, grey ware, 642.
Reconstructed stone vessel with cuneiform inscription, 8737.
Bronze tripod, 14185.
Bronze lion's paw foot, 12126.
Two bronze hoofed feet, 12003.
Bronze ram's head rhyton, 14200.
Another, 11499.
Beak-spouted grey ware vessel on stand.

12. Muscarella and Dyson 1989: 3.
13. Marcus 1996: 43-53.
14. Muscarella 1980: nos. 280-293.
15. Dyson and Voigt 1989:fig. 10a.
16. Albenda 1991.
17. Reade 1995: 38, 41.
18. Gunter 1982.
19. Grayson and Levine 1975; Reade 1977.
20. Sarfaraz 1969; Curtis 1995: col. pl. VI.
21. Levine 1972: pls. VII – XI.
22. Levine 1972: pls. I – VI. See also Radner 2003: 119-121 for textual references to Assyrian kings setting up stelae in Iran.
23. Dyson and Muscarella 1989: 3.
24. Dyson and Muscarella 1989: 2-3.
25. Ghirshman 1954: 88.
26. Contenau and Ghirshman 1935: pl. 4.
27. Reade 1995: 39-40.
28. Kroll 2005: 76,79-80, fig.13.
29. Curtis, V.S., 1988; Mousavi 1994: 7-8.
30. Personal communication from Mr Yusef Hassanzadeh, who is studying this material.
31. Teixidor 1999; Fales 2003. There is some confusion about the size and shape of this stela (see Fales 2003: 132). It is in fact tall and thin, height 178 cm, width 60 cm, and thickness 32.5 cm. The Aramaic inscription is at the top. The stela is now in the storeroom of the National Museum in Tehran.
32. Barnett 1956.
33. Muscarella 1977.
34. During a visit to the site in 1977, we were kindly shown by the excavators some of the small finds. These consisted of about 1000 leaf-shaped iron arrowheads, a few bronze bipartite and tripartite arrowheads, a couple of bronze leaf-shaped arrowheads, a fragment of bowl in Egyptian blue with a bird's head on the rim (now published in Seipel 2000: no.107), a rectangular ivory panel with a crudely-incised Assyrian-style figure, an ivory strip with two lions, a small ivory plaque showing a warrior, three faience seals, one with geometric decoration and two showing archers in the 'Zagros' style, a silver strip incised with pomegranates, a long bronze pin with

projecting bars and globular terminals, and bronze buttons with loop fasteners. For a summary of the excavations in 1995, see *Iran* 36 (1998), p.193.
35. Curtis 1983.
36. See Curtis and Kruszynski 2002: no.193.
37. See Curtis and Kruszynski 2002: no.194.
38. Overlaet 2005.
39. Haerinck and Overlaet 2004: 31, 78-9.
40. Haerinck and Overlaet 1998: 29, fig. 12.
41. Stronach 2003a: 234.
42. Barnett 1962.
43. Eg Muscarella 1987.
44. Eg Razmjou 2005.
45. Rudenko 1970.
46. For other sites with "Median" pottery in the vicinity of Tepe Nush-i Jan in the Malayer Plain, see Stronach 2003: 246.
47. Majidzadeh 2001.
48. Stronach 2003a: 237- 240.
49. Stronach 1969: 15.
50. Curtis 1984: 1-21.
51. Curtis 1984: no.296.
52. Curtis 1984: no.233.
53. E.g. Mallowan 1966: I, figs.134/5, 241.
54. Curtis 1984: no.236.
55. Curtis 1984: no. 234.
56. Curtis 1984: no.237.
57. Moorey 1986: 802.
58. Curtis 1984: no.238.
59. *Ibid*.
60. Curtis 1984: 23.
61. Stronach in Curtis 1984: vii.
62. This matter has been discussed in greater detail, with references, in Curtis 2005.
63. Curtis 1984: no.431.
64. Curtis 1984: no.298.
65. Curtis 1984: nos.377, 477.
66. Stronach and Roaf 1978: 10.
67. E.g. Liverani 2003.
68. Grayson 1991: 147-8.
69. Reade 1976.
70. This idea, implying the presence of Elamite soldiers in the Median army, is being developed by S. Razmjou.
71. Alizadeh 1985; Stronach 2003, 2005.
72. Curtis 1983.
73. Mallowan 1966: II, pl.324.
74. Sarraf 1990; Majidzadeh 1992.
75. Alvarez-Mon 2004.
76. Vallat 1984.
77. Stronach 2003b: 254.
78. Farzin 1993; Bashshash Kanzaq 2000; Seipel 2000: nos.116-117; Henkelman 2003: 214-227.
79. Seipel 2000: no.116.

80. Farzin 1993: cover.
81. Henkelman 2003: pls.13-14.
82. Roaf 2003: 13.

Abbreviations:

Dk, DkM	Denkard
GBd	Greter Bundahishn
RV	Rigveda
Y	Yasna
Yt	Yasht

Bibliographical Abbreviations:

AAASH	*Acta Antiqua Academiae Scientiarum Hungaricae*
AfO	*Archiv für Orientforschung*
AIr	*Acta Iranica*
AMI(T)	*Archäologische Mitteilungen aus Iran (und Turan)*
AOAT	*Alter Orient und Altes Testament*
ArO	*Archiv Orientální*
AS	*Anatolian Studies*
BAI	*Bulletin of the Asia Institute*
BiOr	*Bibliotheca Orientalis*
BSOAS	*Bulletin of the School of Oriental and African Studies*
CHIr	*Cambridge History of Iran*
CAH	*Cambridge Ancient History*
CUP	*Cambridge University Press*
DAFI	*Délégation archéologique française en Iran*
EncIr	*Encyclopædia Iranica*
IrAnt	*Iranica Antiqua*
JNES	*Journal of Near Eastern Studies*
JA	*Journal Asiatique*
JSAI	*Jerusalem Studies in Arabic and Islam*
OIP	*Oriental Institute Publications*
OLP	*Orientalia Lovaniensia Periodica*
OLZ	*Orientalistische Literaturzeitung*
RA	*Revue d'Assyriologie*
RE	*Pauly's Real-Encyclopädie der klassischen altertumswissenschaften*
SEL	*Studi Epigrafici e Linguistici sul Vicino Oriente*
St Ir	*Studia Iranica*
TCS	*Texts from Cuneiform Sources*
UET	*Ur Excavations Texts*
ZA	*Zeitschrift für Assyriologie*
ZDMG	*Zeitschrift der deutschen morgenländischen Gesellschaft*

Bibliography:

Ahn, Gregor (1992). *Religiöse Herrschaftslegitimation im achämenidischen Iran* [AIr 31], Leiden-Louvain.

Alizadeh, A. (1985). "A tomb of the Neo-Elamite period at Arjan, near Behbahan", *AMI* 18: 49-73.

Alram, M. (1999). "The Beginning of Sasanian coinage", *BAI* N.S., 13: 67–76.

Alvarez-Mon, J. (2004). "Imago mundi: cosmological and ideological aspects of the Arjan bowl", *IrAnt* 39: 203–38.

Amarelli, F. (1988). "Il processo di Sabrata", *Studia et documenta historiae et iuris* 54: 110–46.

Amiet, P. (1973). "La glyptique de la fin de l'Elam", *Arts Asiatiques* 28: 3–45.

Andreas, F.C. (1904). "Ueber einige Fragen der aeltesten persischen Geschichte", *Verhandlungen des XIII. Internationalen Orientalisten-Kongresses, Hamburg, September 1902*. Leiden: 93–9.

Badian, E. (1985). "Alexander in Iran", *CHIr* II: 450–61.

Bailey, H. W. (1943), *Zoroastrian Problems in the Ninth-Century Books*, Oxford, 1943.

— (1971). *Zoroastrian Problems in the Ninth-Century Books*, Oxford.

— (1987), "Arya".

Bakker, E.J., De Jong, I., and Wees, H. van (eds) (2002). *Brill's Companion to Herodotus*, Leiden.

Barnett, R.D. (1956). "The treasure of Ziwiye", *Iraq* 18: 111-116.

— (1962). 'Median Art', *IA* 2: 77-95.

Bashshash Kanzaq, R. (2000). *Decipherment of Kalma-Kare Inscribed Vessels*, Tehran.

Beaulieu, P.-A. (1989). *The Reign of Nabonidus, King of Babylon, 556–539 B.C.* New Haven: Yale Near Eastern Researches 10.

Bellwood, P. (2001). "Early agriculturalist population diasporas? Farming, languages, and genes", *Annual Review of Anthropology* 30: 181–207.

Benveniste, Emile (1932). "Les classes sociales dans la tradition avestique", *JA* 221: 117–34.

— (1938). *Les Mages dans l'Ancien Iran*, Paris.

— (1969). Le vocabulaire des institutions indo-européennes, Paris.

Berger, P.-R. (1975). "Der Kyros-Zylinder mit dem Zusatzfragment BIN II Nr. 32 und die akkadischen Personennamen im Danielbuch", *ZA* 64: 192–234.

Bernard, Paul (1972). "Les mortiers et pilons inscrits de Persépolis", *St Ir* 1: 165–76.

Bickerman, E.J., and Tadmor, H. (1978). "Darius I, Pseudo-Smerdis, and the Magi", *Athenaeum* 56: 239–61.

Bivar, A.D.H. (1985). "A Persian fairyland", in *Papers in Honour of Professor Mary Boyce*, Leiden [AIr 10]: 25–42.

Boas, F. (1940). *Race, Language and Culture*. New York.

Bollweg, J. (1988). "Protoachämenidische Siegelbilder", *AMI* 21: 53–61.
Bowman, Raymond A. (1970). *Aramaic Ritual Texts from Persepolis*, Chicago.
Boyce, Mary (1975). *A History of Zoroastrianism*, vol. I, Leiden.
— (1982). *A History of Zoroastrianism*, vol. II. *Under the Achaemenians*, Leiden and Cologne.
— (1987) "Astvatərəta", in Ehsan Yarshater (ed.), *EncIr* II/8, London: 871-3.
— (1989). *A History of Zoroastrianism I* 2nd ed.; *The Early Period*, Leiden.
— (2003). "Preliminary note by Professor Mary Boyce to Agha Homayoun Sanati's translation of her article 'On the calendar of Zoroastrian feasts' ", in C.G. Cereti and F. Vajifdar (eds), *Ātaš-e dorūn. The Fire Within. Jamshid Soroush Soroushian Memorial Volume II*, n.p.: 57–61.
Boyce, Mary, and Grenet, Frantz (1991). *A History of Zoroastrianism*, vol. III: *Zoroastrianism under Macedonian and Roman Rule*, Leiden.
Bresciani, E. (1985). "The Persian occupation of Egypt", *CHIr* II: 502–528.
Briant, P. (1984). "La Perse avant l'empire (un état de la question)", *IrAnt* 19: 71–118.
— (1996). *Histoire de l'empire perse. De Cyrus à Alexandre*, Paris.
— (2002). *From Cyrus to Alexander*, trans. P.T. Daniels, Vinnova Lake, Indiana.
Bunsen, Christian (1857). *Aegyptens Stelle in der Weltgeschichte*, V, Hamburg.
Burn, A.R. (1984). *Persia and the Greeks*, London.
Calmeyer, P. (1979). "Fortuna-Tyche-Khvarnah", *Jahrbuch des Deutschen Archäologischen Instituts* 94: 347–65.
— (1981). "Zur bedingten Göttlichkeit des Grosskönigs", *AMI* 14: 55–60.
— (1982). "Zur Genese altiranischer Motive. VIII. Die 'Statistische Landkarte des Perserreiches' I", *AMI* 15, 105-187.
— (1983). "Zur Genese altiranischer Motive. VIII. Die 'Statistische Landkarte der Persernreich' II", *AMI* 16, 109-263.
Cameron, George G. (1948). *Persepolis Treasury Tablets*, Chicago.
Cantera, A. (2004). *Studien zur Pahlavi-Übersetzung des Avesta* (Iranica 7), Wiesbaden.
Carter, E. (1981). "A summary of the Shimashki, sukkalmahhu, and transitional phases at Tepe Farukhabad", in H.T. Wright (ed.), *An Early Town on the Deh Luran Plain: Excavations at Tepe Farukhabad*. Ann Arbor: Memoirs of the Museum of Anthropology, University of Michigan, no. 13: 218–23.
Cassel, Paulus (1886). *Zoroaster. Seine Name und seine Zeit* [Berliner Studien für classischen Philologie und Archeologie IV/1], Berlin.
Cereti, C.G. (2001). *La letteratura pahlavi. Introduzione ai testi con riferimenti alla storia degli studi e alla tradizione manoscritta*, Milan.
Christensen, Arthur (1933). *Les Kayanides*, Copenhagen.
— (1943). *Le premier chapitre du Vendidad et l'histoire primitive des tribus iraniennes*, Copenhagen.
Contenau, G., and Ghirshman, R. (1935). *Fouilles du Tépé-Giyan près de Néhavend*, Paris.
Curtis, J.E. (1983). "Late Assyrian bronze coffins", *AS* 33: 85-95.

— 1984. *Nush-i Jan III: The Small Finds*, London.
— (2005). "The material culture of Tepe Nush-i Jan and the end of the Iron Age III period in Western Iran", *IA* 40: 233-246.
Curtis, V.S. (1988). "Report on a recent visit to Iran", *Iran* 26: 145.
Dandamaev, M. (1993a). "Cyrus iii. Cyrus II the Great", *EncIr* 6: 516–21.
— (1993b). "Cyrus iv. The Cyrus cylinder", *EncIr* 6: 521–22.
Darmesteter, James (1892–3). *Le Zend-Avesta*, I–III, Paris.
Denyer, N. (2001). *Plato. Alcibiades*, Cambridge.
De Jong, Albert. (1997). *Traditions of the Magi. Zoroastrianism in Greek and Latin Literature* (Religions in the Graeco-Roman World 133), Leiden.
— (2002). "Animal sacrifice in ancient Zoroastrianism: a ritual and its interpretations", in A.I. Baumgarten (ed.), *Sacrifice in Religious Experience* (Studies in the History of Religions 93), Leiden: 127–48.
— (2003). "Dions Magierhymnen: zoroastrischer Mythos oder griechische Phantasie?", in H.-G. Nesselrath, B. Bäbler, M. Forschner and A. de Jong, *Dion von Prusa. Menschliche Gemeinschaft und göttliche Ordnung: Die Borysthenes-Rede* (SAPERE 6), Darmstadt: 157–78.
— (2004). "Zoroastrian Religious polemics in context: interconfessional relations in the Sasanian empire", in T.L. Hettema and A. van der Kooij (eds), *Religious Polemics in Context* (Studies in Theology and Religion 11), Assen: 48–63.
— (2005). "The first sin: Zoroastrian ideas about the time before Zarathuštra", in S. Shaked (ed.), *Genesis and Regeneration. Essays on Conceptions of Origins*, Jerusalem: 192–209.
Delattre, A. (1883a). "Encore un mot sur la prétendue origine susienne de Cyrus", *Le Muséon* 2: 53.
— (1883b). "Cyrus d'après une nouvelle méthode historique", *Le Muséon* 2: 442–59.
Diamond, J., and Bellwood, P. (2003). "Farmers and their languages: The first expansions", *Science* 300: 597–603.
Dickson, H.R.P. (1956). *Kuwait and her Neighbours*. London: Allen & Unwin
Duchesne-Guillemin, Jacques (1962). *La religion de l'Iran ancien*, Paris.
— (1963). "Le Xwarenah", *Annali dell'Istituto Universitario Orientali di Napoli* 5: 19–31.
Dupree, Louis (1980). *Afghanistan*, Princeton.
Dusinberre, E.R.M. (2002). "An excavated ivory from Kerkenes Dag, Turkey: Transcultural fluidities, significations of collective identity, and the problem of Median art", *Ars Orientalis* 32: 17–54.
Dyson, R.H., and Muscarella, O.W. (1989). "Constructing the chronology and historical implications of Hasanlu IV", *Iran* 27: 1-27.
Dyson, R.H., and Voigt, M.M. (1989). "East of Assyria: the highland settlement of Hasanlu", *Expedition* 31, nos.2-3, Philadelphia.
Eilers, Wilhelm (1954). "Der Name Demawend", *ArO* 22: 267–374.
Evans, J.A.S. (1991). *Herodotus. Explorer of the Past. Three Essays*, Princeton.

Fales, F.M. (2003). "Evidence for east-west contacts in the 8th century BC: the Bukan Stela", in Lanfranchi, Roaf and Rollinger 2003: 131-147.
Ferdinand, Klaus (1962). "Nomadic expansion and commerce in Central Afghânistân", *Folk* 4:123–59.
Flower, M.A. (2000). "From Simonides to Isocrates: the fifth-century origins of fourth-century Panhellenism", *Classical Antiquity* 19: 65–101.
Forbiger, A. (1844). *Handbuch der alten Geographie aus den Quellen bearbeitet*, i–ii. Leipzig: Mayer & Wigand.
Fragner, Bert G. (1999). "Der politische Begriff 'Iran' in der Neuzeit und seine historischen Wurzeln", in G. Gnoli and A. Paniano (eds), *Proceedings of the First International Conference of Iranian Studies*, Rome: 365–76.
Frye, R.N. (1962). *The Heritage of Persia*. London.
Fussman, Gérard (1974a). "Documents épigraphiques kouchans" [I], *Bulletin de l'Ecole Française d'Extrême-Orient* 61: 1–66.
— (1974b). "Ruines de la vallée de Wardak", *Arts Asiatiques* 30: 65–130.
Gadd, C.J., Legrain, L., and Smith, S. (1928). *Royal Inscriptions*. London: UET 1.
Garrison, M.B., and Root, M.C. (1996). *Persepolis Seal Studies: An introduction with provisional concordances of seal numbers and associated documents on Fortification Tablets 1–2087*. Leiden: Nederlands Instituut voor het Nabije Oosten [*Achaemenid History* 9].
Geiger, W. (1882). *Ostīrānische Kultur im Altertum*, Erlangen.
Georges, P. (1994). *Barbarian Asia and the Greek Experience. From the Archaic Period to the Age of Xenophon*, Baltimore/London.
Gershevitch, Ilia (1959). *The Avestan Hymn to Mithra* Cambridge.
Ghirshman, R. (1954). *Iran from the Earliest Times to the Islamic Conquest*, Harmondsworth.
Gillman, I., and Klimkeit, H.-J. (1999). *Christians in Asia before 1500*, Richmond.
Gnoli, Gherardo (1980). *Zoroaster's Time and Homeland*, Naples.
— (1985). "Ragha la zoroastriana", in *Papers in Honour of Professor Mary Boyce*, Leiden [*AIr* 10]: 217–28.
— (1989). "Avestan geography", *EncIr*, London–New York.
— (1989*). The Idea of Iran. An Essay on its Origin*, Rome.
— (1998 [2001]). "Xerxès, Priam, et Zoroastre", *BAI* 12: 59–67.
Graf, F. (1996). *Gottesnähe und Schadenzauber. Die Magie in der griechisch-römischen Antike*, Munich.
Grayson, A.K. (1975). *Assyrian and Babylonian Chronicles*. Locus Valley: TCS.
— (1991). "Assyria: Tiglath-pileser III to Sargon II (744-705 B.C.)", *CAH* III/2, 2nd edition, Cambridge: 71-102.
Grayson, A.K., and Levine, L.D. (1975). "The Assyrian relief from Shikaft-i Gulgul', *IA* 11: 29-38.
Grenet, Frantz (1989). "Bal<u>k</u>, vi: Monuments of Balk", *EncIr*.

— (1994). "Bāmiyān and the *Mihr Yašt*", *BAI* 7 (Iranian Studies in Honour of A.D.H. Bivar): 87–94.
— (1996). "Drapsaka", *EncIr VII, 537*.
— (2002). "Zoroastre au Badakhshān", *St Ir* 31: 193–214.
— (2002–2003). "Religions du monde iranien ancien. II. Traditions zoroastriennes sur le territoire actuel de l'Afghanistan", *Ecole pratique des hautes études, Section des sciences religieuses, Annuaire*, 111: 154–8.
— (ed.) (2003). *La geste d'Ardashir fils de Pâbag. Kārnāmag ī Ardaxšēr ī Pābagān*, Die.
Grenet, Frantz, and Rapin, Claude (2001). "Alexander, Aï Khanum, Termez: remarks on the spring campaign of 328", *BAI* 12 [Alexander's Legacy in the East. Studies in Honor of Paul Bernard]: 79–89.
Grillot, F. and Vallat, F. (1978). "Le verbe élamite 'pi(š)ši' ", *Cahiers de la DAFI* 8: 81–4.
Gubaev, A., Koshelenko, G. and Tosi, M. (eds) (1998). *The Archaeological Map of the Murghab Delta. Preliminary Reports 1990–95*, Rome.
Gunter, A. (1982). "Representations of Urartian and western Iranian fortress architecture in the Assyrian reliefs", *Iran* 20: 103-12.
Gyselen, R. (1995). "Les sceaux des mages de l'Iran sassanide", in R. Gyselen (ed.), *Au carrefour des religions. Mélanges offerts à Philippe Gignoux* (Res Orientales 7), Bures-sur-Yvette: 121–50.
Halévy, J. (1883). "Cyrus et l'origine des Achéménides", *Le Muséon* 2: 43–52, 247–60.
Hall, E. (1989). *Inventing the Barbarian. Greek Self-Definition through Tragedy*, Oxford.
Hallo, W.W., *et al.* (eds) (2000). *The Context of Scripture II. Monumental Inscriptions from the Biblical World*, Leiden.
Hallock, Richard T. (1969). *Persepolis Fortification Tablets* (OIP 92), Chicago.
— (1985). "The evidence of the Persepolis Tablets", *CHIr* II: 588–609.
Hansman, J. (1975). "An Achaemenian stronghold", in *Hommages et Opera Minora III. Monumentum H.S. Nyberg* III [*AIr* 6]. Leiden: Brill.
Harlez, C. de (1882). "Même sujet" [rejoinder to Sayce 1882], *Le Muséon* 1: 557–70.
— (1883). "Conclusion", *Le Muséon* 2: 261–8.
Harmatta, J. (1971a). "The rise of the Old Persian Empire: Cyrus the Great", *AAASH* 19: 3–15.
— (1971b). "The literary patterns of the Babylonian edict of Cyrus", *AAASH* 19: 217–31.
Helms, Sven (1982). "The city and famous fortress of Kandahar, the foremost place in all of Asia", *Afghan Studies* 3–4: 1–24.
Henkelman, W. (2003a). "Review of M. Waters, *A Survey of Neo-Elamite History*", *BiOr* 60: 251–63.
— (2003b). "Persians, Medes and Elamites: Acculturation in the Neo-Elamite period", in G.B. Lanfranchi, M. Roaf and R. Rollinger (eds), *Continuity of*

Empire (?): Assyria, Media, Persia. Padua: History of the Ancient Near East/Monographs 5: 181–231.

Henning, Walter Bruno (1947). "Two Manichaean magical texts", *BSOAS* 12: 39–66. [Reprinted in W.B. Henning, *Selected Papers*, 1 *AIr* 14 (Leiden 1977): 273–300.]

Herrenschmidt, Clarisse (1976). "Désignation de l'empire et concept politiques de Darius Ier d'après ses inscriptions en vieux-perse", *St Ir* 5: 33–65.

— (1979). "La première royauté de Darius avant l'invention de la notion d'empire", in *Pad Nam i Yazdan. Etudes d'epigraphie ancien. Travaux de l'Institut d' Etudes Iraniennes* 9, Paris: 23–33.

— (1980). "La religion des Achéménides: état de la question", *St Ir* 9: 325–39.

— (1991). "Vieux-perse *šiyāti-*", in Jean Kellens (ed.), *La religion iranienne à l'époque achéménide*, Gent: 13–21.

— (1995–6). "Histoire du judaïsme à l'époque hellénistique et romaine", *Annuaire de l'École Pratique des Hautes Études, Section sciences religieuses* 104: 230.

— (1996). "Writing between visible and invisible worlds in Iran, Israel, and Greece", in Bottéro, Jean, Herrenschmidt, Clarisse, and Vernant, Jean-Pierre, *Ancestors of the West. Writing, Reasoning, and Religion in Mesopotamia, Elam, and Greece*, Chicago and London: 115–17.

Herzfeld, Ernst (1948). *Zoroaster and his World*, Princeton.

Hinz, W. (1979). *Darius and die Perser*, II, Baden-Baden.

Hintze, Almut (1994). *Der Zamyād-Yašt. Edition, Übersetzung, Kommentar* (Beiträge zur Iranistik 15), Wiesbaden.

— (2004). "On the ritual significance of the Yasna Haptaŋhāiti", in M. Stausberg (ed.), *Zoroastrian Rituals in Context* (Studies in the History of Religions 102), Leiden: 291–316.

— (2004). " '*Do ut des*': Patterns of exchange in Zoroastrianism", *Journal of the Royal Asiatic Society*, Ser. 3, 14: 27–45.

Hoffmann, Karl (1968). "The *Avesta* fragment FrD. 3", *Indo-Iranian Journal* 10: 282–8. [Repr. in *Aufsätze zur Indoiranistik*, vol. 1, Wiesbaden 1975: 221–7.

— (1979). "Das Avesta in der Persis", in J. Harmatta (ed.), *Prolegomena to the Sources on the History of pre-Islamic Central Asia*, Budapest: 89–93.

Hoffmann, K., and Narten, J. (1989). *Der sasanidische Archetypus. Untersuchungen zu Schreibung und Lautgestalt des Avestischen*, Wiesbaden.

Hoffmann-Kutschke, A. (1907). "Iranisches bei den Griechen", *Philologus* 20: 173–91.

Hübschmann, H. (1894–5). "NP Iran", *Indogermanische Forschungen* IV: 119–20.

— (1897). *Armenische Grammatik: I. Armenische Etymologie*, Leipzig.

Huff, D. (2004). "Archaeological evidence of Zoroastrian funerary practices", in M. Stausberg (ed.), *Zoroastrian Rituals in Context*: 593–630, with plates V to XII.

Humbach, Helmut (1985). "About Gōpatšāh, his country, and the Khwārezmian hypothesis", in *Papers in Honour of Professor Mary Boyce*, Leiden [*AIr* 10]: 327–34.
— (1991). *The Gāthās of Zarathushtra*, I–II, Heidelberg.
Humbach, Helmut, and Skjærvø, Prods Oktor (1983a). *The Sassanian Inscription of Paikuli*, pt. 3.1. *Restored Text and Translation*, Wiesbaden.
— (1983b). *The Sassanian Inscription of Paikuli*, pt. 3.2. *Commentary*, Wiesbaden.
Hunink, V. (1997). *Apuleius of Madauros pro se de magia (Apologia)*, Amsterdam.
Hüsing, G. (1908). "Die Namen der Könige von Ančan", *OLZ* 11: 318–22.
Huyse, Philip (1999). *Die dreisprachige Inschrift Šābuhrs I. an der Ka'ba-i Zardušt (ŠKZ)*, 2 vols (Corp. Iscrip. Iran. III, Vol. I, Text I), London.
Jacobs, Bruno (1991). "Der Sonnengott im Pantheon der Achämeniden", in Jean Kellens (ed.), *La religion iranienne à l'époque achéménide*, Gent: 49–80.
Johnston, S.I. (2004). "Magic", in S.I. Johnston (ed.), *Religions of the Ancient World. A Guide*, Cambridge, MA: 139–52 (with references).
Josephson, J. (2003). "The 'Sitz im Leben' of the Seventh Book of the *Dēnkard*", in C.G. Cereti, M. Maggi and E. Provasi (eds), *Religious Themes and Texts of pre-Islamic Iran and Central Asia. Studies in Honour of Professor Gherardo Gnoli* (Beiträge zur Iranistik 24), Wiesbaden: 203–212.
Jullien, C., and Jullien, F. (2002). *Apôtres des confins: processus missionaires chrétiens dans l'Empire Iranien* (Res Orientales 15), Bures-sur-Yvette.
Kellens, Jean (1979). "L'Avesta comme source historique: la liste des kayanides", in J. Harmatta (ed.), *Studies in the Sources on the History of pre-Islamic Central Asia*, Budapest: 41–53.
— (1998). "Considérations sur l'histoire de l'Avesta", *JA* 286: 451–519.
— (1999–2000). "Langues et religions indo-iraniennes: Promenade dans les Yašts à la lumière de travaux récents (suite)", *Annuaire du Collège de France 1999–2000*, Paris: 721–51.
— (2002). "L'idéologie religieuse des inscriptions achéménides", *JA* 290: 417–64.
— (2003) « Le mot « aryen » ou le fantasme contre l'analyse », *Académie Royale de Belgique. Bulletin de la Classe des Lettres,* Brussels, 6ᵉ série t. 14, 1-6 : 99-112.
Kent, Roland G. (1953). *Old Persian Grammar, Texts, Lexicon*, 2nd rev. edn, New Haven.
Kingsley, P. (1990). "The Greek origin of the sixth-century dating of Zoroaster", *BSOAS* 53: 245–65.
— (1995). "Meetings with Magi: Iranian themes among the Greeks, from Xanthus of Lydia to Plato's Academy", *Journal of the Royal Asiatic Society*: 173–209.
Kinneir, J.M. (1813). *A Geographical Memoire of the Persia Empire*, London.

Klima, O. (1967). "The official name of the pre-Islamic Iranian state", in *Sir J.J. Zarthoshti Madressa Centenary Volume*, Bombay: 144–7.
Koch, Heidemarie (1977). *Die religiösen Verhältnisse der Dareioszeit. Untersuchungen an Hand der elamischen Persepolistäfelchen* (Göttinger Orientforschungen III.4), Wiesbaden.
König, F.W. (1965). *Die elamischen Königsinschriften*. Graz: AfO Beiheft 16.
Kotwal, F.M., and P.G. Kreyenbroek, P.G. (1995). *The Hērbedestān and Nērangestān Volume II. Nērangestān, Fragard 1* (Studia Iranica Cahier 16), Paris.
— (2003). *The Hērbedestān and Nērangestān Volume III. Nērangestān, Fragard 2* (Studia Iranica Cahier 30), Paris.
Kreyenbroek, P.G. (1987a). "The *Dādestān ī dēnīg* on priests", *Indo-Iranian Journal* 30: 185–208.
— (1987b). "The Zoroastrian priesthood after the fall of the Sasanian empire", in Ph. Gignoux (ed.), *Transition Periods in Iranian History* (Studia Iranica Cahier 5), Paris: 151–66.
— (1994). "On the concept of spiritual authority in Zoroastrianism", *Jerusalem Studies in Arabic and Islam* 17: 1–15.
— (1996). "The Zoroastrian tradition from an oralist's point of view", in *K.R. Cama Oriental Institute Second International Congress Proceedings*, Bombay: 221–37.
— (2002). "Millennialism and eschatology in the Zoroastrian tradition", in A. Amanat and M. Bernhardsson (eds), *Imagining the End: Visions of Apocalypse from the Ancient Middle East to Modern America*, London/New York: 33–55.
Kroll, S. (2005). "The southern Urmia basin in the Early Iron Age", *IA* 40: 65–85.
Lamberg-Karlovsky, C.C. (2002). "Archaeology and language: The Indo-Iranians", *Current Anthropology* 43: 63–88.
Lamberterie, Charles de (1989). "Armenien *ari* et *anari*", *Etudes irano-aryennes offertes à Gilbert Lazard*, Paris: 237–46.
Lanfranchi, G.B., Roaf, M., and Rollinger, R. (eds.) (2003). *Continuity of Empire (?) Assyria, Media, Persia*, HANE/M-V, Padua.
Lecoq, P. (1997). *Les inscriptions de la Perse achéménide*, Paris.
Lévi, Sylvain (1915). "Le catalogue géographique des Yakṣa dans la Mahāmāyūrī", *JA*, 11è série t. 5: 19–138.
— (1925). "Notes indiennes", *JA* 206: 17–69.
Levine, L.D. (1972). *Two Neo-Assyrian Stelae from Iran*, Royal Ontario Museum Occasional Paper 23, Toronto.
— (1974). "Geographical studies in the Neo-Assyrian Zagros II", *Iran* 12: 99–124.
Liverani, M.(2003). "The rise and fall of Media", in Lanfranchi, Roaf and Rollinger 2003: 1-12.
Luck, G. (1985). *Arcana Mundi. Magic and the Occult in the Greek and Roman Worlds*, Baltimore/London.

Luckenbill, D.D. (1924). *The Annals of Sennacherib*. Chicago: OIP 2.
Lur'e, Pavel (2004). Istoriko-lingvisticheskii analiz Sogdiiskoi toponimii, St Petersburg [unpublished PhD, accessible at www.orientalstudies.ru/pers/z_lurje.html]
Lyonnet, Bertille (1997). *Prospections archéologiques en Bactriane orientale (1974–1978)*, vol. 2: *Céramique et peuplement du Chalcolithique à la conquête arabe*, Paris.
MacKenzie, D. Neil (1989). "Kerdir's inscription", in *Iranische Denkmäler*, Lief. 13, Reihe II: *Iranische Felsreliefs* I. *The Sasanian Rock Reliefs at Naqsh-i Rustam*, Berlin: 35-72.
— (1998). "Ērān, Ērānšahr", *EncIr* VIII: 535.
Madan, Dhanjishah Meherjibhai (ed.) (1911). *The Complete Text of the Pahlavi Dinkard*, Bombay.
Majidzadeh, Y. (1992). "The Arjan bowl", *Iran* 30: 131-44.
— (2001). *The Ancient Ozbaki site, Savoudjbolaqh, Iran*, Tehran (in Persian and English).
Mallowan, M.E.L. (1966). *Nimrud and its Remains*, 2 vols., London.
Marcus, M.I. (1996). *Emblems of Identity and Prestige: the Seals and Sealings from Hasanlu, Iran*, Hasanlu Special Studies III, Philadelphia.
Marquart, J. (1891–3). *Die Assyriaka des Ktesias*. Göttingen: Philologus Supplementband 6.
Marquart, J. (1895). "Beiträge zur Geschichte und Sage von Ērān", *ZDMG* 49: 628–9.
— (1901). *Ērānšahr nach der Geographie des Ps. Moses Xorenac'I* (Abhandlungen der Königlichen Gesellschaft des Wissenschaften zu Göttingen, Philologisch-historische Klasse, Neue Folge, Band III, No. 2), Berlin.
Matīnī, J. (1990). "Īrān dar 'āīnay-e dīgarān", *Majallay-e Iranshenasi* I/1 (Spring): 3–31.
— (1992). "Īrān dar dowrān-e Eslāmī", *Majallay-e Iranshenasi* IV/2 (Summer): 243–68.
Mayrhofer, M. (1973). *Onomastica Persepolitana: Das altiranische Namengut der Persepolis-Täfelchen*. Vienna: Sitzungsberichte der Österreichischen Akademie der Wissenschaften, phil.-hist. Kl. 286.
— (1979). *Iranisches Personennamenbuch, Band I: Die altiranischen Namen*, Vienna.
McNicoll, Anthony, and Ball, Warwick (eds) (1996). *Excavations at Kandahar 1974 and 1975*, Oxford (BAR International Series 641).
Medvedskaya, I.N.(1988). "Who destroyed Hasanlu IV?", *Iran* 26: 1-15.
— (1991). "Once more on the destruction of Hasanlu IV: problems of dating", *I A* 26: 149-161.
Melikian-Chirvani, A.S. (1987). "The wine-bull and the Magian master", in Ph. Gignoux (ed.), *Transition Periods in Iranian History* (Studia Iranica Cahier 5), Paris: 101–134.
Menasce, Jean de (1973). *Le troisième livre du Dēnkart*, Paris.

Meyer, E. (1980). *Geschichte des Altertums*, ed. The Phaidan, Vienna.
Miroschedji, P. de (1985). "La fin du royaume de l'Anšan et de Suse et la naissance de l'empire perse", *ZA* 75: 265–306.
Mohl, Jules (ed. and trans.) (1838–68). *Le livre des rois*, Paris.
Molé, Marijan (1963). *Culte, mythe et cosmologie dans l'Iran ancien*, Paris.
— (1993). *La légende de Zoroastre selon les textes pehlevis*, Paris.
Monchi-Zadeh, Davoud (1975). *Topographisch-historische Studien zum Iranischen Nationalepos*, Wiesbaden.
Moorey, P.R.S. (1980). *Cemeteries of the First Millennium B.C. at Deve Hüyük*, BAR-S87, Oxford.
— (1986). Review of Curtis 1984 in *Bibliotheca Orientalis* 43: 800-803.
Morgenstierne, Georg (1979). "The linguistic stratification of Afghanistan", *Afghan Studies* 2: 23–33.
Moulton, J.H. (1913). *Early Zoroastrianism. The Origins, the Prophet, the Magi*, London (repr. Amsterdam, 1972).
Mousavi, A. (1994). "Une brique à décor polychrome de l'Iran occidental (VIIIe-VIIe s. av. J.-C.)", *StIr* 23: 7-18.
— (2005). "Comments on the Early Iron Age in Iran", *IA* 40: 87-99.
Muscarella, O.W.(1980). *The Catalogue of Ivories from Hasanlu, Iran*, Hasanlu Special Studies II, Philadelphia.
— (1987). "Median art and Medizing scholarship", *JNES* 46: 109-127.
— (1988). *Bronze and Iron: Ancient Near Eastern Artefacts in the Metropolitan Museum of Art*, New York.
Negahban, E.O. (1996). *Marlik: the Complete Excavation Report*, 2 vols., Philadelphia.
Nöldeke, Th. (1887). "Üeber die Namen Persien und Irān", in *Aufsätze zur persischen Geschichte*, Leipzig: 147–9.
Ogden, D. (2001). *Greek and Roman Necromancy*, Princeton/Oxford.
Oppenheim, A.L. (1985). "The Babylonian evidence of Achaemenid rule in Mesopotamia", *CHIr* II: 529–87.
Ouseley, William (1819–23). *Travels in Various Countries of the East, More Particularly Persia in 1810, 1811, 1812*, II, London.
Overlaet, B. (2003). *The Early Iron Age in the Pusht-i Kuh, Luristan*, Luristan Excavation Documents IV, Leuven.
— (2005). 'Chronology of the Iron Age in the Pusht-i Kuh', *I A* 40: 1-33.
Panaino, Antonio (1990). "Calendars i. Pre-Islamic calendars", in Ehsan Yarshater (ed.), *EncIr* IV/6, London: 658-68.
Parpola, A. (2002). "Pre-Proto-Iranians of Afghanistan as initiators of Šāktā tantrism: On the Scythian/Saka affiliation of the Dāsas, Nuristanis and Magadhans", *IrAnt* 37: 233–324.
Pines, S. (1990). "A parallel between two Iranian and Jewish themes", in S. Shaked and A. Netzer (eds), *Irano-Judaica II*, Jerusalem: 41–51.
Porten, Bezalel *et al.* (1996). *The Elephantine Papyri in English. Three Millennia of Cross-cultural Continuity and Change*, Leiden and New York.
Posener, G. (1963). *La première domination Perse en Égypte*, Cairo.

Potts, D.T. (1999). *The Archaeology of Elam: Formation and Transformation of an Ancient Iranian State*. Cambridge.
Prášek, J. (1912). *Kyros der Große*. Leipzig: Hinrichs.
Puig, Jean-José (2005). *La pêche à la truite en Afghanistan*, Paris.
Radner, K. (2003). "A Median sanctuary at Bit-Ishtar", in Lanfranchi, Roaf and Rollinger 2003: 119-130.
Rapin, Claude (forthcoming). "Nomads and the shaping of Central Asia (from the early Iron Age to the Kushan period)", in G. Herrmann and J. Cribb (eds), *After Alexander: Central Asia before Islam*, Oxford (forthcoming 2006).
Razmjou, Shahrokh (2001). "Des traces de la déesse Spenta Ārmaiti à Persépolis", *St Ir* 30: 7–15.
— (2004). "The *lan* ceremony and other ritual ceremonies in the Achaemenian period: the Persepolis Fortification Tablets", *Iran* 62: 103-117.
— (2005). "In search of the lost Median art", *IA* 40: 271-314.
Reade, J.E.(1976). "Elam and Elamites in Assyrian sculpture", *AMI* 9: 97-106.
— (1977). "Shikaft-i Gulgul: its date and symbolism", *IA* 12: 33-44.
— (1995). "Iran in the Neo-Assyrian period", in Liverani, M. (ed.), *Neo-Assyrian Geography*, Rome: 31-42.
Reiner, E. (1973). "The location of Anšan", *RA* 67: 57–62.
Roaf, M.D. (2003). "The Median dark age", in Lanfranchi, Roaf and Rollinger 2003: 13-22.
Roaf, M., and Stronach, D. (1973). "Tepe Nush-i Jan, 1970: second interim report", *Iran* 11: 129-140.
Rollinger, R. (1998). "Der Stammbaum des achaimenidischen Königshauses oder die Frage der Legitimität der Herrschaft des Dareios", *AMIT* 30: 155–209.
— (1999). "Zur Lokalisation von Parsu(m)a(š) in Fars und zu einigen Fragen der frühen persischen Geschichte", *ZA* 89: 115–39.
Roustaei, K. and Potts, D.T. (20040. "The ICAR–University of Sydney Joint Archaeological Expedition in Mamasani, Fars Province: A preliminary report on the fieldwork", *Archaeological Reports* 2: 9–26 (in Persian).
Rudenko, S.I. (1970). *Frozen Tombs of Siberia*, London.
Russell, J.R. (1987). *Zoroastrianism in Armenia* (Harvard Iranian Series 5), Cambridge, MA.
Sarfaraz, A(1969). "The discovery of an Assyrian relief", *Iran* 7: 186.
Sarraf, M.R.(1990). "The bronze bowl of Kidin-Hutran discovered at Arjan, Behbehan", *Athar* 17: 4-61 (in Persian).
Sayce, A.H. (1882). "Cyrus était-il roi de Perse ou de Susiane?", *Le Muséon* 1: 548–56.
— (1886). "La situation géographique d'Anzan", *Le Muséon* 5: 501–505.
Schaeder, H.H. (1941). *Das persische Weltreich*, Breslau.
Schmidt, Erich F. (1953). *Persepolis I: Structures, Reliefs, Inscriptions*, OIP LXVIII, Chicago.

— (1957). *Persepolis II: Contents of the Treasury and other Discoveries*, OIP LXIX, Chicago.
— (1970). *Persepolis*, vol. III. *The Royal Tombs and Other Monuments*, Chicago.
Schmitt, R. (1967). "Medisches und persisches Sprachgut bei Herodot", *ZDMG* 117: 119–45.
— (1991a). *The Bisitun Inscriptions of Darius the Great. Old Persian Text, CII, Pt I, vol. I, Texts I*, London.
— (1991b). "Zu dem 'arischen Ahuramazda' ", *St Ir* 20/2: 189–92.
— (2000). *The Old Persian Inscriptions of Naqsh-i Rustam and Persepolis*, Corpus Inscriptionum Iranicarum Part I, Vol.1, Texts II.
Schwartz, Martin (1985). "The old Eastern Iranian world-view according to the Avesta", *CHIr* II: 648–50.
— (1990). "Viiamburas and Kafirs", *BAI* 4: 251–5.
Seipel, W. (ed.), (2000). *7000 Ans d'Art Perse: chefs d'oevre du Musée National de Téhéran*, Milan and Vienna.
Shahbazi, A. Shapur (1974). "An Achaemenid symbol" I, *AMI*: 135–44.
— (1980). "An Achaemenid symbol II. Farnah 'God-given Fortune' symbolised", *AMI* 13: 119–47.
— (1983). "Darius' Haft Kišvars", in H.-M. Koch and D.N. MacKenzie (eds), *Kunst, Kultur und Geschichte der Achämenidenzeit und ihr Fortleben*, AMI Ergänzungsband 10, Berlin: 242–6.
— (1993). "Cyrus ii. Cyrus I", *EncIr* 6: 516.
— (2001). "Early Sasanians' claim to Achaemenid heritage", *International Journal of Ancient Iranian Studies* I/1 (Spring and Summer): 61–73.
— (2002). "Goštāsp", *EncIr* X: 171–6.
Shaked, S. (1990). "Administrative functions of priests in the Sasanian period", in G. Gnoli and A. Panaino (eds), *Proceedings of the First European Conference of Iranian Studies I. Old and Middle Iranian Studies* (Serie Orientale Roma 67.1), Rome: 261–73.
— (1994). *Dualism in Transformation. Varieties of Religion in Sasanian Iran*, London.
— (1996). "The traditional commentary on the Avesta (Zand): translation, interpretation, distortion?", in *La Persia e l'Asia Centrale da Alessandro al X secolo* (Atti dei convegni Lincei 127), Rome: 641–56.
— (2004). *Le satrape de Bactriane et son gouverneur. Documents araméens du IVe s. avant notre ère provenant de Bactriane* (Persika 4), Paris.
— (2005). "Zoroastrian origins: Indian and Iranian connections", in J.P. Arnason, S.N. Eisenstadt and B. Wittrock (eds), *Axial Civilizations and World History* (Jerusalem Studies in History and Culture 4), Leiden: 183-200.
Shapira, D. (1998). *Studies in Zoroastrian Exegesis: Zand*, PhD dissertation, the Hebrew University of Jerusalem.
Shoberel, Frederick (1828). *Persia: Containing a Description of the Country*, London.

Sims-Williams, Nicholas (1997). *New Light on Ancient Afghanistan. The Decipherment of Bactrian*, SOAS, London.
Sims-Williams, N. and Cribb, Joe (1995). "A new Bactrian inscription of Kanishka the Great", *Silk Road Art and Archaeology* 4: 75–142.
Skalmowski, W. (1993). "Two Old Persian names", *OLP* 24: 73–7.
Skjærvø, Prods Oktor (1995). "The Avesta as source for the early history of the Iranians", in G. Erdosy (ed.), *The Indo-Aryans of Ancient South Asia. Language, Material Culture and Ethnicity*, Berlin – New York: 155–75.
— (1997). "The state of Old-Avestan scholarship", *Journal of the American Oriental Society* 117/1: 103–114.
— (1999). "Avestan quotations in Old Persian? Literary sources of the Old Persian inscriptions", in Shaul Shaked and Amnon Netzer (eds), *Irano-Judaica* IV, Jerusalem: 1–64.
— (2002). "Praise and blame in the Avesta. The poet-sacrificer and his duties", in *Studies in Honour of Shaul Shaked* I [*JSAI* 26], Jerusalem: 29-67.
— (2003a). "Truth and deception in ancient Iran", in Farrokh Vajifdar and Carlo G. Cereti (eds), *Jamshid Soroush Soroushian Commemorative Volume*, vol. II. *Ātaš-e dorun – The Fire Within*, 1st Books Library: 383–434.
— (2003b). "Zarathuštra: First poet-sacrificer", in Siamak Adhami (ed.), *Paitimāna. Essays in Iranian, Indian, and Indo-European Studies in Honor of Hanns-Peter Schmidt*, Costa Mesa: 176–8.
— (2004). "Smashing urine: on *Yasna* 48.10", in Michael Stausberg (ed.), *Zoroastrian Rituals in Context*, Leiden and Boston: 253–81.
Smith, J.Z. (1995). "Trading places", in M. Meyer and P. Mirecki (eds), *Ancient Magic and Ritual Power* (Religions in the Graeco-Roman World 129), Leiden: 13–27 [reprinted in J.Z. Smith, *Relating Religion. Essays in the Study of Religion*, Chicago 2004, 215–29].
Smith, S. (1924). *Babylonian Historical Texts Relating to the Capture and Downfall of Babylon*. London: Methuen.
Spiegel, F. (1871–8). *Erânische Altertumskunde*, i–iii. Amsterdam: Oriental Press (1971 reprint).
Stausberg, M. (1998). "The invention of a canon – the case of Zoroastrianism", in A. van der Kooij and K. van der Toorn (eds), *Canonization and Decanonization. Papers presented to the International Conference of the Leiden Institute for the Study of Religions (LISOR) held at Leiden 9–10 January 1997* (Studies in the History of Religions 82), Leiden: 257–77.
Steblin-Kamenskii, Ivan (1978). "Reka Iranskoii prarodiny", in *Onomastika Srednei Azii*, Moscow: 72–4.
Stolper, M.W. (1984). *Texts from Tall-i Malyan, I. Elamite administrative texts (1972–1974)*. Philadelphia: Occasional Publications of the Babylonian Fund 6.
Stronach, D. (1969). "Excavations at Tepe Nush-i Jan, 1967", *Iran* 7: 1-20.
— (1978). "Excavations at Tepe Nush-i Jan. Part 2. Median pottery from the fallen floor in the fort", *Iran* 16: 11-24.

— (1978). *Pasargadae*, Oxford.
— (1990). "On the genesis of the Old Persian cuneiform script", in F. Vallat (ed.), *Mélanges Jean Perrot*. Paris: 195–203.
— (1997a). "Anshan and Parsa: Early Achaemenid history, art and architecture on the Iranian Plateau", in J. Curtis (ed.), *Mesopotamia and Iran in the Persian Period: Conquest and Imperialism 539–331 B.C.* London: 35–53.
— (1997b). "On the interpretation of the Pasargadae inscriptions", in B. Magnusson, S. Renzetti, P. Vian and S.J. Voicu (eds), *Ultra terminum vagari: Scritti in onore di Carl Nylander*. Rome: 323–9.
— (1998). "On the date of the Oxus gold scabbard and other Achaemenid matters", *BAI* 12: 231–48.
— (2000). "Of Cyrus, Darius and Alexander: A new look at the 'epitaphs' of Cyrus the Great", in R. Dittmann, B. Hrouda, U. Löw, P. Matthiae, R. Mayer-Opificius and S. Thürwächter (eds), *Variatio delectat: Iran und der Westen, Gedenkschrift für Peter Calmeyer*. Münster: AOAT 272: 681–702.
— (2003a). "Independent Media: archaeological notes from the homeland", in Lanfranchi, Roaf and Rollinger 2003: 233-248.
— (2003b). "The tomb at Arjan and the history of southwestern Iran in the early sixth century BCE", in N.F. Miller and K. Abdi (eds), *Yeki bud, yeki nabud: Essays on the Archaeology of Iran in Honor of William M. Sumner*. Los Angeles: Cotsen Institute of Archaeology Monograph 48: 249–59.
— (2005). "The Arjan tomb", *IA* 40: 179-196.
Stronach, D. and Roaf, M. (1978). "Excavations at Tepe Nush-i Jan. Part 1. A third interim report'", *Iran* 16: 1-11.
Tavernier, J. (2002). *Iranica in de Achaemenidische Periode (ca. 550–330 v. Chr.): Taalkundige studie van Oud-Iraanse eigennamen en leenwoorden, die geattesteerd zijn in niet-Iraanse teksten*, 3 vols.
Teixidor, J. (1999). "L'inscription araméenne de Bukân: relecture", *Semitica* 49: 117-121.
Toynbee, A. (1954). *A Study in History*, VII, Oxford.
Tremblay, Xavier (1998). "Sur *parsui* du Farhang-ī-Ōim, *ratu-*, *pərətu-*, *pitu-* et quelques autres thèmes avestiques en -u", *St Ir* 27: 187–204.
— (1999). Etudes sur les noms suffixaux athématiques de l'Avesta, Ecole Pratique des Hautes Etudes, IVe section, Paris [unpublished PhD].
— (2004). "La toponymie de la Sogdiane et le traitement de *$x\theta$ et *$f\theta$ en iranien", *St Ir* 33: 113–49.
Vallat, F. (1980). *Suse et l'Elam*. Paris.
— (1984). "Kidin-Hutran et l'époque néo-élamite", *Akkadica* 37: 1-17.
— (1993). *Les noms géographiques des sources suso-élamites*. Wiesbaden: Répertoire géographique des textes Cunéiformes 11.
Versnel, H.S. (1991). "Some reflections on the relationship magic–religion", *Numen* 38: 177–97.
Vogelsang, Willem (2000). "The sixteen lands of Vidēvdād 1. A[i]ryân[e]m Vaêjah and the homeland of the Iranians", *Persica* 16: 49–66.

Voigt, M. and Dyson, R.H., Jr (1992). "The chronology of Iran, ca. 8000–2000 B.C.", in R.W. Ehrich (ed.), *Chronologies in Old World Archaeology* (3rd edn). Chicago/London: 122–78.
Voigtlander, E.N. von (1978). *The Bisitun Inscription of Darius the Great. Babylonian Version* (Corpus Inscriptionum Iranicarum I.II.1), London.
Waters, Matthew W. (1996). "Darius and the Achaemenid line", *The Ancient History Bulletin* 10: 11–18.
— (1999). "The earliest Persians in southwestern Iran: the textual evidence", *Iranian Studies* 32: 99–107.
— (2000). *A Survey of Neo-Elamite History*. Helsinki: State Archives of Assyria Studies 12.
— (2004). "Cyrus and the Achaemenids", *Iran* 42: 91–102.
Watters, Thomas (1904–1905). *On Yuan Chwang's Travels in India (A.D. 629–645)*, London.
Weidner, E. (1931–2). "Die älteste Nachricht über das persische Königshaus: Kyros I. ein Zeitgenosse Assurbânaplis", *AfO* 7: 1–7.
Weissbach, F.H. (1924). "Kyros 4", *RE* 23: col. 188.
West, M.L. (1993). "Simonides redivivus", *Zeitschrift für Papyrologie und Epigraphik* 98: 1–14.
Widengren, G. (1965). *Die Religionen Irans*, Stuttgart.
— (1977). "The Persian period", in J.H. Hayes and J. Maxwell Miller (eds), *Israelite and Judaean History*, Philadelphia: 489–538.
Wilkinson, C.K. (1975). *Ivories from Ziwiye*, Abegg-Stiftung Bern.
Wilson, H.H. (1851). *Ariana Antiqua*, London.
Wiesehöfer, J. (1999). "Fars ii. History in the pre-Islamic period", *EncIr* 9: 333–7.
— (2002). "Gebete für die 'Urahnen' oder: Wann und wie verschwanden Kyros und Dareios aus der historischen Tradition Irans?", *Electrum* 6: 111–17.
Witzel, Michael (2000). "The home of the Aryans", in A. Hintze und E. Tichy (eds), *Anusantatyai. Festschrift für Johanna Narten zum 70. Geburtstag*, Dettelbach: 283–338.
Yarshater, E. (1985). "Iranian national history", *CHIr*, III: 359-447.
Young, T. C. (1967). "The Iranian migration into the Zagros", *Iran* 5: 11–34.
— (1985). "Early Iron Age Iran revisited: preliminary suggestions for the re-analysis of old constructs", in *De l'Indus aux Bálkans: à la memoire de Jean Deshayes*, Paris 361-378.
— (2003). "Parsua, Parsa, and potsherds", in N.F. Miller and K. Abdi (eds), *Yeki bud, yeki nabud: Essays on the Archaeology of Iran in Honor of William M. Sumner*. Los Angeles: Cotsen Institute of Archaeology Monograph 48: 243–8.
Zadok, R. (1976). "On the connections between Iran and Babylonia in the sixth century B.C.", *Iran* 14: 61–78.
— (1991). "Elamite onomastics", *SEL* 8: 225–37.
— (2002). *The Ethno-linguistic Character of Northwestern Iran and Kurdistan in the Neo-Assyrian Period*. Jaffa.